the FAITH OF AMERICA'S FIRST LADIES

To Jane
a first lady of
faith!

Joe Hampton Cook

the FAITH OF AMERICA'S FIRST LADIES

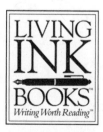

LIVING
INK
BOOKS
Writing Worth Reading

JANE HAMPTON COOK

The Faith of America's First Ladies
Copyright © 2005 by Jane Hampton Cook

Published by Living Ink Books, an imprint of AMG Publishers
6815 Shallowford Rd.
Chattanooga, Tennessee 37421

ISBN 0-89957-088-7
First printing—January 2006
Cover designed by Market Street Design, Chattanooga, Tennessee
Interior design and typesetting by Reider Publishing Services,
    West Hollywood, California
Edited and Proofread by Melanie Rigney, Dan Penwell, Sharon Neal,
    and Rick Steele

Printed in the United States of America
12 11 10 09 08 07 06 –R– 7 6 5 4 3 2

Dedication

To my mother, Granny, Mammaw, and Maw Maw—first ladies who took the distaff in one hand and the spindle in the other to stitch a sample pattern for me.

To my nieces, Julie and Carrie, whose care for my infant son allowed me to work with eager hands on this book. To my other nieces, Corrine, Carissa, Grace, Hope, and Faith, also future first ladies of faith.

And to my husband, Dr. John Kim Cook, a man of strength and support, and my son, Austin, may I bring them "good, not harm" all the days of my life.

Contents

Acknowledgments

WRITING A book begins with a twinkle. As the twinkle becomes a steady ray of light, your heart begins to yearn and your mind begins to churn until you commit to writing. Then the beam brightens when you find the courage to share your idea with those who can shape and polish it into something illuminating for the reader. These are the stars who turned the flicker God placed in my heart into the flame called *The Faith of America's First Ladies*.

I want to first thank Jonathan Clements and the staff at the Nashville Agency for taking the idea for this book, believing in it, and making it a reality. Thanks also to Marita Littauer and the staff of CLASServices, Inc. for planning, hosting, and leading the Glorieta Christian Writers Conference. Thank you for investing and believing in writers and speakers. Thanks to Dan Penwell, who invited me—a sometimes shy woman great with child at the time—to join his table in the cafeteria at the Glorieta Christian Writers Conference. Without his hospitality, I would not have had the opportunity to share the idea for this book with him or the capable team at AMG, Living Ink Books. Thank you, Dan and Gloria Penwell, Melanie Rigney, and Sharon Neal for your editing prowess.

I also want to express appreciation to Stacey Ankele, Carol Blair, Pam Colton, Heather Cooper, Carolyn Greene, Barbara Hill, Deshua Joyce, Bonnie Nichols, Daniel Nichols, Jacqueline Phelan,

Kim Mulkey-Robinson, Holly Rollins, Anne Ryun, and Hilary White for allowing me to write your stories. You are the extra polish that makes this book relevant for women today.

An author writing history relies on the helpfulness of many librarians and historians to check facts and answer questions. I want to extend special thanks to Mary V. Thompson, research specialist for the Mount Vernon Ladies' Association, and Mary O. Klein, archivist for the Episcopal Diocese of Maryland, for their extra willingness to share their expertise. Thanks to John Riley at the White House Historical Association and the Organization for American Historians. Although my White House History Fellowship was focused on another book, the opportunity these organizations provided me opened my eyes to a new world of research at the Library of Congress.

A word of appreciation belongs to President George W. Bush, Laura Bush, Karen Hughes, and Harriet Miers. Thank you, Mr. President and Mrs. Bush, for having faith in me and entrusting me to communicate your message to the public through the Internet. Thank you, Karen, for taking a chance on me when you hired me to develop then Governor Bush's Web site. Thank you, Harriet, for hiring me to work in the White House. The opportunity to serve the Bushes allowed me to grow professionally, especially in writing, and personally in ways I never could have imagined. The experience has inspired me to look toward the sunrise side of the mountain, the side looking at the days to come, not the sunset side of the mountain—an idea the president has often quoted.

A standing ovation belongs to my family, especially to my husband, Dr. John Kim Cook, who often came home from work to find his wife consumed by the screen in front of her eyes and the keyboard under her fingers, madly typing what was churning in her brain. Thank you for loving me with your patience. Thanks to our nieces, Carrie Cook and Julie Parker, for flying to Washington, D.C., to help me take care of our infant son (and to your parents for allowing you to come) so I could finish the book. And a special thanks to my mom for proofing, listening, and most of all, speaking encouraging words, the love language of my heart.

The Proverb of the Wife of Noble Character— Proverbs 31:10–31

[10] A wife of noble character who can find? She is worth far more than rubies.

[11] Her husband has full confidence in her and lacks nothing of value.

[12] She brings him good, not harm, all the days of her life.

[13] She selects wool and flax and works with eager hands.

[14] She is like the merchant ships, bringing her food from afar.

[15] She gets up while it is still dark; she provides food for her family and portions for her servant girls.

[16] She considers a field and buys it; out of her earnings she plants a vineyard.

[17] She sets about her work vigorously; her arms are strong for her tasks.

[18] She sees that her trading is profitable, and her lamp does not go out at night.

[19] In her hand she holds the distaff and grasps the spindle with her fingers.

[20] She opens her arms to the poor and extends her hands to the needy.

[21] When it snows, she has no fear for her household; for all of them are clothed in scarlet.

[22] She makes coverings for her bed; she is clothed in fine linen and purple.

[23] Her husband is respected at the city gate, where he takes his seat among the elders of the land.

[24] She makes linen garments and sells them, and supplies the merchants with sashes.

[25] She is clothed with strength and dignity; she can laugh at the days to come.

[26] She speaks with wisdom, and faithful instruction is on her tongue.

[27] She watches over the affairs of her household and does not eat the bread of idleness.

[28] Her children arise and call her blessed; her husband also, and he praises her:

[29] "Many women do noble things, but you surpass them all."

[30] Charm is deceptive, and beauty is fleeting; but a woman who fears the LORD is to be praised.

[31] Give her the reward she has earned, and let her works bring her praise at the city gate.

First Lady of His Heart

"Many women do noble things, but you surpass them all"
(Prov. 31:29).

W HO IS that woman in the photograph?" The butlers and housekeepers whispered as they fluttered about the White House.

These chitchatting servants walked up and down the mansion's twisting staircases with the curiosity of detectives in their hearts. The mourning period was complete. At last they were free to talk about something other than black crepe swags, and the new president had given them the perfect fodder.

"Is she his mother?" one of them wondered aloud while polishing the silver oval frame of the photograph in question.

"No, she's too young. Perhaps she's his sister," another answered.

The White House servants were more than ready for some lighthearted gossip. An assassin's bullet the previous July had put President James Garfield on his deathbed for weeks. Not even the continual flow of fall's breezes could whisk away the dreariness they felt after his September death. These domestics needed some levity, and the new president did not disappoint them when he finally moved into the White House in December 1881.

Chester Arthur's New York accent, eccentric long sideburns, and hefty frame certainly gave them plenty to whisper about, but the servants were more intrigued with his personal life. Simply by placing a portrait of a beautiful woman on a table, the unmarried president unwittingly gave them a mystery to solve.

The nosiest servants had studied the woman's face, the only obvious clue to her identity. The woman's sleek dark hair was perfectly combed into a chignon or knot resting on her neck. Her smile was slight but her eyes were wide with intrigue. Her jewelry hinted at the wealth of royalty. Teardrop earrings dangled from her earlobes. Encircling her neck was a double strand of pearls joined in the center by a diamond cluster. Although she bore the elegance of Britain's Queen Victoria, this mysterious woman was obviously a gem in her own right.

"Did you notice where he put her portrait?" one said.

"In the state floor hallway," another replied.

"Everyone who comes to visit the executive mansion will see it there."

"The gardener said President Arthur gave him an order. He is to make sure there are always fresh roses next to the woman's portrait. Not a day is to pass without them."

"Quite a romantic executive order if you ask me."

"Maybe the president is courting her."

"Maybe he's in love."

So the White House domestics buzzed about, taking guesses on the identity of President Arthur's lady fair. They did not have to wait long to solve the mystery. A lifelong resident of Washington, D.C., soon visited the White House and instantly recognized the woman. Why, of course; she was the girl who had sung in the choir at St. John's, the church across the street from the White House. As a young woman she had moved to New York to marry the son of a Baptist minister. The servants were thrilled to discover the woman was Ellen Herndon Arthur, the president's wife. But they were sad to learn they would never know the jewel who wore the pearls.

Nell, as Chester had called her, had died suddenly of pneumonia two years before her husband reached the summit of his career. "Honors to me now are not what they once were," the president said of life without her. Chester wanted anyone who came to the White House to know how important she had been to him. By placing her photograph on a table in the state hallway, not in his private residence, he made his declaration public. The scent of newly cut roses drew fresh attention to her each day.

Perhaps Chester most missed his wife's rich alto singing voice, appreciation of the arts, and devotion to their children. Maybe he longed to buy her jewelry again from their favorite store, Tiffany & Co. in New York. Perhaps he regretted not telling her more often how much she had meant to him. He wished he had heeded her warnings about the political corruption surrounding his job as New York customs collector. To honor her memory, Chester decided to use the presidency to pass legislation to end the unethical practices that had plagued his early career. Even after her death, she continued to influence him. Nell was forever the first lady of Chester's heart.[1]

What a great tribute Chester gave to Nell. She probably never knew how valuable she was to him. Her commitment to sing in the choir at St. John's indicates that her faith in God was also important to her. Chester's memorial shows that she made significant contributions as a wife, mother, and community leader. Her life shone brighter than her Tiffany pearls and diamond teardrops. Nell and her legacy were priceless.

I first discovered the story of Nell's photograph when I had the opportunity to work for President George W. Bush and Laura Bush. I served President Bush in the Texas governor's office for three years and then in the White House for two years. My job was to communicate his message by posting, writing, and designing content for his official Texas and White House Web sites.

When I came to the White House, I soon discovered that biographies of the presidents were among the most popular features of the White House Web site— www.whitehouse.gov. United States history united Americans and, in some cases, provided context for current events. So I decided to write a few more pieces for this section. Through my research, I discovered the story of Nell's photograph. What touched me the most was the influence she had on her husband beyond her life span. She left a lasting legacy.

Nell never lived to serve as first lady of the White House, but her marriage to a man who became president places her among a unique group of women. From Martha Washington's leadership to Laura Bush's compassion, our nation's first ladies are a special collection of jewels.

You are probably most familiar with the first ladies who have served in your lifetime. My mother remembers reading as a schoolgirl about Mamie Eisenhower's bangs and her love of pink in the *Weekly Reader*, a newspaper for kids. I remember Rosalynn Carter not as the first lady but as the mother of Amy Carter, who is close to my age. I have more memories of Nancy Reagan, Barbara Bush, Hillary Clinton, and Laura Bush.

"I have admiration for all past first ladies. It's a hard job, and every one of them has made a contribution," Barbara Bush said at the 1992 reopening of a Smithsonian exhibit on first ladies. She then praised the first ladies in her lifetime, from Eleanor Roosevelt onward.[2]

"First lady" is not an official government title. Martha Washington was "Lady Washington." First lady was not used until 1849, when President Zachary Taylor spoke at Dolley Madison's funeral. He said, "She will never be forgotten because she was truly our first lady for half a century." A few years later *Leslie's* magazine described Harriet Lane as the "first lady" because she served so capably as the White House hostess when her bachelor uncle, James Buchanan, became president in 1857.[3]

Today, television interviews and magazine cover stories give us insight into the lives of the women we call "first lady." With a simple click, the media spotlight brings them into our living rooms. Because we have seen their faces and have heard their voices dozens of times, they often seem as familiar to us as our friends and neighbors. Their unique lifestyles intrigue us. When you host a party, you may invite a few friends over for a cookout. When the first lady hosts a party, she may invite the Queen of England.

"People write me and say, 'I know I could talk to you.' And they could. And I could talk to them." Barbara Bush paused and then added, "But I could also talk to the Queen of England. Or . . . Margaret Thatcher. Or Deng Xiaoping. Or Mrs. Sadat."[4]

When you buy a new outfit, you may press a friend for a comment. When the first lady buys a new outfit, she hopes the press doesn't comment. Nancy Reagan wrote about this problem in her memoirs:

> I appreciate good clothes, but they certainly don't rule my life. And I think it's unfair to assume that when a woman dresses well, it means she's not doing much else. I really did have other interests—although in 1981 that wasn't yet clear to the press and to most of the public. During my first six months in Washington, Sheila Tate, my press secretary, told me something like 90 percent of the inquiries she received had to do with fashion. And they say *I'm* obsessed with clothes![5]

First ladies have been stung by criticism of their hairstyles, figures, mannerisms, personalities, decisions, and causes. Criticism hurts, whether it's in public or behind your back at the office or at a PTA meeting.

First Lady Rosalynn Carter remembers the criticism she received for attending cabinet meetings and the days when her typing staff wore gloves after her husband ordered the thermostats set at sixty-five degrees to save energy.

"But I learned you're going to be criticized no matter what you do," she said. "So you might as well do what you want and enjoy it."[6]

Criticism doesn't usually end with the grave. *Smithsonian* magazine called Martha Washington "frumpish" in the late 1980s, which led to a flurry of "Martha bashing" until the ladies overseeing

Martha's home at Mount Vernon came to her defense.[7] Martha lived in a time when petticoats featured paneled boning, which made the hips look stylishly wide. You might look frumpy too if your underwear came with built-in padding.

First ladies have approached their roles differently, but their experiences haven't been too different from the times when life suddenly drops you in a place you never expected to be. Martha wasn't thrilled at first to be the president's wife, even though the opportunity took her to an exciting place, the burgeoning city of New York, which served as the nation's capital.

"I live a very dull life here and know nothing that passes in town. I never go to any public places, indeed I think I am more like a state prisoner than anything else, there are certain bounds set for me which I must not depart from and as I cannot do as I like, I am obstinate and stay in a great deal," Martha said.

Grace Coolidge woke up one day and found out that her husband, Calvin Coolidge, was the president following the unexpected death of Warren Harding. She wrote:

> It is difficult to describe my feelings at this time . . . There was a sense of detachment—this was I, and yet not I, this was the wife of the president of the United States, and she took precedence over me, my personal likes and dislikes must be subordinated to the consideration of those things which were required of her. In like manner this man at whose side I walked was the president of our great country; his first duty was to its people. It therefore became quite natural to refer to him as "the president" and to address him as "Mr. President" in the presence of others.[8]

What I find so fascinating about the first ladies are their uniquely American stories. The more I learn about them, the more relevant and remarkable these women become. Most never set out to be first lady of the United States. They were once little girls with big dreams for their future. Their dreams are ones you and I share—

the desire to love and be loved, to be beautiful, to make a difference, to succeed, to have families, to work, and to find meaning and fulfillment in life.

The first ladies also held roles and responsibilities common to all women. They were daughters, sisters, friends, wives, mothers, neighbors, and volunteers. Some were business savvy, while others minded their own business. Some were teachers and employees. They were often models of the latest fashions and role models of character. Just as you and I experience social pressure today, their culture influenced their choices, and they in turn influenced society. Many of their sacrifices opened doors for future generations of American women to pursue an education, raise families, vote, and launch careers.

The first ladies had moments when their lives were broken, jagged, and flawed. More than anything, they experienced pressure. They often faced the pressure of the nation's spotlight. Sometimes they lived under the heat of their own spotlight. They felt the expectation to marry and have children. They felt pressure to achieve, be perfect, and smile when they were really depressed or worried. Rosalynn Carter described this challenge:

> The whole time we were campaigning and Jimmy was president, one of the worst things that happened to us was Chip's divorce. His wife and baby, who was about a year old, left the White House, and it was the hardest thing in the whole term. I remember having to pretend that I was smiling and happy and greeting people and so forth when my heart was just breaking.[9]

Perhaps the first ladies' experiences were on a different scale or from a different generation than yours and mine. But what they learned and the faith and character they developed can give us insight into our own lives today.

One of my favorite poems is a Hebrew proverb about a remarkable woman of character. Proverbs 31:10–31 in the Bible's Old Testament describes a woman who excelled in all aspects of life.

"Many women do noble things, but you surpass them all" (Prov. 31:29). What a legacy she left!

I first encountered Proverbs 31 when I was a teenager. I longed to emulate this woman and follow her example for success. She was a great wife, mother, businesswoman, community leader, and domestic diva. I wanted to be like her. I soon discovered how difficult it was to maintain such a high level of success in all areas at once. Somewhere along the way, I dropped my study of this passage, but not my desire to have it all.

Years later after working in the governor's office and White House, I saw something in this poem I had never before seen. The Proverbs 31 woman was a first lady. Verse 23 tells us that her husband "is respected at the city gate, where he takes his seat among the elders of the land."

She was a first lady. She was married to a politician, perhaps a city councilman, a judge, or maybe the governor or the president.

I read this passage many times and began to see parallels between the first lady of Proverbs 31 and the first lady of the United States. Perhaps the first rule of first ladies—and of White House staffers— is to "do no harm" to the president. Proverbs 31:12 describes how "she brings him good, not harm, all the days of her life."

One of the most insightful episodes of my White House experience began after lunch one day. I returned to my desk in the Eisenhower Executive Office Building, the grand Victorian building next door to the West Wing. I checked my voice messages and to my complete surprise, Laura Bush had left me a message. I had been working with her staff on the pages for her section of the White House Web site, but she wanted to meet with me to review some of the drafts I had sent over.

The meeting was set up. I had drafted and developed material for Mrs. Bush in Texas, but this was different. I entered a room across the hall from their White House residence. She asked me to take a seat, and with a simple manicure-like table separating us, we went through her Web site drafts.

When we came to one particular sentence, I caught a glimpse of how she approached her role. Because she was speaking and hosting events about President Bush's education initiatives, I wrote a sentence that went something like, "President George W. Bush and Laura Bush's education initiatives . . ." She asked me why I had included her name in that sentence. I was too nervous to say what I was thinking: "You're a former teacher, a champion of education, a librarian; of course you deserve credit here!" She said simply that this was the president's initiative. I omitted her name from that sentence.

I thought about the incident later and realized that I wanted to give her recognition, but she demurred. She could have taken credit, but she didn't want to. Life wasn't about her. She approached her role in a selfless way, similar to the character of the Proverbs 31 woman.

A few years later I read an article during the 2004 presidential election that shocked me. Naomi Wolf wrote a piece for *New York* magazine about the candidates' wives. Because Naomi advised Democratic candidate Al Gore in the 2000 election, I expected her to heap praise on Teresa Heinz Kerry, the wife of Democratic candidate John Kerry, and criticize Laura Bush. Instead, Naomi had put on a pair of Proverbs 31 glasses. Her outlook reflected the concept of bringing good not harm to the person you love the most.

"I am a feminist, but I still believe that a candidate's spouse, male or female, needs to understand something that Republicans get now but Democrats still don't: it's not about them. If you are a president's wife—or husband—your life and imagery do not belong just to you. For the duration, you belong to us, and you need to reflect and respect our own aspirations and dreams," Naomi wrote.[10]

She noted that Teresa's decision to keep Heinz as part of her name only reminded voters of her first husband, who was wealthier than John Kerry. "She is publicly, subliminally cuckolding Kerry with the power of another man—a dead Republican man, at that," she wrote.

Naomi also criticized Teresa Heinz Kerry's convention speech.

"Unfortunately, Teresa Heinz Kerry's speech, which all but ignored her husband, did more to emasculate him than the opposition ever could. By publicly shining the light on herself rather than her husband, she opened a symbolic breach in Kerry's archetypal armor," Naomi wrote.

Naomi pointed out the value Laura Bush brought to the president by speaking in terms to which women could relate and by sharing the personal side of his character. I don't mention this article to disparage Teresa Heinz Kerry, but Naomi made a good point. In her own way, she recognized the good in "bringing good, not harm" (Prov. 31:12).

Proverbs 31 is cherished by both Jewish and Christian teachings. Proverbs are common to many ancient writings and oral traditions, from the Chinese in Asia to the Native Americans of North America. They provide moral lessons for developing character. Many women have found the first lady of Proverbs both inspiring and overwhelming. She achieved success in all areas of life. She had a husband, career, children, work, wealth, and community involvement. Perhaps, like Nell Arthur, her photo hung at city hall. On the surface, the Proverbs 31 woman seems to be similar to Mary Poppins, perfect in every way from her spoonful of sugar to her magic umbrella. Mimicking her accomplishments can be a deflating, unattainable, and impossible task. Not only that, but the Proverbs 31 woman lived in ancient times without modern-day conveniences, spoke another language, and managed servant girls who carried jugs of water from the well every morning and spun wool all afternoon. How can this proverb have anything to offer the twenty-first-century woman?

What makes the first lady of Proverbs relevant today is her character, which was the culmination of a lifetime of pursuits and dreams common to all women. Inside a woman's heart is a desire to be loved and cherished by those closest to her. Women long to be treasured for their beauty and recognized for the beauty they make of their lives. They want their lives to have worth and value. They want their families and friends to appreciate their contributions. This is true for the first lady of the White House or the first lady of a one-bedroom apartment.

As I studied Proverbs 31 again and read interpretations of it by theologians, scholars, and commentators, I began to see this passage differently than I once did. The inspiration of the first lady of Proverbs 31 is best measured by the "how" of her life, not by the "what." This passage's applicable principles are not in what this woman achieved but in how she achieved them. Her character is worthy of study. Proverbs 31 gives us insight into her value to God and the worthiness of the roles God gave her. She was first and foremost the first lady of God's heart, and so are you.

You are a first lady because He created you in His image and gave you a place of prominence in His heart. "In the image of God, he created him, male and female he created them" (Gen. 1:27). God created your inmost being. He knit you together in your mother's womb, and you are "wonderfully made" (Ps. 139:14). In His eyes you are worth more than the rarest of jewels. You are priceless.

You are a first lady to Him because He dearly loves you. He loves you so much that He has a portrait of you hanging in His hallway for all to see. His love for you is abounding, enduring, unfailing, and lavishing. He has poured out His love on you (Rom. 5:5), and nothing can separate you from His love (Rom. 8:39). His love for you gives you intrinsic worth and value. He wants you to understand how much you mean to Him. Because He loves you, He has given you talents, roles, and responsibilities that make you a first lady to others.

He made you a daughter. Perhaps He's given you a husband and children. Maybe He has given you siblings or friends who are closer to you than a brother or sister. Perhaps you are a boss or an employee. You hold a place of prominence and importance in someone else's life. Maybe God has given you responsibilities at home, in the marketplace, and at volunteer organizations. These places demand your time and talent and often require so much of you that you feel like a first lady. All of these things, your abilities, relationships, and responsibilities are valuable, but they are not measures of your worth. Instead, they are opportunities for God to shine through you.

This book focuses on the concept of worth. Proverbs 31 provides a strand of golden principles for better understanding your value to God. The examples of some of our nation's first ladies are the pearls—or whichever gem you prefer—of wisdom, character, and faith along a strand of principles for your appearance, work, experiences, decisions, investments, families, service, and faith. Relevant stories and insights from modern-day women add polish and sheen.

Each chapter features a story of a first lady as the primary example of these principles. I have written these short stories based on actual events in the life of a first lady or president. As much as possible, the dialogue and viewpoints come from quotes, letters, newspapers, autobiographies, videos, and journals about the presidents and first ladies. I chose fictionalized history and this "slice of life" approach to give you a deeper insight into the impressions, emotions, and motivations of these women. Stories and fictional techniques can often touch our hearts more deeply than a list of facts and references. The Bible features stories and parables that illustrate principles.

I hope these biblical principles, first lady stories, and modern-day examples will uncover for you many pearls of wisdom, character, and faith and encourage you to develop a deeper understanding of your intrinsic value. But diving for pearls isn't always easy. You might stumble across a few stones along the way.

CHAPTER ONE

Romancing the Stone

"A wife of noble character who can find? She is worth far more than rubies. Her husband has full confidence in her and lacks nothing of value" (Prov. 31:10, 11).

A KENYAN MAN once offered former President Bill Clinton twenty cows and forty goats to marry Chelsea, Clinton's daughter. Though unrequited, this Kenyan government official had found his ruby.[1] But to find a ruby, you often have to romance a stone.

S till no sign of him," Julia Dent whispered from the crown of the hill overlooking the sparse army barracks. She sat as imperially as a princess, spoiled by the Arabian horse under her saddle, the fancy ribbons on her dress, and her father's other indulgences. But her mind was on another man this Saturday afternoon in 1844.

Will I ever see him again? Julia wondered.

This eighteen-year-old girl had felt strange, riding to the barracks by herself from her father's Missouri farm that morning. For nearly three months she had rarely been without the company of her brothers Fred and John, her sister Nell, their friends, and, of course, the lieutenant. Julia had spent more hours with him than the clock could count. Always chaperoned, they had shared picnics and horseback rides. They had caught glimpses of the farm's chipmunks and cardinals. They had enjoyed the shade of locust trees. The one moment Julia and the lieutenant had shared alone was that fateful conversation on the porch two weeks earlier. Now he was gone, perhaps forever.

"The beat of my own heart, that is the only sound I hear," she said as her slightly crossed eyes surveyed the barracks. But it was her nose that noticed the most obvious change. Gone was the potency of a dozen campfires.

"The burnt fragrance of but one smokestack remains," she whispered.

Julia sat amazed at the quiet surrounding her. Now that the shouts and shots of soldiers were mostly gone, all she could hear were crickets and whip-poor-wills signaling nightfall. Most of the regiment had already obeyed the new orders to report to Louisiana, but the lieutenant had taken leave to visit his parents in Ohio before the orders came. One of the soldiers told her that if the lieutenant did not arrive by today, then he had learned of the new orders and traveled directly to Louisiana.

Why didn't I accept his ring that night? she thought. *If I had, he would surely have returned here first.*

Their meeting had been an ordinary introduction. After all, he wasn't one of the society gentlemen she had met at the parties and balls in St. Louis that winter. Because she loved springtime in the country, she returned wholeheartedly to her father's farm in March. That is when she met him. Fred introduced him as a recent West Point graduate who was stationed at the barracks. Thinking he was coming to see Fred, Julia was delighted when the young man came to visit nearly every day.

Julia was fascinated by the lieutenant's stories of New York. She was pleased when he complimented her warm and lively spirit. This quiet and shy man even admired her ability to dance, although he could not dance himself. Julia had enjoyed his company but had thought nothing more of their relationship until just before he left for Ohio. She nearly rocked off the porch that night when he asked her to wear his West Point class ring as a symbol of their engagement.

"Oh, no. Mama would not approve of my accepting a gift from a gentleman," Julia had replied.

"Will you at least think of me in my absence?" he had said.

"I am so happy when you are near," she had answered.

She didn't know what else to say. She had liked him but had not thought of him as a suitor before then.

The lieutenant left as fast as his horse could gallop. As soon as he was gone, Julia felt something she had never experienced: loneliness. She had met many young society men in St. Louis, but no man's attention had ever affected her this way. This Southern belle's life was carefree, but suddenly her heart wasn't.

Julia surveyed the horizon again.

"The afternoon sun will soon disappear for good," she said.

Her horse began to neigh. Then she heard the crescendo of clip-clopping. Someone in the distance was coming toward the barracks.

"Maybe it's him," she said. Her heart beat faster.

She watched and listened. A farmer driving a wagon soon appeared and rode past the barracks. Disappointment pelted her heart like a hard summer rain. She gave up and rode home.

When she arrived at her father's farmhouse that Saturday evening, she found two friends waiting for her. She was pleased when they told her they would stay until Monday morning.

Their presence will banish all thoughts of the lieutenant, she presumed.

But when she slipped into her bed that night, she thought about him. Her new bed, a gift from her father, reminded her of the lieutenant because she had already followed the old custom of naming the posts after someone special. As she pulled the covers over her, Julia suddenly remembered another adage, "Whatever you dream the first night in a new bed will surely come true."

"Dear God, may I dream of Ulysses S. Grant," Julia prayed. Then she closed her eyes and went to sleep.

"Julia, your dream will not come true," Nell and her friends responded when Julia told them about her dream after church the next day. Julia had thought about her vision so much that she missed hearing the sermon. In her dream, Ulysses wore civilian clothes and came to visit her on Monday at noon. He told her he planned to stay a week.

"Mr. Grant is now calmly sailing down the Mississippi River to Louisiana. Why would he return to the barracks on Monday?" Nell scolded.

Yes, why would he? Julia conjectured. She decided to expel all thoughts of Ulysses Grant from her mind. She spent the rest of the day entertaining her girlfriends without a single thought of the lieutenant.

After saying good-bye to her friends late Monday morning, Julia found herself alone again. She began to loosen her hair from its ribbons when a maid came into her room. The woman went over to Julia's window and began closing the curtains.

"Miss Julia, if there isn't John and, I declare, Mr. Grant, and he has on citizen's clothes and how odd he looks in them, too," she said, pointing out the window.

"He's here? Are you sure?" Julia gasped. Her heart was beating so fast she could barely talk. She ran over to the window.

"Sure enough, there he is," she said.

He is the nicest, most handsomest man I ever saw, Julia thought. *I must find another dress to wear.*

"Go downstairs and tell him I'll be just a moment," Julia said to her maid, who quickly left the room.

Julia chose her favorite dress and changed clothes. She retied her hair ribbons and patted her cheeks to waken her face. She glanced at the mantel clock. Her heart began to beat even faster when she saw the time.

"With the hands of time paused at noon, will the arms of destiny greet me downstairs?" she whispered as she dashed from her room.

Julia bustled into the dining room, where she found Ulysses and her brother John, who lived at a nearby farm, talking to Nell. When she saw Ulysses, she could hardly believe it. Ulysses was wearing civilian clothes, just as she had dreamed. But his pants seemed too long for his short stature. Were her eyes playing tricks on her again?

"How long do you expect to remain, Mr. Grant?" Julia asked, holding her breath.

"I hope to stay a week," Ulysses said.

"You have said the very words of my dream!" she exclaimed.

"Have you been dreaming of me?" Ulysses asked hopefully.

"Yes. Are you also familiar with the prediction? The first dream you have in a new bed will come true. In my dream you came to visit today wearing civilian clothes. And you have arrived at noon. Can you believe it? But where is your uniform?"

"I am wearing borrowed plumage. On my way here, I plunged into a creek and nearly drowned," Ulysses said.

"I loaned him my clothes," John said with a grin.

Julia and Ulysses spent every day together that next week. He escorted her to a wedding in St. Louis where she stood as a bridesmaid. On their return ride, Julia glanced at Ulysses' pinkie finger, where he wore his class ring. She hoped he would have the courage to ask her again to wear it. He did. He told her he loved her and that life would be unsupportable without her. Julia agreed to wear his ring as a symbol of their engagement until a wedding band replaced it.

But when Ulysses asked her father for her hand, Mr. Dent's answer stunned them both.

"If it were Nellie, I would not object, but my Julia is unfitted for being a military wife," Mr. Dent said.

Julia couldn't believe it. Her father was behaving like Laban in the Bible. When Jacob asked for Rachel's hand, Laban offered Leah's instead. Although Julia normally identified with Leah because of her poor eyesight, for the first time she could relate to Rachel. Ulysses assured her that he had no interest in her sister. He loved her the way she was. She had his full confidence.

Julia begged her father to let her marry Ulysses. His refusals were worse than a thousand showers from a skunk on their farm. Perhaps she was a bit spoiled and maybe too young, but she didn't care. She was fit to be the wife of a military man, even if her father disagreed with Ulysses' politics and his opinions of the possible war with Mexico. She knew she could handle the military way of life. Ulysses even offered to resign from the army. Julia pleaded. Nothing swayed her father.

Ulysses finally brokered a Laban-like bargain with Mr. Dent. Although she was disappointed that they could not marry right away, Julia was satisfied with the arrangement. She and Ulysses agreed to write letters while he served in the army in Louisiana. If they still wanted to marry each other after one year of correspondence, then they could marry with her father's approval.

One year turned into two. Two turned into four. The war with Mexico, not Mr. Dent, ultimately kept them apart. This time of uncertainty matured Julia. The spoiled princess earned a crown of character. When the war ended, Ulysses and Julia married in St. Louis. She wore a rich, white, watered silk gown on the day she exchanged Ulysses' West Point ring for his wedding band. He also gave her a gold locket containing a photograph of him in his West Point uniform. She wore his ring and locket the rest of her life.[2]

Ulysses would have paid any price for Julia. Had he lived in Bible times, he would have done just that. According to the ancient custom of betrothal, marriage was the result of a series of steps. If a man and woman met and found a mutual attachment, then the man or his parents asked the woman's father for his consent. Sometimes parents arranged marriages for their children. Then they would have agreed on the price or *mohar* for her hand. Mohar could have been money, property, or even service, which was part of the price Jacob paid for Rachel.

Sometimes the couple married right away. Other times they waited a long time, depending on the circumstances. Whenever they married, the wedding was a symbolic processional followed by a multiday feast. The groom wore festive clothing and led a group of friends to his bride's home. When he arrived, he found his betrothed wearing bridal garments and a veil. She joined her groom and, followed by their friends, they proceeded to his family's house to celebrate.[3]

The first lady of Proverbs 31 most certainly went through the steps of betrothal. Her husband asked her father for her hand, and he paid a price for her. Thank goodness our wedding customs are different today, but we can learn something from the mohar of Proverbs 31. This woman's character proved her priceless, worth far more than rubies.

Ulysses was not the only president to wait for the first lady of his heart. World War II separated "Poppy" from his gal. He missed her so much he painted her name on his plane. George and Barbara Bush married three years after he joined the navy. Theodore Roosevelt had a spat with his childhood sweetheart, Edith. The split was so decisive that he married another woman. After she died, Theodore returned to Edith. They had five children together.

Another president and first lady met as children. Harry Truman once wrote about his ruby in his diary:

> I only had one sweetheart from the time I was six. I saw her in Sunday school at the Presbyterian Church in Independence when my mother took me there at that age and afterwards in the fifth grade at the Ott School in Independence when her Aunt Nannie was our teacher and she (Bess) sat behind me. She sat behind me in the sixth, seventh, and high school grades, and I thought she was the most beautiful and sweetest person on earth—and I'm still of that opinion after . . . [many] years of being married to her. I'm old-fashioned, I guess.[4]

Harry waited twenty-eight years before he was able to marry beautiful blue-eyed Bess. His struggle to earn enough money to support them and his World War I service delayed the pair's marriage.

Julia, Barbara, Edith, and Bess were worth the wait. And in God's eyes, so are you.

Shortly after Ulysses Grant became president in 1869, mining for jewels became a booming enterprise. Mining companies sprang up in

North Carolina, where entrepreneurs discovered rubies and sapphires in the Blue Ridge Mountains. These companies capitalized on the commercial value of the red, blue, purple, and yellow stones. They used them for jewelry production and industrial abrasives. Years later when scientists invented cheaper synthetics to replace these stones, the mines lost both their luster and lucrative business. Most of them closed. Today, some of these mines have reopened as tourist sites. You can visit them and search for gems. Finders are keepers.

What does it take to uncover a ruby or sapphire? Just as Ulysses pursued Julia, you have to romance the stone. The process takes determination and work. At the Sheffield Mine in Franklin, North Carolina, you start by purchasing a bucket of natural dirt. Then you pour an eighth of it into a tray provided by the mine owners. You dunk the tray into water to break up any mud balls. Then you separate the rocks and roll them around to scrub them. You rinse. You scrub. Rinse. Scrub. Rinse. Scrub. Because the rocks look clean before they really are, you have to scrub and rinse at least twice as many times as you might expect.

To look for jewels, you spread the stones on a tray. You hold them up to the sunlight and look for glossy surfaces of pink, purple, red, yellow, or blue hues. Without the sun, you can't see the jewels. If you find a gem, a jewelry expert will validate it. You can keep the rock as is or take it to a jeweler, who can turn it into a beautiful necklace, ring, or bracelet.

What's amazing about searching for gems is how many people give up before they find any jewels. Unlike Ulysses Grant, they end the romance too soon.

"Too many of our customers half clean the rocks, decide there isn't anything worthwhile in the tray, throw out the half-washed rocks, and leave discouraged," the mine managers claim. "Then when a heavy rain comes to finish the washing job, we find the discarded gems."[5]

Rubies are a metaphor for the first lady of Proverbs 31. "A wife of noble character who can find? She is worth far more than rubies. Her husband has full confidence in her and lacks nothing of value"

(Prov. 31:10–12). Most translations of the Bible use the term "rubies" in this verse. The Hebrew word is *peniyniym*, which translates to "precious stones." Diamonds, rubies, sapphires, and emeralds are all precious stones. You could use any valuable jewels to describe her worth as priceless.

All jewels start in the same place: mud covered. No matter how thick the mud encases them, they retain their ability to shine. But only when someone rinses off the mud and polishes them can they truly shine. Too often gems remain stuck in the mud. When they are romanced through a rinsing and scrubbing process, they not only shine, they sparkle.

God places circumstances in our lives to help rinse off the mud covering the jewel inside of us, the one he created in his image. I love the story of Julia and Ulysses' courtship, which she wrote in her memoirs and also explained to a reporter for *Ladies' Home Journal* in 1890. Ulysses discovered something in Julia that was worth far more than rubies when they met that spring of 1844. He saw past her flawed eyes and into her soul. He had full confidence in her. But he missed what her father saw. Julia was a diamond in the rough. Though partly responsible for overindulging his daughter, Mr. Dent knew that Julia's spoiled nature was unfit for a military marriage that would result in long separations, unsteady income, and dangerous travel.

Julia's four-year separation and courtship correspondence with Ulysses gave her an opportunity to rinse off her mud mask. Their long courtship gave them time to decide if they were truly committed to each other and willing to confront whatever life brought them. God used Ulysses and Julia's separation to grow and mature both of them. Perhaps he saw that Julia needed some rinsing and scrubbing.

Different areas of our lives need rinsing at different times. Sometimes God needs to do a little cleaning of our relationships. Sometimes it's our talents or our work. Sometimes it's our body or appearance that needs improving. No matter which area is the weakest in your life, God made you as a beauty to be uncovered, a gem designed to sparkle. Sometimes all it takes is removing the mud mask.

One mud mask moment stands out in my memory. When I became a graduate student at Texas A&M University, I accepted a part-time job as a writer and designer for a newsletter. Writing was not a passion for me back then, but I'd had high school teachers who had complimented my ability, so I was quite confident I could do the job. My boss was disappointed in my writing. She had a journalism background and spent hours pruning and redoing my work. I was mortified at all of the red marks she placed on the articles I wrote. It became such a problem that I worried I would lose my job. Because my husband was also in graduate school and working part-time, my employment was critical to our meager income stream.

I ultimately decided to accept the criticism and learn from it. My boss was trying to tell me that my writing style was too academic. I needed to economize and write more simply. So I began to study all of those red marks as clues for how I could get better. My writing improved enough for me to keep my job. I also took a few journalism and writing classes.

At the time I hated those red marks. They were painful to me and quite embarrassing. But now I see that God used my boss to help me. I had no desire to become an author back then, but God needed to remove a mud mask so he could reveal a talent hidden inside.

A few years later, when President Bush was governor, the Lord opened a door for me to develop my talent and interests in a new direction. Because Sam Houston was one of then Governor Bush's favorite Texas heroes, I decided to do some research on him. I eventually discovered enough material to write a book for older children about Sam Houston and his daughter.

I was in the middle of researching and writing the book on weekends when the press office deputy director sent me over to the governor's mansion at the end of February 1999 to staff a photo shoot of the governor for *Fortune* magazine. The resulting photo also appeared on the first printing of *A Charge to Keep*, George W. Bush's autobiography. The shoot took place in the adjoining parlors of the governor's mansion. The photographer had set up a screen in one part of the room, where he took most of the pictures. Near the end, the photographer asked Governor Bush to move to the other side of the room, which happened to include a portrait of Sam Houston on the wall, so he could take pictures in the mansion's natural setting.

"Why don't you get me with Sam Houston in the background?" the governor kidded.

I was there in case anyone needed anything, but the shoot was going well, so I had kept silent up to that point. Because of my research, I realized that Sam Houston's birthday was in a few days.

"Sam Houston's birthday is coming up," I said.

The governor looked at me with surprise.

"When is it?" he asked.

"March 2," I replied.

"What else happened that day?" he asked knowingly.

I froze. He was quizzing me about Texas history.

"It's Texas Independence Day," I replied. When Texans declared independence from Mexico in 1836, they made it official on Sam Houston's birthday.

"March 6?" he asked.

"Alamo," I said, hoping I was right. I was.

"April 21?" he asked.

"San Jacinto," I answered confidently, which was the day Sam Houston defeated the Mexican army in the Battle of San Jacinto.

After I passed his quiz, he told me that reporters began asking him Texas history questions when he first announced his candidacy for governor. He probably enjoyed being the one giving the history quiz instead of receiving it.

From there my interest in writing and history grew exponentially. The Lord has been placing me in situations ever since then to develop my skills. I am sure I'll read this book in a few years and think of ways of improving it.

By the time Julia became first lady, she had encountered many mud-scrubbing moments. She and Ulysses survived poverty and malaria early in their marriage. She endured criticism from his parents that she was "unpardonably extravagant" while they were overly frugal. Those she loved the most were divided during the Civil War.

Her father supported the Confederacy, sharply opposing the "accursed Lincolnites," while Ulysses became the commanding general for the Union. She often traveled to dangerous places to support and encourage Ulysses during the war. She narrowly escaped capture by Confederate soldiers and survived the shelling of a boat she boarded after a battle in Mississippi. Through all of these experiences, she maintained her love for Ulysses and her faith in God.

Of her life she said, "I do not complain. Mine has been a happy, happy life. I have drunk deep from the cup of joy and from the cup of woe. The Lord knows best."[6]

Julia proved her father wrong. The daughter of a gentleman farmer had become an excellent military wife and first lady. She proved the value of romancing the stone. Her life went through many mud-mask moments that polished the jewel inside of her.

Any sparkle in our lives is the result of rinsing and scrubbing. As first ladies of God's heart, we can return His love by confessing our sins and giving Him every part of our lives: our work, families, relationships, decisions, appearance, time, and treasure. He wants us to love Him with "all our heart and with all our soul and with all our mind" (Deut. 6:5).

And sometimes He wants us to wear purple or maybe a pair of stiletto boots.

CHAPTER TWO

Extreme Makeovers

"She is clothed in fine linen and purple" (Prov. 31:22).

SECRETARY OF STATE Condoleezza Rice knows how to put her best foot forward. She usually wears a sensible pump, but she also knows when to don a high heel or clad a high-styled stiletto boot.

"I like clothes. I always have," Condoleezza said in response to a reporter's question for the *Washington Times* in March 2005. The inquiry about her fashion sense came after she answered a series of hefty questions about her political views.

"When I was five years old, my poor father would go off to work on his sermon on Saturday—he was a Presbyterian minister—and my mother and I would go shopping. Shopping is fun," Condoleezza said.[1]

Condoleezza shops very well. She loves clothes, and clothes love her. The day after that interview, she became the belle of the ball by wearing a red Oscar de la Renta dress to the annual Gridiron dinner in Washington.[2] Earlier that year, she chose to wear a black skirt and jacket with a band collar and seven gold buttons, similar to a marine's dress uniform, to greet soldiers at an army airfield. Combined with a pair of striking stiletto boots reaching her knees, her ensemble projected an image of power and confidence.[3]

Condoleezza's appearance appropriately reflects her diplomatic position. This secretary of state understands the value of image. And so did another woman with a diplomatic role. This first lady's ability to charm the queen of England turned her into a Republican princess.

If beauty is in the eye of the beholder, then a beholder knows a gem when he sees one.

"What color are her eyes?"

"Is she brunette or blonde?"

"Is she tall?"

"Is she thin?"

"How old is she?"

"Have you met her?"

Dozens of sweet feminine voices danced around Patrick Lynch faster than the serenading notes of the Marine Band in the White House's East Room the night of March 6, 1857.

I came to write about the president, but some lovely lady has caught everyone's attention tonight, Patrick thought.

Who is she? He wondered as he felt the crowd crush against him. He took a small step forward. The line to meet the nation's newest president, James Buchanan, moved more slowly than the rhythm of an Irish ballad.

Patrick pulled out his pocket watch.

Quarter to ten. I hope I make it before the president retires, he thought. *He's probably been shaking hands all day.*

Patrick's mature journalistic eyes instinctively led him to survey the faces and fashions surrounding him.

"Never has such an astonishing scene met my gaze before," he whispered in his distinctive Irish accent. Although he had lived in New York for a decade, his voice still revealed the rhythm of an immigrant.

"Republican royalty. Congressmen. Senators. Judges. Governors. Even a Polish prince and a Russian nabob, all in one place," he whispered. "Great color for my newspaper. But which woman has caused such a stir?"

Patrick took mental notes of the brilliant chandeliers that made the scene of flitting fairy forms and men of power glow. But he was dismayed as he searched for one woman to stand above the rest. Each wore a bell-shaped hoopskirt, a garment that only grew more fashionably wider with each passing year. Patrick noticed the gentlemen tried to protect the ladies from injury, while the ladies attempted to preserve their dresses, jewels, flowers, and ornaments. With such common extravagance, no lady appeared to be grander than any other.

Oh, well. I'm here to write an article about the president. It would be inappropriate to describe a lady in the article, he thought.

The line advanced forward, and Patrick took a larger step than before, placing him closer to the ladies in front of him. He was so close that he could plainly hear their conversation. He could also smell their perfume, more pungent than pleasant.

"She was presented to the Queen of England," one of the ladies said.

"Really, how exciting," the other replied.

"I hope to meet her."

Who is this woman? And where is she? Patrick mused, feeling more tension over the mystery than an unresolved band cadence.

"Oh, I do wish to be introduced to Miss Lane," a belle blurted in a pitch that exceeded a trumpet's treble pitch.

Ah, Miss Lane, the president's niece of course, he conjectured, feeling a decrescendo of relief.

The line advanced. Patrick watched in amusement as the ladies lifted their gigantic skirts to take a few tiny steps forward.

What if I wrote about Miss Lane? The readers, especially the Irish, would be interested in her.

He dwelled on the concept for a moment.

No, I cannot. Writing about a lady, especially for my advanced years, would exceed the bounds of propriety.

But the idea gnawed on him worse than a beetle infestation of Irish potatoes. As the line inched forward again, he tried to determine a proper way to justify including Miss Lane in his story.

I don't have much time, but maybe I could find out more about her, went through his mind.

"Excuse me, ladies. May I introduce myself?" he said.

The ladies nodded.

"I'm Patrick Lynch, the editor for *The Irish American* newspaper in New York. I also sometimes contribute to the *New York Times*. May I ask you a few questions?"

"Yes, of course," one answered excitedly.

"Tell me, what do you know about Miss Lane?" he asked.

"She's said to be a beauty, formal but elegant. Evenhanded in her manners, treating everyone the same. Even the Southern ladies approve of her," one said without taking a breath.

"Miss Lane wore the most exquisite gown last night at the inaugural ball," the other answered.

"Her dress was stunning. White, silk I believe, trimmed with artificial flowers and matching ones in her hair."

"She also wore a necklace, many strands of seed pearls," the other added.

"We wanted to meet her, but she was too busy shaking hands next to the president last night. So we hoped to meet her tonight."

Patrick quickly glanced at the head of the line to see if a woman was standing next to the president. Because the room was so congested, he could barely see the top of the president's head; much less observe if Miss Lane was at his side.

"You said she was standing next to the president last night?"

"Yes, so we expect her at her uncle's side this evening. She's overseeing the social functions for him; he's a bachelor, you know."

"Thank you, ladies, for your time. Enjoy meeting the president and I hope you are introduced to Miss Lane as well," he said, wishing the same for himself.

Soon he reached the crest of the line, bringing President Buchanan into full view.

"At length, I have reached the Republican sovereign ruler, but where is Miss Lane?" he whispered with dismay.

President Buchanan was shaking hands by himself with only the commissioner of public buildings beside him. Miss Lane was nowhere in sight.

Patrick watched as the commissioner introduced the ladies in front of him to the president. He chuckled silently when President Buchanan's baritone voice became even more gentle and musical when he greeted the ladies.

The president is truly a gentleman, in looks and demeanor, Patrick mused.

The commissioner turned to Patrick.

"I'm Patrick Lynch of New York. How many have come through the line?" Patrick asked, his voice cracking nervously.

"Not sure, perhaps five thousand," the commissioner said, gesturing for Patrick to move in front of the president. "Mr. President, I am pleased to introduce Patrick Lynch of New York."

"So good to meet you, Mr. Lynch. I always enjoy meeting an American with an Irish name," the president said as he shook Patrick's hand.

Patrick nodded and attempted to speak. He had so much to say, but his voice suddenly stopped like a musical score reaching a double rest.

What a moment! The president is so courteous, even after shaking thousands of hands today. But my emotions rendered me silent, he thought as he walked away. *What happened to her?*

"Mr. Lynch," a man called.

"General Burnett," Patrick replied, smiling as he smelled his friend's familiar tobacco scent.

The men stopped and shook hands.

"Good to see you. I trust you are here with your Irish eyes and journalistic pen."

"Of course. I plan to write about tonight, such an enthusiastic crowd. The *Times* may carry my piece."

"Have you met the president?" Burnett asked.

"Just had the pleasure," Patrick said. "General, have you met Miss Lane? Seems she is the most talked-about star this evening."

"I was briefly introduced to her earlier. She was receiving guests in the oval parlor. Shamed to admit it, but I've circled past her a couple of times. Don't think I'm the only gentleman who has taken more than one opportunity to look at her face. She is one in ten thousand."

"Do you know much about her?"

"Not much, although I know she joined him in England when he was an ambassador. She made quite an impression on Queen Victoria, I understand. The queen was so impressed that she gave her the court status of an ambassador's wife."

Patrick looked at his watch. Just a few minutes remained until ten o'clock.

"Is it too late to introduce me?"

"Let's try. Follow me."

The pair squeezed by hundreds of satin bustles, cockades, and brass buttons to exit the room. General Burnett led Patrick into the small parlor between the East Room and the oval parlor.

Patrick glanced through the doorway of the oval room and saw a woman of medium height standing with an erect posture.

Miss Lane! He mulled this over in his mind. His spirits brightened faster than a burst of fireworks.

Patrick noticed her sweet smile as she spoke to a pair of guests. With all the talk about her, he was surprised that she did not appear to be as extravagant as the other belles. Her dress was elegant yet simple.

"Mr. Reed," General Burnett called to a man who was standing nearby. "I have a friend here who would like to meet Miss Lane. You were so kind to introduce me earlier, would you do the same again?"

General Burnett introduced Patrick to Mr. Reed, who was from Pennsylvania, Miss Lane's home state. Mr. Reed then escorted Patrick into the oval room.

"Miss Harriet Lane, it is my pleasure to introduce you to Mr. Patrick Lynch."

"Pleased to meet you, Mr. Lynch," Miss Lane said as she shook his hand.

Patrick noticed how her violet blue eyes looked confidently into his. He guessed she was in her twenties. Her hair was ash blond, plainly worn but faultless. Her complexion was as clear as a lily. Her cheeks were as pink as a rose. He could smell her perfume, light and floral, not unpleasantly pungent.

"Mr. Lynch is a nonpartisan member of the press," Mr. Reed said.

"Yes, Miss Lane, I defend everything democratic and Irish with equally earnest zeal. I will certainly give an enthusiastic and exuberant account of this evening for the paper."

"I hope you will. Thank you for coming. I know your presence means so much to the president," she said. "A pleasure to meet you."

Then another guest stepped forward for an introduction, and Patrick stepped away.

"What do you think of Miss Lane?" General Burnett asked, leading Patrick into the hallway toward the entrance.

Patrick's heart was beating so fast that he paused briefly to consider the question and catch his breath.

"Miss Lane occupies a position similar to that which Queen Victoria occupies at Buckingham Palace," Patrick said, as if he were penning the phrase. "I do believe those in the American fashionable world will consider her a Republican princess."

The pair collected their frock coats. As Patrick prepared to depart, he turned to General Burnett.

"How did you know about Miss Lane's success in England?" he asked.

"I believe I read something about her in a newspaper," the general said.

"Ah," he said with a smile. "Precedence. Precedence, of course."

Patrick said good-bye to his friend and left the White House more exuberant than ever. If another editor had already written about Miss Lane, then he could too.

Patrick returned to New York and wrote about the reception. His article appeared in the *New York Times* on March 20, 1857. He devoted a single short paragraph to President Buchanan and then wrote one five times as long about Miss Lane. He apologized for breaking any social proprieties about discussing the beauty of a lady, explaining the precedence in the press for doing so. The Irish American reporter summarized Miss Lane's presence in the White House this way:

"Her beauty reminds me of that mixed Celt and Saxon in Ireland which Lord Byron has immortalized by calling the most exquisite in the world; and her artlessness and grace, sweetness, and goodness of heart and manner make her a generous and noble American girl," he wrote.[4]

More than 130 years later, another inaugural reception took place in the same oval parlor, known as the Blue Room today, where Patrick Lynch met Harriet Lane. Unlike the public reception of 1857, this affair was private. However, the circumstances also called for everyone to put their best foot forward or anywhere except in their mouths. The meeting of an outgoing and incoming president isn't always easy, especially if the two ran against each other in the prior election.

After twelve years of service, eight as vice president and four as president, George Bush spent his last hours in the White House welcoming the new president. President Bush, First Lady Barbara Bush, Vice President Dan Quayle and his wife Marilyn greeted incoming President Bill Clinton, First Lady Hillary Clinton, Vice President Al Gore, and his wife Tipper in the White House's Blue Room. Three of the ladies—Barbara, Marilyn, and Tipper—had two things in common: they had all been married to a vice president of the United States, and they all wore purple to the reception.[5]

Hillary donned her purple dress later that evening. She danced at eleven inaugural balls wearing a beautiful violet beaded gown with a blue-velvet silk overskirt by a New York designer. Her overcoat was violet and gold velvet.

Purple was also one of Mary Todd Lincoln's favorite colors. She often wore a purple velvet day and evening dress made by her African American dressmaker, Elizabeth Keckley. Martha Washington loved purple so much that she wore a pair of purple satin shoes with silver trim when she married George Washington.

Perhaps these ladies chose purple because of its vibrancy. Maybe they loved its symbolism as the color of royalty and kings. The woman of Proverbs 31 also loved the color purple. Verse 22 tells us: "She is clothed in fine linen and purple."

In trying to better understand the meaning behind "fine linen and purple," I turned to an expert, Jacqueline Phelan. When I first met Jacqueline at church several years ago, I immediately admired her style. She really knows how to look her best by wearing vivid colors and striking silhouettes that accentuate her dark hair, olive skin, and statuesque height.

I knew Jacqueline had taught fashion history (as well as fashion business and psychology) at Marymount University in Virginia, but I didn't know until we met for coffee to talk about this verse just how much she loves fashion and the extent of her expertise. Jacqueline has worked as chief curator at the Fashion Café Museum Collection and as an educational assistant for the Costume Institute at the Metropolitan Museum of Art in New York. She also has a graduate degree in museum studies of costume and textile from New York's Fashion Institute of Technology. Jacqueline understands fine linen, and she knows purple.

She also has something in common with the first lady of Proverbs 31, a love for material, which Jacqueline describes as "a womanly art" because of its softness and comfort. She helped me to understand that textiles were big business in the ancient world.

"She's spinning the flax and wool and she is making the fabric and selling the fabric [Prov. 31:13, 24]. This was obviously something she loved. People who love fabrics and textiles, even in the museum world, they're like a class unto themselves. They're their own breed," Jacqueline said. "She was doing what was appropriate for enriching her family, not only money-wise, but also image-wise."

Jacqueline pointed out something I had not noticed about verse 22: "She is clothed in fine linen and purple." What is interesting is what this verse doesn't say. It's missing a pronoun.

"Interestingly it doesn't say she wears her fine linen. It doesn't identify that the fabric she is wearing is the fabric she has made. So there's something there because otherwise wouldn't they—if fabric is her trade—say she is clothed in her fine linen? Why isn't she wearing her fine linen?" Jacqueline asks.

Because she was a seamstress, the first lady of Proverbs 31 must have made her own clothing. She must have worn homespun. However, she also wore fine clothing made and dyed by someone else. She chose to wear something that was better than she could make. Perhaps she saved up enough money to buy something she admired at the market. Or maybe she made a deal and traded a multitude of wool cloaks for a fine linen tunic or a purple silk scarf. Regardless, she wore couture, something just right and appropriate for her. She found a fabric that helped her to put her best foot forward. She did it by draping herself in purple.

"It obviously wasn't disrespectful that she was dressed in purple. If it was too much of a royal color, it would have been disrespectful. Purple was a color of status," Jacqueline said.

"What makes that particularly interesting is it doesn't say fine linen of purple it says 'and purple.' I don't think it's differentiating between the linen and purple; most likely they're the same, although often when it's purple fabric, it's silk fabric."

Purple was also expensive. Purple dye was costly to produce. It did not adhere to fabric easily, and the process for dying material purple was difficult and somewhat mysterious.

"Purple in ancient times came from a shellfish, a mollusk specifically called the murex, and it was very difficult to get out. It was a secret process that has virtually been lost to the ages," Jacqueline said.

Although historians can't replicate the process, they know that dying purple was difficult and distasteful. Each shell secreted mere drops of the dye, which made the process tedious. To make 1.4 grams of pigment required 12,000 murex.[6] Tyre, a southern port in Lebanon, is an area known for manufacturing purple dye.[7] Because Solomon traded with the King of Tyre, it's reasonable to conclude that the first lady of Proverbs 31 wore purple fabric dyed in Tyre.

"You really didn't want to make the purple. You wanted to wear it, not make it," Jacqueline said.

Purple was very valuable. By choosing purple, a rare and expensive color, and selecting fine linen made by a better seamstress, the first lady of Proverbs reveals an important beauty principle. She saw herself as a person of value, worthy enough to wear valuable, even expensive clothes. We know that she took care of her body because "Her arms are strong for her tasks" (Prov. 31:17).

One of the principles behind wearing fine linen and purple is that God wants you to value your appearance. He created you in His image, so why wouldn't He want you to care for your body? He wants to polish the jewel He has created. Because He has placed you as a first lady to others, your appearance is also important to those around you.

"The Proverbs 31 woman was someone who really was putting her best foot forward and by supporting the image of her family, her husband is well respected," Jacqueline said. "She is like a first lady dressing appropriately, supporting her presidential husband's image by having a proper image for herself."[8]

Mamie Eisenhower is a good example of a woman who valued her appearance and her clothes. She struck a balance between wearing fine purple linen and inexpensive garb. Her closet was a rainbow spanning the arc from made-to-order couture to off-the-rack clothes. I loved the way Susan Eisenhower described her grandmother's wardrobe. She wrote, "There was a democracy to her closet." She noted that Mamie wore a wide range of hats, handbags, gloves, dresses, and gowns from J.C. Penney to New York couture. She treated each the same, hanging them on padded hangers perfumed with sachets.[9]

Mamie was aware of how her image reflected on her husband, his policies, and the nation's reputation of strength. When her husband, President Dwight Eisenhower, decided to host a White House dinner for the chairman of the Soviet Union, Mamie turned to a New York designer, Arnold Scaasi, for help. She needed the right attire for hosting the enemy during the cold war.

"Why don't you wear a gold dress to emphasize that we are a rich and powerful country," Scaasi said when they met to discuss her dress.[10] He designed a strapless gold damask dress. Mamie wore it, adding long white kid gloves to the ensemble.

Mamie was attracted to Scaasi's work not because it was expensive, but because he understood and valued her uniqueness.

Since then, nearly fifty years later, Scaasi has created custom clothes for very different women. From movie stars to nuns, he has designed dresses with an eye for their inclinations and special occasions. His design philosophy underscores the meaning behind wearing fine linen and purple. "You have to know their lifestyle and, very often, become part of it," he wrote.[11]

You don't have to wear Scaasi or expensive clothes to show that you value your appearance.

"It [fine linen and purple] doesn't mean you have to wear designer clothes. It doesn't mean that you have to curl your hair every time you go out the door. But it just means, I think, putting your best foot forward and taking a healthy pride in your appearance for yourself, for your family, for your husband, for the image you are projecting to the world," Jacqueline said.

"It doesn't have to be expensive. You can take the most humble item of clothing and make sure it's washed and pressed. If you have only one piece of clothing, you can do that every day."

Valuing your appearance doesn't mean that you have to have a supermodel figure. Movie stars are not more valuable because they are fit. The principle is that your image, your body is valuable to God, regardless of who you are, what shape you have, or what flaws you may see. Your body is precious, a gift from God. "Do you not know that your body is a temple of the Holy Spirit, who is in you, whom you have received from God?" (1 Cor. 6:19).

Barbara Hill is an image consultant based in the Washington, D.C., area. She has analyzed many faces and figures to help people learn their best colors and styles. Through her business, Bridal Artistry, she helps brides-to-be choose the best makeup colors to match their complexion, their gown, and the color scheme of the wedding. Her wardrobe and makeup clients range from stay-at-home moms to business execs. She once held a private consultation with a member of the Saudi Arabian royal family.

Before becoming a mom and starting her own business, Barbara worked for a nonprofit organization that received grants from the U.S. State Department to plan events and trips for foreign leaders who visited Washington at the invitation of U.S. embassies abroad. Meeting dozens of foreign leaders of tremendous influence clarified her understanding of people and their value.

"One thing that job taught me was that we are all people created by God. There are no special people (who) are born to be president of a country. Every person has assets and flaws. It takes a lot to get me awed with a person just because of (his or her) position," Barbara said.

As an image consultant, Barbara has seen many women who lack confidence in their appearance. "They often don't understand that when you look nice and present yourself well, you are more approachable," she said.

People are attracted to you when you are confident in your own skin, the skin that God created.

"Some people don't see themselves made in the image of God. They see themselves somehow as inadequate in different ways. They don't see themselves created uniquely. Many people don't see themselves as a beautiful person. They don't feel like they can be made beautiful," she said.

When you value your image and understand that your physical body comes from God, then you have a responsibility to care for it and wrap it in beauty.

"We're honoring God's creation and we're honoring ourselves as the creation of God by taking care of ourselves as well as our family," Barbara said.

If you owned the largest, rarest diamond in the world, you wouldn't put it in a Ziploc bag or hide it in a bright orange Tupperware bowl. No, you would display it over black velvet in a locked glass case for everyone to see, but not touch. The purple linen principle is much the same way. "Do not give dogs what is sacred; do not throw your pearls to pigs. If you do, they may trample them under their feet, and then turn and tear you to pieces" (Matt. 7:6). Your body is precious and unique.

"What image are you projecting? What message are you sending? Are you sending the message you want to send?" Barbara said. She asks these same questions of her clients because they are helpful in evaluating image and appearance.

"Some people want to project a flamboyant persona. Now, if you are flamboyant and want to send that message, then have at it. But don't expect people to see you as a more subdued person or as a professional who can be trusted to give a thoughtful and well-thought-out reply," she said.

When choosing makeup and clothing, one question to ask is, "Does it cross over the line of being a distraction?"

"If something is tasteful and well done, it will not be a distraction. You won't think, 'All I remember is that her eye makeup was too dark.' Or 'All I remember is that she wore the most ridiculously heavy jewelry,'" Barbara said.

Doing too little or nothing at all is also a distraction.

"Have you ever talked with someone who didn't wear any makeup and their skin was all uneven or there was something distracting about them . . . their eyes were very big but their eyebrows were so blond they didn't show up. All you could see were big irises. There was no shaping to the eye," Barbara said.

"The expectation in a professional environment is that a person will look professional. And you look professional when you look put together," she said.

Striking a balance between distraction, too much on one end and too little on the other, helps people to see the real you. Extreme makeovers need not be extreme.

An example would be "if you remember the person and you say, 'She was just charming.' Like people said about Jackie Kennedy. She was just charming. She was a good listener, reached out to other people. She certainly was one who had a quiet confidence. I don't know if she was a believer (in Christ) or not, but she lived in a reasonable way, and a way that was honoring to her husband,". Barbara said.

Another way to think of your image is to use your appearance to tell a story, your story, highlighting the unique assets that God has given you.

When Hollywood costume designer Oleg Cassini became Jacqueline Kennedy's primary designer, he learned that designing clothes for the first lady was different from designing costumes for the dozens of movies he had made. She had her own distinct story.

"I was trained to dress the individual," he told *Women's Wear Daily* in 1964. "I learned that the story dictates the fashion. The Kennedy story was an extremely elegant one, and you could not experiment."[12]

Cassini started Jacqueline's fashion story by making suggestions for her inaugural wardrobe. She chose one of his gray-beige suits for the swearing-in ceremony. This understated suit set her apart from the other women and men on stage. Their jeweled-tone suits looked dark on the black-and-white television sets of the 1960s. Jackie's light beige suit with two oversized buttons made her stand out among the crowd. She "popped" on television.

Jackie's wardrobe continued to tell her story. She chose fabrics and colors that were appropriate to the occasion. They spoke loudly and served as a perfect foil to her whispery voice and private personality. Jackie talked with her wardrobe, showing she valued herself and others by what she wore.

On her first international trip, she greeted the Royal Canadian Mounted Police in Canada. Jackie wore a five-year-old red wool twill suit by Pierre Cardin. Her ensemble created a picture-perfect moment because it matched the mounted police, famous for their vibrant red uniforms and gold buttons. The images showed up well in color photographs, and the editors of *Life* chose to showcase the event on the magazine's cover.[13]

Jackie's story took her all over the world. President Kennedy suspected the Soviets were making under-the-table deals with India, and he needed to send a message that the United States was also interested in India. So he sent Jackie on a "cultural tour." Her wardrobe spoke what she couldn't say. While taking a boat ride on Lake Pichola to the palace in Udaipur, India, Jackie wore an apricot suit with a matching coat. The material was silk zibeline, a sturdy but shiny fabric that could withstand the heat while reflecting the sun. The color and texture of her dress made her instantly identifiable to the Indian onlookers who crowded the distant shore. Through her wardrobe, the first lady made her presence, and America's interest in India, known.[14]

Today, American women often pay big bucks to put their best face forward. The resources to do so are incredible. From surgical face-lifts to nonsurgical chemical peels, U.S. physicians and surgeons performed nearly 11.9 million cosmetic procedures totaling $12.5 billion in 2004. Ninety percent of their patients were women. The most popular nonsurgical procedure was Botox injections, which increased by 764 percent from 1997 to 2004.[15] The desire to look youthful and beautiful is intense and expensive.

Now I'm not saying that Botox is bad or that you shouldn't splurge on facials or cosmetic treatments. But don't work so hard on your outer appearance that you forget to focus on the beauty that doesn't fade with age. Inner beauty has the potential to get better as the years go by. Harriet Lane was beautiful on the outside, in large part, because she took care of the inside.

Harriet also lived during a time of extreme makeover pressure. She survived the era of Scarlett O'Hara extravagance. Much like the pressure to have a supermodel figure today, the 1850s were years of extremes in beauty, particularly in fashion.

Before she was first lady, Harriet accompanied her uncle and supported him in his role as U.S. ambassador to England. He advised her to buy her dresses from Paris because the women of Europe dressed less extravagantly than the women in America. He wrote, "You will, of course, have no dresses made in the United States. I am not a very close observer or an accurate judge, but I think the ladies here of the very highest rank do not dress as expensively, with the exception of jewels, as those in the United States."

Harriet described one of these "less extravagant dresses" to a friend after she wore it to a party hosted by the Queen of England.

"I wore a pink silk petticoat, overskirt of pink tulle, puffed and trimmed with wreath of apple blossoms; train of pink silk trimmed with blond and apple blossoms and so was the body. Headdress— apple blossoms, lace lappet, and feathers. Her Majesty was very gracious to me yesterday as was also the Prince," Harriet wrote.[16]

If this dress was less extravagant than American clothes, can you imagine what the high society ladies of Washington and New York wore to a party? The Southern aristocracy ruled the social and fashion world, especially in the nation's capital. Many members of Congress felt the pressure to out-entertain and outdress. This cost some of them a small fortune, as much as $750,000 a year.[17] That Harriet, not a Southerner, was able to assume the role of first lady without criticism, and even flattery, from the society ladies of her day was a remarkable achievement.

Mrs. Roger Pryor, a contemporary of Harriet's, complimented her in a book that she wrote about the Civil War. "And she (Harriet) had exquisite taste in dress. She never wore many ornaments, many flowers, nor the billows of ruffles then in fashion. I remember her in white tulle, with a wreath of clematis; in soft brown or blue silk; in much white muslin, dotted, and plain, with blue ribbons run in puffs on skirt and bodice."[18]

Harriet knew how to put her best foot forward, and she learned it from an unusual source: her uncle. He taught her the virtues of balancing outer and inner beauty.

By the time Harriet was nine years old, she had lost both of her parents. Harriet and her siblings went to live with their mother's brother, Uncle Nunc, at his home in Wheatland, Pennsylvania. He soon discovered that Harriet's mischievous and fun-loving personality needed shaping and taming for her to become a proper young woman. James Buchanan sent his "out-setting" niece to a private school.

When he learned of her misbehavior at the school, he corrected twelve-year-old Harriet by writing, "Education and accomplishments are very important, but they sink into insignificance when compared with the proper government of the heart and temper."[19]

He later sent Harriet to finishing school at the convent at Georgetown while he lived nearby in Washington and served in Congress. Here, her inner beauty matured her heart. She "acquitted herself so handsomely"[20] from the convent that Buchanan trusted his niece to enter Washington society, but not without a warning. He wrote:

> Keep your eyes about you in the gay scenes through which you are destined to pass, and take care to do nothing and say nothing of which you have cause to repent. Above all be on your guard against flattery; and should you receive it, "let it pass into one ear gracefully and out at the other." Many a clever girl has been spoiled for the useful purposes of life and rendered unhappy by a winter's gaiety in Washington. I know that Mrs. Pleasanton (a family friend) will take care of you and prevent you from running into an extravagance. Still it is necessary that, with the blessing of Providence, you should take care of yourself.[21]

Harriet's inner beauty won her uncle's trust. He relied on her in England and asked her to serve as his White House hostess. He called upon her to help him host the first Japanese delegation to visit the United States. Harriet's Japanese guests called her a "queen of beauty." She also joined her uncle in hosting Prince Edward VII, the first member of the British royal family to visit the White House. The prince's visit was a symbol that the United States and Britain were friends and no longer enemies. Harriet carried herself so well that she again earned high praise from Queen Victoria, the prince's mother. Perhaps Harriet charmed the prince in the first seven seconds of meeting him.

"In the first seven seconds the first impression is made through our outer appearance," Barbara Hill told me. "Taking care of one's outer beauty really 'buys time' so that, hopefully, others will come to recognize the inner beauty and character that the Lord has been refining. To me, that is a very good reason to pay particular attention to your appearance."[22]

Barbara says the inner beauty will trump the outer beauty every time, but it takes longer for people to see the inner beauty. It's a balance between both, but as inner beauty ages, the wrinkles fade. "It (your beauty) should be that of your inner self, the unfading beauty of a gentle and quiet spirit, which is of great worth in God's sight" (1 Pet. 3:4).

When I first worked in the White House, I had recently moved from Texas. It didn't take me long to discover the fashion differences between Washington, D.C., and Austin. The most striking difference was color. I could walk down the halls to my office in the Texas capitol in a red or teal suit and fit right in. But walking down the halls in the White House in either color made me stand out too much. I love wearing red.

Although Bill Blass once said, "When in doubt wear red," I still doubted. I began to wonder if my red suits were a distraction when so many White House women staffers wore neutrals and shades of black, brown, and blue. I didn't have the clout of a senior officer who could get away with wearing brighter colors more easily. I eventually decided that I would save my red skirt and jacket for my last day on the job!

Red is a color many first ladies have turned to over the years. This vivid color also has brought recent first ladies together for a cause that uses outerwear to draw attention to innerwear, the heart. The red dress is the symbol for Heart Truth, a national campaign to inform women about heart disease. Cardiovascular disease is a leading cause of death among women. Each year nearly half a million American women die from cardiovascular disease, about 60,000 more than men. Democrat and Republican first ladies all donated one of their favorite red dresses for the First Ladies Red Dress Collection to draw attention to this national campaign for heart health.

Laura Bush hosted Nancy Reagan at the unveiling of the First Ladies Red Dress Collection at the Kennedy Center in May 2005. Nancy donated a red lace Oscar de la Renta evening gown that she wore when Queen Elizabeth presented President Ronald Reagan with the Order of the Bath. Hillary Clinton wore her donated red dress on Valentine's Day and to one of her husband's speeches to Congress. Barbara Bush wore her red dress, designed by Arnold Scaasi, to a state dinner. Rosalynn Carter and Betty Ford wore their dresses many times to everyday events, while Lady Bird Johnson wore hers to celebrate her eightieth birthday. Laura Bush wore her red suit to the Bolshoi Ballet in Moscow.[23] The First Ladies Red Dress Collection also featured information about heart health. Viewers of the display could enjoy seeing the dresses while learning that taking care of your heart never goes out of style.

The heart truth about beauty is much the same. The outer appearance points the way to the heart, revealing the jewel within.

One of the most beautiful portraits of a first lady is of Grace Coolidge. In her official portrait, she wore a rich ruby red 1920s gown with the White House in the background and her dog by her side. Her husband was originally supposed to sit for the artist, but he was too busy. Grace agreed to pose instead. She had learned long ago that her husband didn't tolerate idleness for very long. He taught her that sometimes in life, you have to hackle flax.

CHAPTER THREE

Eager Beavers

"She selects wool and flax and works with eager hands"
(Prov. 31:13).

W HEN GRACE married Calvin Coolidge, she knew she had hitched herself to a man of thrift. But she had no idea just how frugal the Coolidge clan was until she had children.

"Savings accounts were started with a five dollar gold piece placed in a fist of each baby by Grandfather Coolidge as a test. If the child held it tightly clasped, he would be frugal; if he allowed it to slip from his fingers, the propensities of a spendthrift were indicated," she wrote.[1]

Grace also discovered the Coolidges were a colony of eager beavers. When her son, Calvin Jr., became a young teen, his father arranged for him to work in the tobacco fields. He was working there when his father became president. A boy said to him, "Gee, if my father were president of the United States, I wouldn't be working in the tobacco field." Calvin replied, "If my father were your father, you would."[2]

A hundred dollars will not purchase what ten formerly would," Abigail wrote as she opened her latest letter to her husband.

The wife of John Adams sat alone at a table in their house with only her pen, paper, and accounting diary to keep her company.

Abigail wrote a few more lines and then pulled her homespun shawl more tightly around her shoulders to comfort her. She wasn't sure which was more chilling, the December cold outside or her finances.

Even Cousin Tufts has had to raise the prices on the goods he sells me, and he only recently became a merchant, she reasoned.

Although Abigail lived within the booming cannons of Boston, her personal war was as much for financial solvency as it was for independence from Britain. Her daily battles were clashes of plus and minus signs. Whenever possible she employed frugality as her weapon against debt's red line.

I never will borrow if any other method can be devised.

Abigail had repeated her pledge as often as she had breathed since John asked her to manage their farm four years earlier. His frequent absences seemed longer to her than a century.

Abigail rested her pen in the inkwell. Then she picked up her accounting diary from the table.

The best smell in the world, she thought, catching a whiff of the ledger's leather binding. She smiled. Since she was a girl perusing her grandfather's library of Shakespeare and Milton, book covers were her favorite scent.

Abigail opened the book and scanned her log's most recent entry. "Common sugar is 200 pounds per hundred, cider is 12 pounds a barrel. I can't purchase a single sixpence worth of anything," she said with frustration. Abigail picked up her pen and copied the information into her letter to John.

She knew her accounts merely mirrored the Revolution's swells of inflation, but she took her responsibility seriously. When John became a delegate to the Continental Congress in 1774, he had to give up his law practice. Someone needed to manage their four children and the farm, their only other source of income. At times Abigail felt more yoked to husbandry than to her husband.

She had written John that she hoped to be as good a farmeress as he was a statesman in Philadelphia. But her problems attacked her faster than weeds could pop up in untilled fields. For four years she had endured labor shortages, terse tenants, price inflation, and disease. Nothing, not even John's compliment that their neighbors were more pleased with her management than his, could make her enjoy farming.

Her problems had worsened earlier in the year when Congress sent John to France to negotiate a peace treaty with Britain. Not only was her love and best friend overseas, but his absence also meant more farming for her. She made a decision. Abigail employed her Yankee ingenuity and rented the farm to a more qualified caretaker.

Abigail stared at her accounting diary. She felt she could not complain. Heaven had blessed her with fine crops. But the minus signs worried her. Inflation threatened to send her into poverty. She had to do something to improve her finances. She had to find more plus signs.

"Frugality, industry, and economy are the lessons of the day. At least they must be so for me or my small boat will suffer shipwreck," she said, snapping shut her accounting log.

Abigail stood, picked up the diary, and carried it to a nearby cabinet. As she placed the book on the shelf, a coin fell to the floor. She picked up the nickel, which felt as cold as the icicles on her window. Then she tossed it into the air.

"There's no sort of property that is held in higher estimation than money. I must find a way to earn more of it," she whispered.

She caught the coin as it succumbed to Newton's law and rubbed her fingers over its solid surface.

"Hard money like this is what I need. Paper money is not even worth the paper," she said, trembling.

Her arched eyebrows rose even higher into her forehead as she thought about her terrible encounter with paper money. A band of villains had dispersed counterfeit money last year. When she discovered she had five pounds of it in her pouch, she felt ill, knowing that greed and corruption had touched her innocent fingers. She vowed to only trust hard money after that.

Abigail glanced at the cabinet, which held her treasure chest of books, china, and ink bottles. A piece of paper containing the familiar handwriting of her husband caught her eye. She pulled it from the shelf. As she read the letter, dated August 27, 1778, one phrase caught her attention.

"I have several times sent some things to you and shall continue to do so," she read aloud.

She paused.

Of course! Parisian goods, French merchandise, Abigail thought.

Abigail scanned the room. Her eyes darted to a cup and saucer that John had shipped to her from Paris. Then she scurried throughout the house, collecting all of the items John had sent. She returned to her table. Her hands eagerly sorted them into two categories: essentials to keep and goods to sell.

"We don't need all of these," she said hurriedly, placing more items in the sales pile. "One new dress and a handkerchief for me will do. The children can keep one item as well. We have what we need. The rest will earn hard money, and I know who will help me sell them."

Abigail sat at her table and grabbed her pen and another sheet of paper. She made a list of items that John could purchase for her, such as calico dresses of different colors, tea, china, and other products.

"In your last letter you mention having sent some articles," she added in her letter to John. "There is no remittance you can make me which will turn to a better account than goods, more especially such articles as I enclose a list of."

She refreshed her pen and continued.

"Doctor Tufts' son has lately set up in trade; whatever I receive more than is necessary for family use I can put into his hands, which will serve both him and myself," she wrote.

After penning a few more lines, Abigail closed the letter and dated it December 13, 1778.

Ingenuity has won the day's battle. I'm going to be a merchant, a woman of wares. Abigail smiled as she continued to ponder. *Now I can afford to relax and read a good book.*[3]

Onc December afternoon when I was working for the White House, I decided to find a vending machine. I walked into the wide hallway of the Eisenhower Executive Office Building and realized that no one else was around. As I approached the intersection of the hall and the base of the arched stairway leading to the second floor, a nickel literally fell from the ceiling and hit the floor in front of me. My first thought was that someone walking down the stairs dropped the nickel. I glanced up and saw a robust man with thick white hair descending the stairs. I recognized him as Newt Gingrich, the former Speaker of the House of Representatives.

"Did you drop a nickel?" I called when he reached the bottom of the stairs.

"No," he said as he came over to me. I picked the nickel off of the floor and explained how it had fallen from the ceiling.

"It doesn't work that way," Speaker Gingrich said. "Money from the government doesn't fall from the sky and into your pocketbook."

I laughed, and he walked away. I concluded that the nickel had been lodged among some of the computer wires concealed in the grooves of the ceiling. Somehow it came loose and succumbed to gravity's grip.

Abigail Adams also knew that money was not going to fall from the sky and into her accounting diary. Her hard work and courage during the Revolutionary War have inspired generations of Americans. When John Adams became the first vice president and second president of the United States, Abigail became one of the most admired women of her generation in part because of her character. Her work ethic reveals several principles found in Proverbs 31, such as eagerness, entrepreneurship, and excellence. She shows what it means to "select wool and flax and work with eager hands" (Prov. 31:13).

Wool and flax were the raw materials of the ancient world. Selecting wool and flax was similar to many ordinary tasks today— fun the first few times, but boring after time. Choosing flax meant hackling fibers or separating the longer strands from shorter ones. The longer ones were suitable for spinning and making linen. Hackling was monotonous.

Choosing wool and flax also stunk. Buying wool required bartering with a wool carder, who smelled like sheep. Wool carders cut the wool from sheep, washed it in hot water, and then untangled or combed it. They were also often viewed as being on the raw end of society because they sold wool to women. Imagine working with a man who was considered a lowlife because he traded with you, a woman.[4]

By eagerly selecting wool and flax, the Proverbs 31 woman approached the most boring, unpleasant part of her work with eagerness. "She sets about her work vigorously" (Prov. 31:17).

Although Abigail discovered she didn't like being a farmer, she approached it diligently. Farming to her was as tedious as selecting wool and flax was to the woman of Proverbs 31. Abigail's stick-to-itiveness showed her eagerness and commitment to perform a mind-numbing job as long as she had to.

The U.S. Department of Labor estimates that women will make up 48 percent of the workforce by 2008.[5] With so many employed women, no wonder our society often supersizes our value and importance based on where we work and what we do. Among the first questions people often ask when they meet someone new is, "What do you do?" or "Where do you work?" First-time expecting moms often face questions of what they plan to do about their job when their baby comes. Will they continue to stay employed? Will they be a stay-at-home mom? Is there an option somewhere in between?

The work of your hands matters to God. The debate in Proverbs 31 is not where this woman worked. She is not praised because she works at home. She is not praised because she works in the textile business outside her home. She is praised because she does her work vigorously and eagerly. The emphasis is not on where she works, but on how she works. The value for work is not found in a location. You give value to your work by how you approach it.

What I find refreshing about Proverbs 31 is that the primary principle for work, no matter what you do or where you do it, is simple. God asks that you approach your work eagerly. He cares about your work. Your value is not in the job you hold or which rung of the career ladder you grasp. It doesn't matter if your boss is your best friend or your worst enemy. Whether you're the CEO of a jewelry company or merely minding the store, your attitude about work reveals your heart. You give value to your work by performing it with a willing heart and an eager attitude. Ecclesiastes 9:10 puts it this way: "Whatever your hand finds to do, do it with all your might." If you can't do your job eagerly, then maybe it's time to either change your attitude or find something you can do with all your might.

When Abigail Adams realized John wasn't coming home anytime soon to take over their farm, she outsourced the responsibility to another manager. In this way she kept her promise to John to manage the farm while finding other sources of income. Abigail became a successful merchant. Much like commerce today, she took what was unique to her, Parisian goods, and matched it with a need in the marketplace. The venture provided her with hard money while giving her purpose in her work. Her family survived the Revolution because of her resourcefulness and eagerness. By taking advantage of the opportunity God gave her, she employed another principle for work found in Proverbs 31: entrepreneurship.

The Jewish economy was mostly self-sufficient. Each household grew and made all of the food and clothing it needed. Had the Proverbs 31 woman simply made enough clothes for her family, she would have met society's expectations for her, but she went further. She turned her hands to the marketplace. Verse 24 says, "She makes linen garments and sells them, and supplies the merchants with sashes." She employed the principle of entrepreneurship or opportunity.

Perhaps one day she walked through the marketplace and saw a merchant selling his sashes. Maybe she stroked a blue sash with her fingertips to study the grain of the cloth. She picked it up and held it to the sunlight to check the dye's saturation. Then she had an idea. She had some extra cloth and knew she could make a better product. She saw an opportunity to work with eager hands and seized it.

"She is using the wool and the flax to make the linen, and she is selling the fabric and things of that nature. So you know you're talking about a lady who is a tradeswoman who is adding financially to her family," Jacqueline Phelan told me.[6]

Just as she explained to me the significance of fine linen and purple, Jacqueline also helped me understand the significance of textiles in biblical times.

"In ancient times, textiles, fabrics such as linen, were part of your portfolio of wealth. It's not like today where people have clothing and blankets," she said. "It's not even the same as having a Chanel suit. Your textiles were actual items of wealth, such as your landholdings or your herds of cattle. Textiles were very expensive."

The Proverbs 31 first lady was not simply a spinner of wool who filled her family's closet. While working with eager hands, she took advantage of unexpected opportunities that God gave her to make linen garments and sashes for the marketplace. She employed the principle of entrepreneurship. It's easy to assume that entrepreneurship means running your own business. It does, but the principle behind it is much broader. A spiritual principle for entrepreneurship is learning to take advantage of the opportunities God opens for you.

First ladies have often found themselves in a unique position to lasso unexpected opportunities. A new president and first lady often hear the ticking clock as soon as they step into the White House. They know they have a once in a lifetime chance to serve the American people, and they had better make the most of it. Never again will they have this much influence, power, and visibility.

The media starts evaluating the president's success at the end of his first one hundred days. Then they write about his first year. Then they measure his popularity based on the outcome of the midterm election the following year. Television reporters hype the

next presidential election through the lens of the current administration, and so on. There's an urgent pace, knowing that four years is
never enough time to do all that a president and first lady would like
to do. As a result, many first ladies work with eager hands while
keeping their eyes focused on opportunity.

When President George W. Bush was running for reelection in
2004, his wife evaluated the job of first lady. At a campaign stop at
the University of Nevada, Laura Bush described the importance of
working eagerly and taking advantage of opportunity.

"As we've lived (in the White House) for three years and as I've
studied more and more history and looked into the lives of the
women who lived (there) before me, I've sort of developed this idea
of responsibility that the first lady has to be constructive, to use the
time she has to be as constructive as she possibly can be for our country," she said.[7]

Laura was a teacher in the late 1970s when she met George W.
Bush, a charismatic young businessman who shared her West Texas
accent. They both grew up in Midland, Texas. Their personalities
are opposite. He's kinetic, and she's calm. They share a great sense
of humor and the bond of common values.

The Bushes remind me of another president and first lady, a
couple who served exactly a century before them. Like Laura, Edith
Roosevelt was married to a man with endless energy. She was the
calm to Theodore Roosevelt's whirlwind. Edith's days as first lady
were not only constructive but also filled with new construction.

When Theodore and Edith Roosevelt moved their six children
into the White House, they found a cramped, hundred-year-old
building dripping with heavy Victorian furnishings. Their living quarters were located on the same floor as the president's office and his
staff's offices. Edith described the situation as "living over a store."

The Roosevelts took advantage of Congress's unusual willingness to pay for a renovation. Edith worked eagerly with the architect to update and renovate the White House interior. The architect
also separated the president's living quarters from his office space.
The president and his staff moved into a new building adjacent to

the White House. You've probably heard of the extension. It's now called the West Wing.

With the renovation complete, Edith could have easily relaxed and enjoyed her success. Theodore described Edith as ". . . wise as mistress of the White House and is very happy with it."

But an opportunity came along in January 1905 that Edith couldn't refuse. She employed the Proverbs 31 principle of entrepreneurship. She stepped out of her domestic bounds and into diplomatic ties. This time, she eagerly worked to construct peace.

Russia and Japan were at war. Theodore Roosevelt wanted to find a way to solve the conflict before it became a world war involving the United States. He turned to a friend he and Edith had met on their honeymoon in London years earlier. Cecil Spring Rice was a British diplomat to Russia. Roosevelt invited Cecil to a private dinner at his summer home in New York. Roosevelt discovered that his British friend's knowledge of what was going on in Russia was exactly what he needed. There was a problem. Because Cecil was a foreign diplomat, any written correspondence with him had to go through official channels.

Theodore, Cecil, and Edith devised a plan. When Cecil obtained new information about Russia, he wrote a letter to Edith. By writing Edith instead of the president, he could bypass the British foreign office and the U.S. State Department and, at the same time, provide Roosevelt with the information he needed. Edith passed on each letter from Cecil to her husband.[8]

Through her quiet work, this pearl helped her husband to shine. President Roosevelt hosted peace talks with Japan and Russia. His success earned him the Nobel Peace Prize. Without Edith's willingness to participate, he might have failed. By taking advantage of an unexpected opportunity in the realm of diplomacy, Edith employed the broader principle of entrepreneurship.

So often we plan our lives. We go to school, we choose a career, and off we go with high expectations. Sometimes life disappoints us. Bosses, human resource directors, and coworkers frustrate our plans or make life difficult. Sometimes a major merger results in losing a job we love. God's purpose for us is more than we can imagine. Our job is to be open to the opportunities He places before us. We are to accept that His ways are not always our ways. "No eye has seen, no ear has heard, no mind has conceived what God has prepared for those who love him" (1 Cor. 2:9).

When my husband and I became engaged, we planned our lives and careers. We enjoyed college so much that we decided to spend the rest of our lives working as college administrators. We went to graduate school to earn advanced degrees in university administration. I was going to work in a university's press or communications office, and my husband was going to focus on university recruiting and admissions. We married and four months later we went to graduate school at Texas A&M University. When we got there, we discovered God had prepared something different for us, something I never dreamed or wanted to do.

One night my husband shared with me his desire to work in politics. I was not happy. My family had always "voted for the man, not the party," and I had no interest in politics. When I realized how serious my husband was, I decided to explore the possibility. I began to read about politics. I listened to lectures, including a speech at Texas A&M given by the governor of Texas. George W. Bush talked about his family, faith, and views on education, welfare, and tax reform. God planted a seed that night, and I became more willing to employ the principle of entrepreneurship. The idea grew on me, and I became open to my husband's dream and the opportunities God placed before us.

After I finished my master's degree, I became an event planner for the university's media office. I worked so my husband could finish his PhD. At the time, the campus was abuzz over a construction project. Former President George H. W. Bush was building his presidential library at Texas A&M. I had the opportunity to serve on a committee to plan some of the opening events for the presidential library center.

This and other experiences led me to work in the governor's office and my husband to work for a state representative and then for an agency housed in the governor's office, which ultimately led to opportunities in Washington. Because we were open to God's plan for our work, He blessed us. Our eyes could not see what God had planned for us.

Sometimes God's opportunities are quiet and simple. He often uses our work to rinse and scrub our talents and character. Sometimes He gives us opportunities to make a difference in the lives of our coworkers, employees, or bosses. He doesn't want us to barricade our brains or hide our jewels in a box. He wants us to keep our eyes open for opportunities to be used by Him so we can shine.

Eagerness and entrepreneurship wouldn't be complete without excellence, another Proverbs 31 principle for work. "She is like the merchant ships, bringing her food from afar" (Prov. 31:14).

Most of the book of Proverbs comes from the sayings of King Solomon. Although some scholars suggest that someone else wrote Proverbs 31, likely the Proverbs 31 woman lived during or after the times of Solomon. King Solomon was quite the entrepreneur. He sent his trade ships throughout the Mediterranean. These ships brought gold, silver, ivory, and even baboons to the Proverbs 31 woman's world.

The ancient Hebrew diet of bread, fruits, and vegetables probably became a little stale after a while. Trading with merchants gave the first lady of Proverbs 31 an opportunity to expand her family's food palette. Through trade she became a gourmet cook. Maybe she bartered bundles of linen for some exotic fish. The principle here is that she infused something special, something excellent into her cooking when she could.

God values excellence. His instructions to the Jews for building the temple included fine and valuable materials, such as gold, silver, and bronze. He asked skilled craftsmen, embroiderers, woodworkers, stonecutters, and goldsmiths to build the tabernacle and its curtain, poles, tents, and bases. If God expected excellence in His home improvement project, why wouldn't He want us, created in His image, to pursue excellence in constructing our lives? He delights in excellence. "Whatever is true, whatever is noble, whatever is right, whatever is pure, whatever is lovely, whatever is admirable—if anything is excellent or praiseworthy—think about such things" (Phil. 4:8).

Helen Taft is a great example of a woman who incorporated excellence into her work. Helen turned the White House inside out in her first six weeks as first lady in the spring of 1909. She had lived in Washington for several years as a cabinet secretary's wife, which gave her the chance to observe White House operations. One of her first decisions was to hire a new housekeeper to tidy up the mess left by the rambunctious Roosevelt children. Another problem she saw was the confusion tourists had about visiting the White House. Helen ordered a livery to stand guard twenty-four hours a day at the north door to answer questions and direct tourists to the correct entrance.[9]

Helen was also a techie of her time. She eagerly embraced the new world of motorcars and machines. She saw how new technologies could add quality and efficiency to life. As a result, she saved time by changing the way the housekeepers cleaned the silverware, not by hand but by machine.

Helen's taste for quality literally led her to bring her food from afar. "Afar" in her case was New York. She made some inquiries and discovered that one of the best chefs in the nation worked for one of the wealthiest men in the nation, J. P. Morgan of New York. Helen hired away Morgan's Swedish chef to oversee the White House menus.

Her quest for excellence earned her high praise, jewels in her crown, from a critical source. The *Washington Post* said she was the "best fitted woman to ever hold the position."[10]

Today, we live in a world of gadgets and gizmos. We can easily confuse excellence with the perfection found on our computers and phones. Perfection and excellence are not the same. God wants us to pursue excellence in our work, but He doesn't want us to obsess over the chip in a stained-glass window. Philippians 4:8 doesn't say, "if anything is *perfect* or praiseworthy." It says, "if anything is *excellent* or praiseworthy—think about such things."

Pam Colton of Vienna, Virginia, is a wife and mother of two grown children. When I first told Pam about this book, she explained that Proverbs 31 has been a sample pattern for her. I admire Pam because she strives to honor God through all areas of her life, especially the work of her hands. She understands how hard it is to work with eager hands at both work and home. She also knows how to keep her eyes on the Lord for His opportunities in life and to serve Him with excellence.

Pam's career spans thirty-five years. For the past nine years she has worked for Coopers and Lybrand, which became Pricewaterhouse-Coopers Consulting, which became part of IBM Consulting. She also worked for twenty years in the government, including nine years at the Pentagon. In between her work at the Pentagon and the corporate world, Pam worked with eager hands as a homemaker and as a president, secretary and treasurer, and manager of three separate but simultaneous small businesses.

"It is still a man's workplace. In order to be in a senior position, you quite often have to choose work over family. You have to be reachable by cell phone at all times. Vacations quite often have to be canceled. If you choose not to take on extra work assignments, you are viewed as not being a team player. The old saying (is that) those who do the work continue to be asked to do more," Pam told me, noting that she prays, plays Christian music on her computer, and often bites her tongue to keep her attitude in check at work when the pressures mount.

"When I forget my priorities, the Holy Spirit very gently reminds me that I am taking on too much and I need to let go and spend more time with the Lord. It is amazing and yet comforting to know that I am never alone and His purpose will come forth if I remember that I am here to do His work and enjoy the journey," she said.

Pam explained that her hands are always moving. If she gets a chance to sit down without a computer, she crochets or creates one of her fabric corsages. Although she's never really bored, she understands how to tackle and hackle jobs that are dry and difficult.

"My advice about eagerly taking on a boring job: make it a game of how quickly and accurately you can get it accomplished. If you can figure out a way, divide it up among your workmates. Idle hands are the devil's workplace, and he has no place in my life," she said.

Sixteen years ago, an opportunity came to Pam that she never expected. She was already a mother to her son, but the Lord answered her prayer for another child. She faced the decision of whether to continue working in the marketplace or to stay at home with her daughter.

"I have been blessed in the workplace. I was on a career ladder when God told us to adopt a little girl. The month I was to be again promoted, I told my boss that God's calling on my life came before a career and that (God) would provide the finances for the expensive adoption and our new season in life," Pam said. "My boss understood and wished me well. I worked for one month after we returned home with Kelly."

In that same year, an opportunity came along that provided for their finances. Their home was sold in a land deal. This was yet another example of God's provision. The settlement allowed her family to move into a home that was more than they ever dreamed of owning. Even though they didn't have much money for decorating or vacationing, they were happy.

"I have never tried to go through the door when (God) closed it. And so many times, I have seen where my obedience has saved me from heartache. Some jobs were abolished. In one instance, I broke my leg. My job let me work from home whenever I needed to, whereas starting a new job and working from home would not have been an option," Pam said.

Pam believes the key to being a Proverbs 31 worker and woman requires a non-me attitude in a world where the prevailing philosophy is "it's all about me."

"It can't be all about me. God's children need to be all about him," Pam said, explaining that her work habits affect those around her, particularly her bosses, and serve as a witness of her faith in God and Christ. Excellence matters.

"Whatever I do, I do it as unto God as if He were in the room and visible by everyone," she said.

I have one more story to share about working with eager hands, entrepreneurship, and excellence. When I was working for President Bush in the White House, my first book, *Maggie Houston: My Father's Honor,* was published. I had signed the contract before joining the White House staff, but the book was not available until the fall of 2002. I was scheduled to speak about it at the Texas Book Festival in Austin, but I didn't receive my copies of the book until the night before I was to fly to Austin. I took one book with me to work the next morning. I was so excited that I decided to go upstairs and show it to my friends in the White House Photo Office.

I left my office and walked onto the first floor hallway of the Eisenhower Executive Office Building, which houses an auditorium where the president often speaks to large groups. The hall was empty except for a man with a curlicue cord running down his neck. He was a Secret Service agent. His presence meant that either the president or vice president was coming. Now when you are a White House staffer and the president or vice president walks down the hall, you are to stand quietly to the side and let him pass without interrupting him. However, that day I was excited, even eager, about my book! Sure enough, within seconds, President Bush bolted through the door and started walking straight toward me. An entourage followed behind him.

What should I do? I thought.

I wanted to show him my book, but I didn't want to breach protocol. I stood still but grabbed my book with both hands, held it up in front of me with the cover facing outward and then thrust it away from me for him to see it.

"What's that?" he asked as he came right up to me.

"It's my book, sir," I said. I was so nervous I forgot to address him as "Mr. President."

I quickly added, "It's about Sam Houston and his daughter," because I didn't want him to think I had written some inappropriate tell-all book about him.

He took it from me and started flipping through it.

"I need an autograph," he said.

I froze. He was asking me to sign it. Excitement and reality hit me at the same time. This was the only copy of my book, and I needed to take it with me to the airport that afternoon so I could use it at the book festival. I reasoned, if you're going to give your only copy away, I guess a good person to give it to is the president of the United States.

Then I had an idea.

"Would you like me to sign it now or later, sir?" I asked.

He stared at me with his trademark pensive look.

"Later," he said with a nod and bob of his head.

Whew, I thought as he went on his way.

I realized what a great blessing that encounter was from the Lord. He used my eager hands and heart to provide a serendipitous opportunity. The first person, other than my husband, to see my first book was the president of the United States. When I returned from the book festival, I photocopied the inside cover of my book about ten times. I practiced what I wanted to write on those copies. When I was ready, I used a Sharpie pen to write a brief message to the president, thanking him for the opportunities he had given me. With many books now at my disposal, I also wrote a short message to Laura Bush and sent a separate copy to her.

God cares about our work. He knows that more than ever, women feel pressure in today's workforce. Deadlines, performance reviews, time sheets, bosses, promotions, glass ceilings, conflicts, and even the clock itself create an environment of pressure. Whatever work God has given you, it's encouraging to embrace His simple job description of the three Es: work with eager hands, with an eye on entrepreneurship, and a heart for excellence.

Sometimes working for our families takes us to another place. Sometimes we live life on our knees.

CHAPTER FOUR

Family Focus

"She speaks with wisdom, and faithful instruction is on her tongue. She watches over the affairs of her household and does not eat the bread of idleness" (Prov. 31:26, 27).

DURING HIS service to President William Howard Taft as his chief military aide, Major Archibald Butt wrote a letter to his sister-in-law that would have made his mother proud. It also would have made her cry.

> It is Sunday, and I have been to church and feel so much better for it. Sometimes I feel compelled to go to church. I do not know whether it is superstition, fear of something to come, or merely to keep in touch with what I have been associated with so long, or merely that the atmosphere of the church brings me in closer touch with mother. I know I never think of her without thinking of her faith and her church and her desire to have us keep in touch with it. Isn't it wonderful how the wishes of a good woman survive so strongly after she has gone?[1]

As with all mothers, Archie's mom had no idea what her son would face in life, but she left him a legacy of faith that he could draw upon wherever hc went. One place Archie decided to go was

Europe. He took a vacation there and purchased a first-class ticket for the maiden voyage of Britain's latest luxury ship. Archie died when the *RMS Titanic* sank on April 14, 1912.

"Major Butt was devoted to his mother, whom he brought here to live with him," said Lieutenant Commander Palmer, a friend who found pictures of Archie's mother hanging on the walls of Archie's home after his death. "His devotion to his mother while she lived and his affectionate memory of her after her death were always touching."[2]

Archie's mother focused on her family. Another mother's focus also left behind a legacy of faith.

S urely he will not depart before coming to see me," Anna Harrison said as she eased her antique body upright in bed one morning in early May 1862. Although she now spent more time on her back than on her feet, the day reminded her of past partings when she stood on her porch and watched her loved ones go off to battle. She had seen many Harrisons depart for war in her eighty-five years, too many.

Anna stretched out her arm toward the bedside table. Her hands shook as she picked up the latest Cincinnati newspaper. She read an article about the Union forces and then, as usual, skipped to the names of the casualties beginning with the letter "H." She felt her chest tighten as she read, holding her breath until the end.

"No Benjamin," she whispered with relief. "And now Carter returns to his company today."

I wish I could do something for him before he leaves, but I feel I have little left to offer in my condition, she thought.

Anna put the newspaper aside. She glanced at the miniature painting of her husband, William, which held a permanent place on the table next to her Bible, still warm from an early morning use. Its pages were worn from the wear of a lifetime.

"All soldiers, just like their grandfather," she said.

With my sword and my good right arm, she thought, remembering William's response when her father asked how he would support her in marriage more than sixty years ago.

If Papa had only known he was giving my hand to the ninth president of the United States, he might not have objected so much, she mused, laughing out loud.

Anna smiled at the memory of finishing school in New York and traveling with her father to the Ohio River Valley, where she met the most handsome man in the military. William came from good Virginia stock. His father had signed the Declaration of Independence. Nothing, not her father's overprotection or the threat of Indian raids, would keep her from marrying William and living out west. The Lord worked so much to their good. William became governor of the Indiana territory, the most northern and western part of the United States in those days. She survived the pains and peril of childbirth, not once, not twice, but ten times.

Anna heard a firm knock on the door.

"Come in," she said, but her voice cracked worse than parched wood in the fireplace.

The knock came again, louder this time.

"Come in," she said as strongly as she could.

Anna smiled when Carter, her grandson, appeared in the doorway.

"I was hoping you would come," she said.

"I couldn't leave for war again without saying good-bye," Carter said as he walked to her bedside.

"You fill your blues well. Your uniform reminds me of your grandfather."

"Thank you, but my shoulders are a bit bare. Ben is the one who's made captain," he said.

"You will, too," she said.

"Perhaps. If I survive, that is."

Both paused. The silence between them spoke more loudly than any word they could utter. His wartime service and her age were an ominous combination. They didn't know if they were merely crossing the River Jordan or crossing the River Styx. Anna knew they had a better chance of seeing each other in heaven than again on earth.

"May I?" Carter said.

She nodded while he pulled a chair from a desk and moved it next to her bed. He sat in the chair and leaned so close that she could smell the scent of breakfast coffee on his breath.

"You look lovely today. The newspapers were right to name you the most handsome woman of the northwest," he said.

"You are so kind, but that was more than twenty years ago," Anna said.

She remembered how she had laughed at the newspaper's compliment of her brown eyes, liberal lips, and petite figure when William ran for president. She had thought it was quite a statement for a woman who was as old as the nation itself.

"I feel I won't live much longer," Anna said.

"You've been saying that since you were seventy. All for the good, now. All for the good," he said cheerfully.

For those who love and fear the Lord, all things shall be ordered for their good, she believed in her heart.

Anna knew she had a million reasons to repeat that Scripture throughout her life. Her mother had died when she was just a year old. Her father, a Colonial soldier, had risked his life by dressing in a British soldier's uniform to take her to her grandparents, who lived under British occupation on Long Island during the Revolutionary War. Her grandmother had taught her reading, arithmetic, and the Bible. She insisted that Anna finish her schooling at a fashionable New York school. Anna always believed her grandmother was the good that came out of her mother's death. She was the pearl hidden inside an oyster.

Anna also saw the Lord's hand in bringing good out of difficult times. When William rose as a popular American hero after winning the Battle of Tippecanoe, the publicity earned him the presidency. She had been so proud of him. Her William was the ninth president of the United States. But the greatest challenge to her faith came when he died of pneumonia a month after his inauguration. Why, after eluding death so many times in war, had he died after grasping the presidency in peace? Why him and not her? She was the one who had been too sick to travel to Washington, D.C., for the inauguration.

While the country found comfort in ceremony and public tributes, Anna found comfort in her private faith and the arms of her fellow Presbyterian parishioners in Cincinnati. She clung to the hope that her grief and faith would give her sensitivity to encourage others in times of need.

"What I regret most about returning is leaving you," Carter said.

Anna heard gravity in his voice.

"I hope you will be as understanding as your brothers if I do not write often. My hand is unsteady. I can't write as I could when I taught your father his lessons."

"You were a good teacher and you are the best of grandmothers. Papa credits you for the fact that he is a Christian," he said.

Anna smiled at the thought of Carter's father, Scott, who asked her to live with him at his home overlooking the Ohio River after her home burned. She often wondered why she had lived so long, surviving all but one of her children. But she knew the Lord had provided for her good.

Carter reached out and took her hand into his.

Anna didn't realize her hands were colder than a block of ice until she felt the warmth of his youthful hand.

"If you're feeling so poorly, perhaps I should stay and take care of you?" he asked. "After all, if I am well enough to return to war, then I am well enough to care for you."

"Oh, no, my son. Your country needs your service; I do not," Anna immediately replied. "You are serving in the footsteps of your grandfather."

She paused. Like the sudden appearance of the moon on a cloudy night, her mind brightened at the memory of praying with William before he went off to war.

Prayer, that's it. The promise of prayer, that is what I have to offer to Carter, she thought.

The matriarch of the northwest gripped Carter's hand as tightly as she could. She took a deep breath, inhaling an extra measure of strength in her spirit.

"Go and discharge your duty faithfully and fearlessly. I feel that my prayers on your behalf will be heard, and that you will be returned to safety," she said with more confidence than a preacher delivering a sermon.

"I hope that is the case, to see you again, here, in this house, under this roof."

"I parted so often with your grandfather under similar circumstances of war, and he was always returned to me in safety. I feel it will be the same with you."

The two gripped hands more tightly. Then they prayed, each for the other.

"I must go now. My commander is expecting me," he said, rising to his feet. He walked to the doorway.

"Thank you, Grandma, for your prayers. I shall carry them with me, wherever my life takes me."

As she watched Carter close the door, Anna's liberal lips widened into a gigantic smile. Her life still had purpose. She had given him the only gift she had left to give: the promise of prayer.[3]

When First Lady Barbara Bush accepted an invitation to serve as the graduation speaker for the class of 1990 at Wellesley College, she received protest, not praise, from dozens of students and a chorus of reporters. Barbara's philosophy was well known. "Being a parent is the most important job you will ever have," she had often said. Her only career had been serving as a professional mom to her five children and as a grandmother to seventeen. Barbara's critics openly wondered what qualified her to address a group of highly driven, career-seeking graduates. How could Barbara dare speak to, much less inspire, the women of Wellesley?

Inspire she did. To a cheering crowd of six hundred, Barbara overcame the feminist fracas. Wearing a strand of her signature pearls, she told the women of Wellesley that they could choose any career role they wanted, but family and friends still came first.

"Your success as a family, our success as a society, depends not on what happens at the White House but on what happens inside your house," Barbara said to deafening applause.[4]

Barbara Bush and Anna Harrison have something in common: a commitment to placing family first. They, along with Abigail Adams, are also sisters in an exclusive sorority of three. They are the only first ladies to be married to a president and to have one of their direct descendants become president. Abigail Adams was the first, although she did not live to see her son, John Quincy Adams, become the sixth president. Barbara Bush beamed with pride the day her oldest son took the presidential oath. Anna died in the spring of 1864 before her grandsons Carter and Benjamin returned from war. White House historian William Seale noted that President Benjamin Harrison carried the legacy of his grandfather and grandmother with him into the White House in 1889. Seale wrote, "He had held in reverence the withered saint who always sat closest to the fire, her head haloed by a frilled cap."[5]

Whether potty training their children or training them to love their neighbors, these women added daily to a bank account of wisdom from which their children and grandchildren would draw. They had no idea the influence they would have on the nation simply by focusing on their family. Like the Proverbs 31 woman, each of these first ladies "watched over the affairs of her household" while "speaking with wisdom and faithful instruction" (Prov. 31:26, 27).

A quick read of Proverbs 31 reveals that this woman had three circles of influence: her family, coworkers, and the needy. Her worth was not found in the size of her family or the number of friends who came to her parties. Her value did not come from the people around her. But she saw her relationships as opportunities to positively influence and encourage others, especially her extended family.

The woman of Proverbs 31 watched over the affairs of her household. A household in ancient times was much broader than today's concept of the nuclear family. Parents, children, sons- and daughters-in-law, and their children lived under the authority of a common male ancestor.[6] The Proverbs 31 first lady was married to the head of such a household. As a result, she roomed in the innermost apartment of the house. From there she fulfilled her duties as overseer of many generations. She was not only a first lady to God, but she was also a first lady to others, primarily those in her household. She brought value to her household because she watched over them and helped them to become the people God wanted them to be.

Today, households are a bit different. Families are often much smaller in size. But no matter how big or small, your family looks to you for oversight and wisdom. You are a first lady to your family, whether or not your family includes a husband, children, or grandchildren. Perhaps your family is a sister or brother, parents, or grandparents. Often women find themselves taking care of multiple generations—their parents, husband, children, or grandchildren—all at the same time. The Proverbs 31 woman influenced those closest to her. Her tools were her eyes and tongue. With her eyes, she watched over her household. Then she used her tongue to speak words of wisdom.

She observed her family's comings and goings. She knew when they needed new clothes and shoes, when they needed to eat, sleep, and play. She understood their emotional needs. She knew when to talk and when to listen. I suspect she also spent a lot of time on bended knee at the tabernacle.

How can you and I watch over the affairs of our household? How can we support the members of our families? How can we help them to discover the jewel within and let their God-given talents shine? We can do what Anna Harrison did. We can start by praying.

When Barbara's firstborn, the future President George W. Bush, became governor of Texas in 1995, he asked her to do three things. "Pray for me. Don't brag," he said, and then added with a grin, "and don't talk to Connie Chung"—a reference to an embarrassing television interview given by the mother of Newt Gingrich, then the Speaker of the House of Representatives.[7]

When her son became president, Barbara continued to follow his advice. She sometimes asked others to pray for him, especially during times of national crisis. She happened to be speaking to the Charity Guild of Catholic Women at a For God & Country luncheon in March 2003 just after her son sent U.S. troops into Iraq. She asked the group to pray for him as he led the nation at war.[8] Barbara was one of hundreds of praying mothers. Many mothers were praying for their sons and daughters, including Bonnie Nichols of Cranberry Township, Pennsylvania.

My husband met Bonnie's son, Lieutenant Daniel Nichols, in 2001 at the U.S. Department of Labor where they both worked. Daniel also served in the reserves as a navy chaplain. They became friends and prayer partners. They met once or twice a month before work to pray until Daniel was called to active duty and sent to Iraq. His wartime story showed me the tremendous value of a mother who prays.

"My earliest memories are times when I would awake in the very early morning and steal out into the living room of our house where I would always find my mother deep in prayer. This had a lasting impact that continues to this day," Daniel said.[9]

I later shared Daniel's perspective with Bonnie. She laughed because she remembers those mornings differently. Just as she would find a quiet moment to pray, five-year-old Daniel would appear, and she didn't do much praying.

"Somehow children pick up on what you really want to do. Kids are going to pick up on what you really believe, in spite of what you might say or teach. It's more of a life thing," Bonnie said. "Prayer has always been very, very important to me. You never feel like you do enough."

I was surprised to learn that the focus of Bonnie's prayers was mainly missions, not her family. Although she prayed for her family and believed God was taking care of them, she wanted to expand her focus. She decided to spend more time lifting up those in need, those who didn't have anyone praying or caring for them. She read books that mapped a plan for praying around the globe in a year.

"I felt if I upheld the needs of the people who had devastating needs around the world that God would take care of the little things here," she said.[10]

The world's needs circled back to Bonnie and Daniel in a real way when Daniel was called to active duty. As part of Operation Iraqi Freedom, he served as a chaplain to the Third Marine Aircraft Wing. Navy chaplains support both the U.S. Navy and the Marine Corps. Leaving behind his pregnant wife and three children, Daniel went to Iraq. Both Daniel and his mother couldn't help but notice the coincidence. Bonnie had named him after Daniel in the Bible because "he had trusted in his God" (Dan. 6:23). The Old Testament's Daniel faced many dangers, such as surviving a night in a lion's den in Babylon. The irony was clear. Babylon is modern-day Iraq.

"It was frightening. You don't want to see your son go to war. On the other hand, I knew that he was gifted to be that very thing. I knew if God wanted to send someone special, He would send Dan. He was really gifted to lead a group of men," Bonnie said.

The marines whom Daniel served found themselves facing threats to their survival or the possibility of severe injury. Many of them also felt the strain of serious domestic problems, such as divorce or ill family members, tugging at them from home. Sometimes the weight was so great that a few contemplated suicide. Daniel's primary job was to counsel these marines and direct them to both practical and spiritual resources. He was to be a leader among them.

As a marine colonel once told him, "Chaplain, there's something you need to understand: I don't care how good a soldier you are. What's important to me is not the rank that's on your shoulder. What I need from you is what that cross symbolizes. To our troops you are a person who has some kind of connection to God. That's really what they want. They want to know there's somehow, some way to reach God. And so you are to be the presence of God here for my people."

Daniel followed the colonel's advice and ended each counseling session by asking the marines if he could pray for them. He took his prayer responsibility seriously. He prayed for each need and marine by name. But soon the prayer needs weighed heavier on him than a hundred military backpacks. His caseload had grown to more than a thousand, and he didn't have time to pray for each request. Then he had an idea.

"It was to Mom whom I turned when the prayer burden became too much for me to handle alone. She organized for me a growing network of faithful believers who prayed fervently for my marines and sailors, and I kept them updated with regular and very intimate details of the men and women I came across," Daniel said.

With the network in place, Daniel ended each counseling session by offering to have someone back home pray for the marine's specific needs. He e-mailed the requests to his mother, and she enlisted people at churches from Idaho to Africa to pray specifically for those needs. The network also supported Daniel's wife and children by praying for them. He followed up and let Bonnie know how the prayers were answered.

A really tough marine reluctantly approached Daniel at camp one day. He insisted that Daniel make it look like they were just hanging out. He didn't want anyone to think he needed the chaplain's help. He told Daniel he didn't really believe in God, but he had some problems back home to resolve. Daniel gave him practical advice on how to use the military's legal channels available to him. Then he offered to have someone in the prayer network pray for him. Daniel also encouraged him to try prayer himself. A few weeks later this same marine, the one who didn't want to be seen with a chaplain before, ran up to Daniel and hugged him. He told him that one bullet-strewn, starlit night had led him to pray to God. A few days later, he received a letter from home that solved his problem, answering his prayer.

Another marine, who had stopped practicing his faith, walked past Daniel's tent one evening. He heard Daniel talking about Babylon and the Bible's Daniel, who was the marine's favorite character when he was a child. The marine later talked with Chaplain Daniel and decided to renew his faith.

"The stories of God changing hearts and lives go on and on, some of them absolutely amazing, others far more mundane but no less touching," Daniel said.

"Marines love to have the chaplain pray, so long as it's short and meaningful, and I found myself with ample opportunity from hardened warriors to scared young men and women. Prayer is nothing less than an invitation of the presence of God and nothing more than opening one's heart wide for others to see the magnitude of the love and care you have for them."

A few months later, Daniel's reserve admiral came to Iraq for an on-site visit. The admiral asked Daniel why his cases had lessened in number and decreased in intensity. Daniel thought about it and told the admiral about his mom and the prayer network.

"I guess it helps to have Mom praying," Daniel said.

Bonnie had no idea as a young mother that her example and commitment to pray would affect her son and thousands of marines in the years to come. Like Anna Harrison, she watched over her household by directing her eyes toward heaven in prayer. She fulfilled the meaning of Colossians 4:2. "Devote yourselves to prayer, being watchful and thankful."

Watching over your family doesn't mean you have all the answers. But one way to fulfill your responsibility as a first lady to your family is to pray for them. Pray for your parents, your siblings, and their children. If you are married, pray for your husband, children, and grandchildren. Your commitment to prayer can make a difference to those in your innermost circle of care.

Also pray for yourself. The only person you can change is yourself. "Watch and pray so that you will not fall into temptation. The spirit is willing, but the body is weak" (Matt. 26:41). Come to God in humility, asking Him to make the necessary changes and remove any dirt and sin in you so you can shine more brilliantly and watch more effectively over the affairs of your household. Becoming a first lady to your family is a priceless gift whose value can never be counted.

If childhood is the season of life when we gather wisdom and old age is the season of life when we share wisdom, then motherhood is the season where the two are intertwined.

Another way to focus on your family is to train your tongue so it can be a tool for training.

When I was expecting my firstborn, I heard one piece of advice more often than I had morning sickness. "Children don't come with instruction manuals." One woman I met during this time had a different take on the instruction manual metaphor. Carolyn Greene is a mother of ten, a grandmother of four, and a preacher. She shared this wonderful word of wisdom with me after my son was born.

> A good mother makes all the difference in the world. I get upset when folks say their kids didn't come with instruction books! To them I say, "Oh dear, what a shame! Mine did. They came with a complete interactive instruction system that I can connect with via telephone within minutes. If I need to, I can arrange an in-house consultation and conference without charge. I call my interactive instruction book Mother. If you didn't get issued a good manual, you can still become a good manual for your children."

The first lady of Proverbs 31 was likely a woman of age and maturity because of her ability to impart pearls of wisdom and character to her children. Verse 26 tells us that "she speaks with wisdom, and faithful instruction is on her tongue." She had trained her tongue to speak wisely. She had found ways to make sure her family understood the value of following God's instruction manual.

Moral and religious training were responsibilities of Hebrew households. Parents were the natural teachers of their children. The primary focus of their teaching was the Torah or the Jewish law.[11] Speaking with wisdom and faithful instruction meant that the Proverbs 31 woman passed along religious and moral teachings to her household. She would have known and lived by this passage in the law: "Fix these words of mine in your hearts and minds; tie them as symbols on your hands and bind them on your foreheads" (Deut. 11:18).

One of the most poignant reflections on Anna Harrison's life came from her son, Scott, the father of Carter from this chapter's short story. "That I am a firm believer in the religion of Christ is not a virtue of mine. I imbibed (it) at my mother's breast and can no more divest myself of that than I can my nature."

As a young mother, Anna Harrison found herself raising her ten children without many community resources. They lived in the then unsettled territory of Indiana. She was her children's only teacher and, often, their only preacher. Occasionally a traveling minister came by their house, but she was responsible for her children's religious instruction. I suspect she relied on her grandmother's example, which filled many pages of her instruction manual and added many pearls to Anna's strands of wisdom. Anna's letters reveal a strong understanding of Scripture. Her knowledge of the Bible helped her to speak wisely.

Another first lady wrote about the value of sharing God's instruction manual with her children. "There is no insurance which parents can give their children comparable in value to that of a policy of firm religious conviction. It should be administered as naturally and as regularly as three meals a day. There are bound to be times when they will be compelled to draw upon the account heavily, and it should be made adequate for every need," Grace Coolidge wrote.[12]

I can just picture Grace scrambling a few eggs for breakfast in their Vermont cottage while correcting her sons' manners. Perhaps she encouraged them to show respect so they could "love their neighbor as themselves" when they went bike riding with the boys down the street. Not only did Grace take advantage of teachable moments at home, but she also made sure her children received weekly faithful instruction at church.

Spiritual training for the Bush family was also rooted in church attendance. In his autobiography, *A Charge to Keep*, President

George W. Bush reflected on the inspiration he received by attending church as a child.

"My family had attended the First Presbyterian Church in Midland; with the move to Houston we began attending the Episcopal Church, the denomination my dad was raised in. I served communion at the 8 a.m. service at St. Martin's. I loved the formality, the ritual, the candles, and there, I felt the first stirrings of a faith that would be years in the shaping," Bush wrote.[13]

Laura Bush shared a similar experience with her husband. She talked about it with CNN's Larry King in 2001. "Church has always been important to him, and he went with his family to church every single Sunday just like I did, you know, from childhood on. So . . . faith has a lifelong importance to both of us."[14]

One of the characteristics of a wise woman is the ability to recognize the needs of your family members. As Grace Coolidge's sons grew into teenagers, she realized that they needed encouragement from outside the family. She saw that her pastor had a knack with children. Grace encouraged him to stop by and talk with her sons as they played in their yard.

"I have seen him halt in front of our house when the boys were out at play, sit down on one of their sleds, and have a friendly chat about things that were of interest to them at the moment," she wrote. The influence paid off, and the boys made a public commitment of their faith one Easter Sunday when they were twelve and thirteen years of age.

A modern-day example of a woman who speaks with wisdom and faithful instruction is Deshua Joyce, a mother of four. As her children became teenagers, she recognized they might not listen to her as much. This navy wife called in the reinforcements. When each child turned thirteen, Deshua and her husband sent a letter to their child's friends, teachers, past teachers, pastors, and others. She asked them to write letters of encouragement to her child, describing characteristics they saw and qualities that God could use in their future. Deshua wanted her children to receive encouragement from how other people viewed them.

"I always grew up with the idea that your mom and dad had to say nice things about you," she said. "But it was what other people said that was really going to count at that stage in your life."[15]

Deshua also took advantage of the teachable moments. She didn't contrive moments or do it too often, so her children wouldn't tune out. Many times the teachable moments would start with nature.

"I had the idea that nature was God's way of thrilling us. One time I remember we had a pumpkin vine growing behind our home . . . I asked, 'Would you like to be a pumpkin on the vine or a grape on the vine?'"

They wrestled with the idea of bearing a lot of fruit, like grapes, or bearing large fruit, like pumpkins. She used the moment to talk about the principle that bearing fruit in life comes from remaining in the vine. She drew upon John 15:5, "I am the vine; you are the branches. If a man remains in me and I in him, he will bear much fruit; apart from me you can do nothing."

Another way she and her husband imparted faithful instruction was to have regular devotion time as a family. They also kept notebooks on their children, documenting the characteristics they saw in them. If a child was a little short on compassion, they would place that child in an environment, such as serving meals to the homeless, to give them an opportunity to discover the value of compassion.

The Joyces also used bedtime as moments to pray a blessing over their children. They consistently prayed the same Scripture out loud each night before their kids went to bed. This was their way of blessing them, of giving them a verse to remember for life. They chose a Scripture the first lady of Proverbs 31 would have known: "The LORD bless you and keep you; the LORD make his face shine upon you and be gracious to you; the LORD turn his face toward you and give you peace" (Num. 6:24–26).

When it comes to speaking with wisdom, Deshua believes that more is caught than taught.

"You can't give what you don't have. You can't fake your own spiritual walk with the Lord. You can't teach your own children to have a spiritual life, have a prayer life, their own devotions, if you're not doing it yourself," she said.

My friend Carolyn Greene came face-to-face with the reality that motherhood is about modeling behavior. She wrote:

> When my son was born, I grew up. I found myself repeating the same things my mother did. I told the same stories, I gave the same warnings, quoted the same scriptures, and I gave the same evil looks and tickled the same tickles. With each passing day I became aware that I was becoming my mother. One day while I was sweeping through the house I looked up and caught a look at myself in the hall mirror, where to my amazement, instead of my own face I saw my mother's face looking back at me.

I have a great mother. She knows when to offer insight and when to hold her tongue. She has been a teacher, nurse, cheerleader, editor, cook, seamstress, tour guide, photographer, personal shopper, and first lady to me. She has provided many pearls of wisdom from her instruction book. Now that I am a mom, I appreciate her more than ever. I know that as I mature as a mom, I'll look in the mirror and see her looking back at me because she modeled motherhood for me.

When your children or other family members see your face in the mirror some day, what do you want them to see? Perhaps you'll want them to see you holding a distaff in one hand and a spindle in the other.

CHAPTER FIVE

Follow the Leader

"In her hand she holds the distaff and grasps the spindle with her fingers" (Prov. 31:19).

HARRY TRUMAN estimated that he shook 25,000 hands in 1949 but his wife, Bess, shook 50,000. In a letter to her daughter, Bess wrote about hand-shaking fatigue after a White House event: "The reception, of course, was horrible—1,341 and my arm is a wreck this A.M."

The best way to avoid the big squeeze is to follow President Harry Truman's advice. Seize the other person's hand first. Slide your thumb between the other person's thumb and index finger, so that you, not the other person, do the squeezing. In other words, lead by example.[1]

Mrs. Troupe carefully stepped from the carriage and onto the muddy ground, still wet from the melted snow of a late winter's storm. She walked as delicately as a kitten to ensure that her best pair of satin shoes and silk stockings remained as clean as possible.

What a grand opportunity, to finally meet her ladyship, she thought, stopping a few feet from the coach.

Mrs. Troupe waited while the other women in her party, less than a half dozen, disembarked. To match the anticipated grandeur of the hostess, each woman wore her finest dress. Beautiful bibs and bands ornamented their garments, all imports from Europe. For a pack dressed more perfectly than peacocks, they walked toward the most unlikely of destinations, a tavern. But the ladies in their finery approached the pub with the same wonder and excitement of entering a castle to meet a queen.

Smoke from the tavern's detached kitchen swirled into the sky. Mrs. Troupe took a whiff, hoping to inhale the comforting aroma of seasoned boiled chicken or pork, but a disappointing blandness greeted her nostrils instead.

"The undesirable effects of the Revolution," she whispered in a slightly resentful tone. She knew the food shortage and all of Morristown's troubles were the direct result of the welcomed intruders: the Continental army.

At first Mrs. Troupe and the residents of New Jersey's Morristown had been elated when General George Washington and his troops took refuge in their humble hamlet that winter. A spirit of excitement had followed the soldiers, who boasted of their fresh success of crossing the Delaware River under the bloated noses of the British. Mrs. Troupe's family and her neighbors had opened their homes and sheltered as many men as possible. However, the soldiers had ravaged their farms for food and killed most of the game available in their forests.

Perhaps worst of all, she was horrified to learn that the soldiers had carried with them smallpox, a contagious deadly disease. Two of the three spires in town, the Presbyterian and Baptist ones, had been turned into infirmaries to care for the sick and dying. Mrs. Troupe wondered which was more strained, the town's hospitality or their patriotism.

Mrs. Troupe and the other women in her party walked into the tavern. A servant greeted them and escorted them upstairs to the quarters of General and Mrs. Washington.

When they reached the top of the stairs, the ladies walked into a sparse hallway with a low ceiling.

Such a modest dwelling place for a woman of her stature, Mrs. Troupe reflected.

The servant led them to one of the bedrooms along the hallway's axis.

Mrs. Troupe's eyes immediately focused on the room's only occupant, a petite woman with snow white hair. The woman wore a plain brown dress with a checkerboard print apron. The click clicking of her knitting needles echoed in the room.

Must be the tavern keeper's wife, Mrs. Troupe presumed.

"Come in, come in," the woman's high musical voice called out.

"So good of you to come and visit," she said warmly. "I'm the general's wife, Mrs. Washington. Please come in and have a seat."

Lady Washington is dressed more like a lady in waiting than the general's wife, Mrs. Troupe thought.

The shock she felt was stronger than the bolt of lightning that struck Benjamin Franklin's kite. She was simply stunned that this tiny woman wearing a homespun dress was the grand dame married to General Washington.

Mrs. Troupe and the others introduced themselves and then sat in the simple wooden chairs arranged in a semicircle around Mrs. Washington.

"Isn't this cupboard an excellent one? And so is the rod for my clothes," Mrs. Washington said, directing the ladies' attention to the basic shelving along the wall.

"Two of Morristown's kindest souls built these for my comfort here. They went so far as to smooth the boards' corners to rid them of worm rot."

Mrs. Troupe studied the threads and half-formed shell dangling from Mrs. Washington's needles.

Stockings. She's making stockings, went through her mind.

"I see you are making stockings for General Washington," Mrs. Troupe said.

"Oh no, these are for the soldiers," Mrs. Washington replied.

Mrs. Troupe felt embarrassed. She worried that her cheeks were flusher than a pig's nose.

Mrs. Washington continued to knit while leading the ladies in a genteel conversation. She talked about the soldiers and their desperate need for stockings, shirts, and shoes because the provisions of the Continental Congress had been limited. The more Mrs. Washington talked about the soldiers, the more she knitted. And the more she knitted, the more mortified Mrs. Troupe became at her own idle hands.

None of us has brought a stitch of work with us!

Mrs. Troupe participated in the ladies' polite conversation as best as she could, trying to hide her growing discomfort. She couldn't have been more self-conscious had she served French wine to the King of England. She wished she could change into plainer clothes and sit at a spinning wheel herself.

Another woman then introduced the topic of the smallpox epidemic into their conversation.

"Have you been inoculated?" the woman asked Lady Washington.

"Yes, last year in Philadelphia. The general was perhaps surprised at my decision, because I had been so fearful of it," she said. "But he was pleased when I came through it after a month."

Mrs. Troupe shuddered at the thought of inoculation, which required a small cut on the arm. The doctor took a tiny amount of mucus from an open sore on a patient who had smallpox. Then the doctor placed the mucus into the cut of the person receiving inoculation. The hope was that only a mild case of the smallpox would emerge, enough to prevent death and inoculate against future exposure.

"One of the soldiers told me that the general had issued an order forbidding smallpox inoculation," the woman said.

"That is true, but the order was last year, before the summer campaigns, when he couldn't afford to have large numbers recovering from the inoculation. General Washington took to smallpox as a young man and he believes in inoculation. The soldiers are now being inoculated," Mrs. Washington replied.

Mrs. Troupe felt uncomfortable when no one responded. She certainly did not know what to say.

"Do you not think it is important that American ladies be patterns of industry to their countrywomen?" Mrs. Washington asked declaratively.

Again none of the ladies answered. Mrs. Troupe wondered what the others thought of Lady Washington's suggestion.

Are they as embarrassed as I am? she wondered.

"The separation from our mother country will dry up the resources of comfort. Shouldn't we become independent by our determination to do without those items we cannot make for ourselves?" Mrs. Washington said, seemingly unbothered by their silence.

"As our husbands and brothers are examples of patriotism, we must be patterns of industry," she said.

Mrs. Troupe tried to smile, but Mrs. Washington's words convicted her worse than a sermon or a moral lesson she had ever heard at church. As she glanced at Lady Washington's eager knitting hands, she decided Mrs. Washington's statement was merely a reflection of her thrifty habits and personal virtues. Lady Washington embodied the pattern of industry that she proclaimed. Her character illuminated her pearls of wisdom.

The conversation soon subsided. The ladies politely concluded their visit and left the tavern. Mrs. Troupe walked without care over the muddy ground, no longer worried about soiling her skirt or stockings. As she boarded the carriage to return home, she decided to leave behind her doubts about the Revolution and her embarrassment. Mrs. Washington had inspired her and strengthened her spirit. Mrs. Troupe couldn't wait to return to her house to start the tapping and whirling of her own spinning wheel.[2]

Ancient Jewish oral tradition taught that a wife was obligated to grind, bake, wash, cook, nurse the children, make the bed, and spin wool. If the wife had one maidservant, then she didn't have to grind, bake, or wash. If she had two maidservants, then she wouldn't have to cook or nurse. If she had three, then she didn't have to make the bed or spin wool. If she had four, then she could spend her time leisurely. But even if she had a hundred maids, she should spin wool, because leisure led to "idiocy," as one old rabbi put it.[3]

Martha Dandridge Custis was the wealthiest widow in Virginia when she met George Washington. Because her children were very young at the time, Martha had received control over an enormous amount of land and money. She also inherited more than two hundred slaves from her deceased first husband's estate, including two maids and four "waiters."[4] With so much wealth and help, she didn't have to sew a stitch, but she chose to knit. Like the Proverbs 31 woman, she let go of leisure to lasso leadership instead.

Martha literally and symbolically embodies verse 19 of Proverbs 31. "In her hand she holds the distaff and grasps the spindle with her fingers." The distaff and spindle were the tools of spinning. To spin in ancient times, the Proverbs 31 first lady would wrap wool or flax around a small reed called a distaff. Next, she would thread a hook attached to a twelve-inch reed called a spindle. Then she would begin to spin, glancing occasionally at the clay ball attached by a ring to the spindle to make sure the ball was keeping the spindle upright.[5]

Spinning wasn't much different in Martha Washington's day. By taking the tools of sewing into her hands, Martha, like the Proverbs 31 woman, showed those around her that she was willing to get her hands dirty or at least risk pricking her fingertips. Martha grasped the significance of her marriage to George Washington, the commanding general of the ragtag army of the Revolution. She traded her imported dresses for homespun attire. She understood the value of leading by example. She stitched the sample pattern.

As Martha shows, leading by example means being willing to sacrifice. Proverbs 31:15 tells us that "she gets up while it is still dark; she provides food for her family and portions for her servant girls." This woman certainly did not need to get up that early. Her servant girls were fully capable of the early morning shift. My guess is that she wanted to set an example for them. Through her actions she said, "If I can do this, you can too!"

When asked about the best mode of parenting and disciplining, Laura Bush told a reporter, "By example, I think we always know that by example is the best way to teach. It's hard to tell people things, you know, especially the finger-point. 'You should do' lines never work very well for anybody. I mean, I don't think we like that either, even as adults, and children don't either."[6]

Jenna Bush, one of Laura's twin daughters, is proud of her mother's example. While campaigning for her father in 2004, Jenna described her mother as "a role model for women across the country."[7] She also followed in her mother's footsteps by choosing to teach after graduating from college. Jenna was not the first daughter of a president to follow the career choice of her mother. Another first daughter also learned from her mother's example of leadership and sacrifice.

Mary Fillmore had heard the stories of how her parents met. Her mother, Abigail, was the daughter of a poor Baptist preacher in western New York. She was trying to pull herself out of poverty by teaching when she met Millard Fillmore, a meager clothier's apprentice. Mary had heard Millard's compliments of Abigail's willingness to keep teaching after they married—an unusual decision for a married woman in the 1820s. Mary knew her mother's sacrifice eventually gave their family enough security to allow her father to serve as a member of the New York state legislature. Abigail made it possible for Millard to become vice president and then president of the United States.

Mary had also seen her mother read. She had crawled into her lap more often than the sun rose just to catch a glimpse of her mother's latest book. It came as no surprise to Mary when her mother carried her passion for reading and books into the White House when she became first lady in 1850. Congress appropriated the funds, and Abigail purchased reference books and maps to establish a library for the White House.[8]

Abigail's sacrifice and leadership showed Mary that she could do what few women were doing back then, go to college. Mary graduated from the State Normal School of New York and became a public school teacher in Buffalo. She could speak French, German, and Spanish and was proficient in music. Mary benefited from her mother's ability to lead by example.

Mamie Eisenhower was another first lady who led by example and sacrifice. She was a vivacious woman, full of life and lightheartedness. The very social Mamie married Dwight Eisenhower, an amiable but tough man who became president in 1953. During World War II, Ike served as the brilliant commanding general of the allied armies. This top post forced Ike and Mamie to live apart during the war. While he served in Europe, she lived in an apartment in Washington, D.C. From military wives to nosy news reporters, almost everyone watched her every move. She displayed model behavior.

Her granddaughter Susan wrote, "Mamie had developed a code of conduct for herself, which included an uncompromising personal policy about being seen in public."[9]

Before the war, Mamie had often enjoyed social outings in Washington. But during the war, she gave up public socializing. As the wife of a general who was sending men into harm's way, she knew she had no business going to restaurants and enjoying the good life.

Her sense of sacrifice and love for her husband forced her to make a decision. Mamie shared an apartment with an officer's wife and daughter. Her roommate started inviting over friends who became drunk and disorderly. Mamie knew her own inner ear disorder caused her to stumble from dizziness, which fueled false rumors that she was an alcoholic. Mamie decided to protect her own reputation from further gossip and asked her roommate to move into an apartment across the hall.[10]

Mamie knew she was in the spotlight. A top U.S. milliner was among many businessmen who tried to send her gifts. He wrapped up a box of stylish hats and sent them to her. Although she loved hats and jewelry, she promptly returned them. She believed extravagance set a bad example during wartime and opened her to criticism by the press. Mamie also deftly handled nosy reporters, often turning down their requests for interviews. One reporter sent her roses to lure her into talking to him. She promptly sent the flowers to a nearby military hospital and declined the man's interview request.[11]

Ike appreciated Mamie's sacrifices. "I do have time to tell you again that I'm prouder of you every time someone brings me news of the way you handle yourself—of the serene way that you (my mother, too, God bless her) brush off the chance to indulge in cheap publicity. You are a thoroughbred," he wrote.[12]

"She had the most extraordinary sense of the right thing to do—how and when to do it—than any woman I have ever known," Kate Hughes said of her friend.

Mamie's sacrifices also gave her credibility to speak to others when necessary. At a gathering of military wives, her friend Janie Howard openly worried about her husband's safety and survival.

"Well, Mamie, you don't have to worry, because your husband is a general," Janie said.

Mamie later took her aside and gave her a Martha Washington-like admonition. "Nobody's safe, Janie, and Ike's got the whole burden on his shoulders. Never let me hear you complain about anything, because your husband is a professional soldier and we're the ones who have to hold up. We're the ones who can't complain."[13]

Perhaps Mamie remembered the criticism another first lady faced when she failed to live sacrificially during a crisis. Like Harriet Lane immediately before her, Mary Lincoln lived in the era of Scarlett O'Hara extravagance of the 1850s. Mary entered the White House under the worst of circumstances but she failed to respond appropriately. Instead of demonstrating frugality, she spent extravagantly during the Civil War, which brought her husband more harm than good.

Leading by example is more than just sacrifice. Leading by example also means treating others with the same respect you would give yourself or your closest family members. The Proverbs 31 woman not only got up early as an example to her employees, but she also took care of them as if they were family. Verse 15 tells us that "she gets up while it is still dark; she provides food for her family and portions for her servant girls." She showed them they had value by providing them with the same fruits, vegetables, and lentils she gave her family. She practiced the golden rule: "So in everything, do to others what you would have them do to you, for this sums up the Law and the Prophets" (Matt. 7:12).

Pat Nixon often led by example in this way. Her hardscrabble background gave her a deep appreciation of equality. One of her first events as the White House hostess gave her an opportunity to lead by example. Within a month after becoming first lady in 1969, Pat held a luncheon for women members of the press corps. Many of these women had attended events in the White House, but they usually had to compete with the men in the press corps to get a good seat or standing position in the room. Pat treated them to a luncheon served at the elegant long table in the State Dining Room. Each reporter drew a number for a seat at the table. Pat surprised them when she also drew a number.[14]

Treating others the way you want to be treated requires getting into their heads. No one can read anyone else's mind, but leading by example requires thinking about other people's needs and then coming up with creative ways to help them succeed. Leadership is not self-focused. Leaders allow other jewels to shine in the spotlight.

Julia Grant had come a long way from the spoiled Southern belle of Missouri by the time she became first lady in 1869, exactly a century before Pat held the job. At her first few receptions, Julia and her closest friends greeted all of the guests who came through the receiving line. She soon realized that the job required more of her. Just as her husband led his cabinet members, she also set an example for their wives. Julia wondered how she could help them to succeed. She soon had an idea.

At the next series of receptions, Julia had a new plan. When members of the diplomatic corps came through the line, Julia arranged for the wife of the secretary of state to stand next to her and shake hands. Then when those who served under the secretary of the navy came through the line, Julia asked the navy secretary's wife to stand next to her, and so on. Julia gave these women a chance to sparkle.

Julia continued this practice in other ways. Whenever they were greeting guests from a particular state, she arranged for the wives of the senators representing that state to greet with her. She shared the joy and helped other women to be successful in their roles as wives of elected officers and government officials. She had learned that life wasn't all about her.[15]

One first lady who best exemplifies the idea of leading through this kind of humility was Dolley Madison. She was perhaps the most gracious hostess in Virginia when her husband became president in 1809. Dolley was the first wife of a president to live in the White House long enough to make it a home and place for entertaining. The White House was finished in 1800, when John Adams was completing his one and final term. Abigail only lived in the house a few months. Thomas Jefferson, who followed Adams, was a widower. Although Jefferson entertained, he usually dominated the conversation and held partisan parties. Jefferson rarely invited guests from opposing parties to the same dinner or reception. The White House needed a woman who led by example and considered the needs of her guests. The White House needed Dolley.

Dolley had a knack for equality. She quickly realized that she could bring her husband great good by hosting both political parties at the same White House party. She knew James would benefit by hearing different opinions through the banter of a healthy debate in a relaxed, social atmosphere. But she didn't want to cause a high society riot by breaking Jefferson's rules and inviting Federalist and Republican guests to the same party. She also didn't want her guests to be uncomfortable. Dolley decided to host a different kind of party, an open house that didn't require an invitation. Soon everyone in Washington knew that Wednesday evenings at the White House were open to most anyone. Guests also knew they were taking a chance of meeting someone with opposite political views. This made for quite an eclectic mix of people and required a hostess who considered her guests' needs above her own.

One party in particular tested Dolley's skills. A young man, who was new to town, came to one of her open house receptions. He was drinking a cup of coffee when Dolley came into the room. Her appearance made him so nervous that he dropped the saucer and thrust the cup into his pocket. This mishap would have distressed many hostesses, but Dolley pretended not to see it and instead chatted away with him. She talked about the weather, the crowd attending the reception, and then about his mother, an acquaintance. She talked long enough for the man to regain his composure. Then she offered him a cup of coffee, as if it was his first cup. Ignoring the bulge in his pocket, the man accepted.[16]

Dolley's ability to think about the needs of her husband and her guests won her praise from the public. She demonstrated the value of Philippians 2:3, "Do nothing out of selfish ambition or vain conceit, but in humility consider others better than yourselves." Dolley was the "Queen of Hearts." To this day she is considered one of the best first ladies to ever serve.

What does leading by example mean for women today? What type of leadership are you modeling? Whatever position of leadership God has given you, he wants you to lead by example and treat those under your guidance the way you want to be treated.

"I lead others the way I want to be led," Holly Rollins of Oakton, Virginia, told me. She is a senior associate for Booz Allen Hamilton. "I tell the managers working for me to never apologize for having a life outside of Booz Allen. If Booz Allen stopped giving out paychecks, none of us would show up. It's therefore not a calling."

Perhaps leading by example also means expecting more of yourself than of those around you. Holly explained that responsiveness is one area of leadership that is often overlooked. Responsiveness is a great way to model leadership in today's world.

"Often senior people hide behind the veil of busyness as a way to pick and choose things they want to do. I think they hold staff to a higher standard of responsiveness than they themselves deliver, such as returning calls, e-mails, providing data, or approving expense reports. I try to respond within twenty-four hours of a request, even to say, 'I can't get to this until next week.' I've tried to let things falling through the cracks be an exception and not the norm."

Sacrificial leadership is a valuable way to reflect humility and show a sincere respect for others.

"I think it's also important to know staff, what makes them tick, their hobbies, interests, and family situation. I ask about spouse and kids by names and acknowledge when staff is having a stressful situation outside of work," Holly said.

For Holly, leadership translates into work performed. She does this by actively mentoring and coaching.

"Going into a client meeting I will use the Socratic Method to draw out of staff (in a lead-the-horse-to-water way) as to the goals and objectives of the meeting, how we will measure if it's successful, etc.," she said.

"I'll come out of the meeting and ask them how they think we measure up. I then offer my perspective. Staff are frequently too tactical and don't see the big picture. I avoid making them feel that their perspective is wrong but rather augment their understanding with mine so they can begin to think more like senior management. I've gotten very, very positive feedback on this approach."

As some of the first ladies have illustrated, sometimes leadership requires sacrifice. In today's world of me-ism, this can be done through a willingness to allow others to express their opinions in a meeting, even if they differ from yours.

"If I'm facilitating a meeting, at the end I go around the table and ask each person individually if they have any questions or anything they want to add. I find way too many meetings dominated by windbags who talk too much. Sometimes the most thoughtful ideas come from the quieter folks in the room," Holly said.

I admire Holly because she pursues excellence at both work and home. She is the mother of two children, ages three and one.

"I actually changed my work status over the issue of excellence because I knew that I couldn't fulfill the responsibilities of a senior manager at a level of excellence and raise two kids effectively," she said. "I therefore rescoped my role and told my company, 'I can do these few things and maintain a level of excellence. If that reduced role is okay with you then that's what I want.' I had a very favorable reaction and lots of support from partners."

Maybe leading by example is a pattern of living that you demonstrate to those closest to you. Just as Abigail Fillmore's sacrifice and work ethic inspired her daughter Mary to become a teacher, the way you fulfill your talents may inspire those around you to fulfill theirs. Your children may not share your talents, but they will absorb the work ethic they see in you. They will remember how you lived your life and how you worked. Your way of living leaves an imprint on those around you.

Leading by example leads to opportunities to give pearls of wisdom to others. Martha, Mamie, Julia, Abigail, Dolley, and Pat effectively led because they understood the value of sacrificial leadership and humility. They were first ladies to their families, and they were first ladies to their guests.

Others beyond your family will remember your life as well. George H. W. Bush reflected on Pat Nixon's special touch when he toured a medical center. He told about a time when she visited a similar hospital. Pat stopped to embrace a little girl blinded by rubella. She talked to the girl, holding her close for several minutes. Then someone came over to tell her that the child couldn't hear her. She was deaf as well as blind. Pat, already aware of the girl's disabilities, said, "But she knows what love is . . . She can feel love."[17]

When your cup overflows, don't stuff it into your pocket. Set the example and pour a cup for someone who is thirsty.

CHAPTER SIX

Charity Choices

"She opens her arms to the poor and extends her hands to the needy" (Prov. 31:20).

T HE CAMERA focused on the man in NBC's New York studio. Through the lens's limited point of view, the broadcaster's orange tie was a vivid contrast against the newsroom's cartoon-blue background. His tiger-speckled glasses took up most of his face, while his coat's lapels were as wide as his chest. To the viewer, the newsman's clothing merely reflected the times, silently scream-ing, "It's 1970."

When he saw the camera's signal, the broadcaster looked directly into the lens. "Mrs. Richard Nixon ended her visit to Peru. She said she found the earthquake destruction incredible," he said simply, with no emotion.

Another camera instantly burst Technicolor's rainbow, taking the viewer to the gray bumpy streets of Lima, Peru. There the camera panned over endless lines of uniformed men along a drab street. They stood at attention, flanking the city's ancient plaza and cathedral.

Out of the camera's eye but within its ear, the reporter's reso-nant voice began to narrate the story.

"Elements from all three Peruvian armed services were arranged around Lima's Plaza de Almas Monday morning. It was the feast of St. Peter and St. Paul," he said.

The reporter's name, Tom Steinhorst, flashed in white block letters over the plaza scene, a magic trick of newsroom editing, while the camera showed a limousine speeding from left to right along the street next to the plaza.

"The first lady arrived with Consuelo de Valasco, the wife of Peru's president, to attend mass in the cathedral," Steinhorst continued.

Then the camera changed its point of view, filming from a position in front of the cathedral's doorway. It held steady and showed the two first ladies, who wore black lace mantillas in their hair, as they walked up the steps. When they entered the cathedral, they disappeared from the camera's eye.

"Later the Peruvian president, General Juan Valasco, arrived at the head of his government," Steinhorst narrated while the camera showed Valasco following the same path as the women—up the steps, into the cathedral, and out of sight.

Although the camera showed their separate entrances, it failed to explain why President Valasco did not accompany his wife and his country's most important guest, the wife of the president of the United States, into the Mass remembering the fifty thousand Peruvians who died in the earthquake. Steinhorst also didn't mention that it was Consuelo, not her husband, who had greeted Pat at the airport the day before.

But twelve years earlier, other cameras had captured the reason for President Valasco's hostile hospitality. Pat and Richard Nixon, who was vice president of the United States at the time, had visited Lima. Leftists had mobbed their car and threatened their lives. President Valasco had recently overthrown Peru's government. He dared not welcome Pat, at least not in front of the cameras. He was a leftist.

Steinhorst and his camera also failed to explain why Pat had decided to return to the nation whose president could not shake her hand in public and whose people had thrown rocks at her years earlier. But sometimes a camera with a limited point of view can answer the most important question, even if someone forgot to ask it.

Steinhorst continued to narrate while his camera switched from the cathedral and showed a scene with rubble in the foreground and mountains in the distance.

"After Mass, Mrs. Nixon with Mrs. Valasco flew to the disaster area with tons of American supplies. This town was one of the hardest hit. Huarez had been a city of thirty-five thousand. Mrs. Nixon was given the estimate that about a third of the population perished in the quake," Steinhorst stated without emotion.

Steinhorst did not report what Pat, the locals, and other reporters knew. Half a dozen helicopters and planes flying relief missions into Huarez had crashed in the treacherous mountain air currents. He didn't explain that Pat's visit was dangerous. He also didn't describe the supplies she brought, the two planes full of blankets, tents, medical kits, and fifteen thousand dollars in donations from individual Americans.

The camera showed Pat and Consuelo as they climbed over boulders and chunks of concrete in Huarez. Surrounding them were reporters, relief workers, and local Peruvians. Consuelo kept her eyes focused on her guest, offering her hand to make sure Pat didn't fall. But the first lady didn't need the help. The camera showed Pat stepping around the debris easily, as if she were wearing tennis shoes and not pumps.

Pat focused her attention on the hopeless faces of the Peruvians and the aid workers. She didn't appear to notice what the camera's color film detected brilliantly. Her blue suit matched the sky above, causing her to stand out among the gray and lifeless hues around her. Her smile and warm handshakes lit their faces. She was their rainbow after the storm.

"Mrs. Nixon was obviously impressed with the extent of the devastation. She seemed to pay special attention to the children," Steinhorst said, his voice hinting at emotion for the first time.

His voice dropped away for a few seconds, allowing the natural sounds of the scene to take over his story.

The camera zoomed to a close-up of Pat and a young girl.

"Oh, my," Pat said while the girl handed her a bouquet of daisies.

Pat smiled and hugged the girl tightly, as if she were clinging to her own daughter.

"These are beautiful," Pat said.

The camera flashed for two seconds to a scene of hundreds of tents, where thousands of Peruvians had taken refuge. More than eight hundred thousand had lost their homes.

"The tents here were provided by American relief. In this camp, Peace Corps teams are working with Peruvian volunteers," Steinhorst narrated.

The camera seemed eager to get back to Pat and cut to another close-up of her. Steinhorst again stopped his narration to allow the sounds of the scene to tell the story. A man showed Pat his festive tan sombrero, trimmed with red fringe. He gave it to her and said, "Even though it's old." Pat smiled and eagerly put the sombrero on her head.

The camera's narrow perspective couldn't show each hand that Pat touched. It didn't have enough tape to record Pat as she listened, with the help of a translator, to the Peruvians tell their stories of where they were when the earthquake hit. No camera captured her raspy voice as she asked relief workers where they were from. One answered Germany, another South Africa. She commended them all for their efforts to help and hugged as many as she could.

"One major purpose of the trip clearly was to reawaken American interests. And most Peruvians were still suffering from the consequences of last month's earthquake," Steinhorst said, while the camera panned from left to right over a scene of Peruvian bystanders sitting on fences. What stood out the most were their faded black farmer's hats, one of the few items they now owned.

For the first time, the camera turned to the mustached and leisure-suited Steinhorst, who stood and held his microphone in front of a group of Peruvians holding a leftist banner.

"And one Washington official said, 'Peru needs help. Who's the president more apt to listen to than his own wife?'" he reported. "Tom Steinhorst, NBC News, Huarez, Peru."

Then he sent the camera's eye back to the man in the brightly colored New York studio.[1]

In its own limited way, Steinhorst's camera answered the question of why Pat returned to Peru. When the earthquake created boulders out of buildings, Pat was there to extend her hands to those who once threw stones at her. She came because they needed her. They needed hope.

L ima's newspaper editors praised Pat for her courage, tenderness, and sacrifice.

> Certainly an act like Mrs. Nixon's is not common in an age in which the rules of international protocol are limited to form and a conventional response such as a telegram, as befits the high station of a first lady of a nation. In her human warmth and identification with the suffering of the Peruvian people, she has gone beyond the norms of international courtesy and has endured fatigue in an example of solidarity and self-denial.[2]

When Pat entered the White House as first lady in 1969, she brought with her memories of official life from 1952 to 1960. She discovered that much had changed in America since she was the wife of the vice president. By the time she was first lady, most households owned television sets, and the media had defined a new role for the first lady: news maker. With the spotlight on her more than ever, Pat knew that her charitable choices would be a topic for television. Her daughter explained how she approached this challenge.

"As Mother considered the various suggestions for projects, she was aware that any first lady's influence must be wielded cautiously and responsibly," Julie Nixon Eisenhower wrote.[3]

Helen Thomas, the veteran United Press International White House correspondent, observed that Pat's own childhood and young adulthood—which were lean, difficult, and grieving years—also impacted her choices.

"She is warm and kind and she goes the extra mile to shake a hand and greet a stranger," Helen said. "She is concerned about people's feelings. Mrs. Nixon is a very strong woman, and sometimes a very stubborn woman. As a hostess, she has kept her promise of not entertaining just the big shots. She never forgets her days of poverty when she was growing up."[4]

Pat's charity choices led her to open the White House doors to the disabled and arrange for special tours for the blind. For the first time, visually impaired visitors ran their hands along the silk walls, carved sofa legs, and cool silver urns. One camera filmed a White House Christmas party that Pat hosted for children from a blind school. It showed her warm hugs and captured a touching close-up of a blind teenage boy in a red sweater. He smiled while carefully touching the side of the White House gingerbread house to feel its hardened dough walls and the outlines of the icing stars on the rooftop.

"While always dignified and gracious, Mrs. Nixon was also a passionate believer in volunteer service and the importance of Americans helping one another. The appearance of the White House today and its accessibility to visitors at special times each year owe themselves in large degree to her generous and creative efforts," President Bill Clinton said in a tribute to Pat after her death in 1993.

"During her first Thanksgiving as first lady, she invited 224 senior citizens from area nursing homes to the White House for a special meal. She invited hundreds of families to nondenominational Sunday services in the East Room. And she offered the White House as a meeting place for volunteer organizations dedicated to solving community problems," Clinton said.[5]

Pat also spent much of her time as first lady on missions of personal diplomacy, such as her visit to Peru. By the time she left the White House, she had visited seventy-eight nations through her role as the wife of the president and vice president. She is the most widely traveled first lady to date. She also promoted volunteerism and opened the White House doors to the poor and needy. Pat modeled a life of service.

If one quality unites the first ladies of the United States, it is service. The pattern began under the first first lady. Mary V. Thompson, a research specialist for the Mount Vernon Ladies' Association, found a humorous way to describe Martha's commitment to charity.

"George Washington's cousin, Lund, who managed Mount Vernon during the Revolution, once remarked that, 'Mrs. Washington's charitable disposition increases in the same proportion with her meat house,'" Mary said.[6]

Mary also explained why Martha extended her arms to those in need.

"As a public expression of her faith, Mrs. Washington took concrete steps to care for those less fortunate than herself by giving money and food to the poor. Charities such as these were, to a certain extent, probably expected for someone of her social class," she said.

In the chapter on leadership, we saw how Martha led by example when she employed her eager hands to sew for soldiers. She discovered in the Revolution what other first ladies encountered. When a woman becomes first lady of the United States, she sees the world with new eyes. Her role takes her to places she might not have ever visited. Her husband makes decisions that impact the masses. As a result, service often becomes more important to her than ever before. Because the title of first lady is unofficial and doesn't come with a set of rules and laws, first ladies have much freedom in how they spend their time. No law dictates how they extend their hands, but most of them have found ways to serve.

Unlike today, personal charity was a command in ancient times. The Hebrew law said, "If there is a poor man among your brothers in any of the towns of the land that the LORD your God is giving you, do not be hardhearted or tightfisted toward your poor brother. Rather be openhanded and freely lend him whatever he needs" (Deut. 15: 7, 8).[7] The book of Ruth shows us that poor women were legally allowed to follow behind wheat harvesters and collect grain for bread.

Because the Proverbs 31 first lady spoke with faithful instruction, she knew the law's decree to take care of the poor and needy. Verse 20 tells us "she opens her arms to the poor and extends her hands to the needy." Notice the imagery. The hands that eagerly held the spindle and distaff or sewed clothing for her household also extended to those in need. Hands imply action. They are more than just words of the tongue or feelings of the heart.

The woman of Proverbs 31 served God by serving others. Her instruction book taught that "he who is kind to the poor lends to the LORD, and he will reward him for what he has done" (Prov. 19:17). Likewise, "he who oppresses the poor shows contempt for their Maker, but whoever is kind to the needy honors God" (Prov. 14:31).

The concept of serving God by serving others also appears in the New Testament. "If anyone has material possessions and sees his brother in need but has no pity on him, how can the love of God be in him?" (1 John 3:17). A parable for charity is found in Matthew 25:31–46. Jesus told His disciples that when the King comes into his glory, he will sit on his heavenly throne and separate people into categories, just as a shepherd separates sheep from goats. The King will praise the people on his right and give them their inheritance because they fed, clothed, and cared for him. But these people will ask, "Lord, when did we see you hungry and feed you, or thirsty and give you something to drink? When did we see you a stranger and invite you in or needed clothes and clothed you? When did we see you sick or in prison and go to visit you?"

The King will reply, "I tell you the truth, whatever you did for one of the least of these brothers of mine, you did for me." Then he will tell the group on his left to leave and be cursed. By not caring for the least of these, they did not care for him.

In giving the 2003 commencement address for Georgetown University's School of Nursing and Health Studies, Laura Bush spoke about the correlation between faith and service.

As a Jesuit university, Georgetown's tradition of social teaching inspires you to respect and cherish life, to love and serve your neighbor, and to use faith and service to others as guiding principles.

But the fact is, I get to take part in memorable moments like this and try to pass along any pearls of wisdom. And, of course, a commencement speaker is supposed to give some grand life advice—or issue a call to action to make the world a better place. I don't have to do either for this class—you are the advice I would give to others and you are already making a difference in the world.

Remember your faith and your commitment to serve God and each other. Your faith and service to others defines your humanity. It is what gives life meaning. You are about to begin one of the most noble and honorable forms of public service. Every one of you has a calling—a calling true to yourself, and true to your aspirations. Answer that calling with the skills and values you've gained here—with leadership, with a continual search for knowledge and with service to others. You've been led by your heart and it will be your compass throughout your career and your life.[8]

She ended her address by reminding the graduates of this quote: "The grand essentials of happiness are: something to do, something to love, and something to hope for."

Choosing charity gives your eager hands something to do, out of love for God, while giving others hope for their future.

One of the challenges of service is deciding where to begin and how to identify the needs. So many people need help that it's often difficult to choose where to start. Extending your hands to the poor and needy requires developing an eagle eye for opportunity. Before you can reach out your hands, you have to see the need and match it with your abilities. You have to listen for your calling.

In her autobiography, Rosalynn Carter talked about her top charity choice. She made the decision to focus on mental health issues when her husband was governor of Georgia. She explained the difficulty of identifying needs among a multitude of choices:

The problem is sorting out priorities: which causes to be involved in, what to do, and how much to do. I was approached by many organizations and many good causes, but my first choice was mental health . . . I had learned first hand in the campaign that (state public) services were not adequate. I had asked Jimmy for a commitment that he would do all he could for mental health programs, so I had to be willing to work on them, too.

Jimmy appointed a commission, and Rosalynn went to work. She knew she had a lot to learn. When she cried throughout a tour of a mental hospital for children, the superintendent told her that she needed to get over her tears of sympathy. He told her that most mentally retarded people are happy. They do not know they should be sad. Rosalynn took his advice. She worked one day a week at a mental health hospital in each area of care. She engaged children in activities, followed the progress of alcoholics, and planted flower beds with geriatric patients. She toured other hospitals and attended commission meetings. Her support of mental health programs resulted in a 56 percent increase in care for those who needed it.[9]

Most people don't have the time and energy to devote so much to a cause. But Rosalynn's decision to focus on a major issue shows the value of identifying just one need and giving your all to it.

Heather Cooper of Fairfax Station, Virginia, is a wife and mother of two who has been volunteering for twenty-five years. She understands what it means to extend a hand to the needy and the challenge of choosing from so many needs. Her vast experience ranges from volunteering as a seventh grader on youth mission work trips in the Appalachian Mountains to leading service organizations, such as Key Club in high school and Circle K in college. When she moved to Virginia as a young adult, she became involved in the Campagna Center, a local organization that supports most of Alexandria's hometown charities such as Wright to Read and Head Start. She also chaired the annual Scottish Christmas Walk, which attracts thirty thousand to the city of Alexandria for a weekend of events. Because of her vast experience, I asked Heather to share how she sorts through an array of needs and service opportunities.

We were e-mailing back and forth about volunteerism when Hurricane Katrina struck the Gulf Coast in August 2005.

"As I watch the TV and see the countless families devastated by Hurricane Katrina, and see all the work that needs to be done in Iraq, I feel overwhelmed at the great need that exists for all of us to reach out and help our fellow man," Heather said. "It is excruciating to watch all of the suffering, and when you are called to serve, it is hard to say 'no' and also hard to decide where your help is most needed."[10]

Just as mental health issues tugged at Rosalynn Carter's heart and the Peruvian earthquake victims gripped Pat Nixon's, Heather explained the power of answering the call of your heart.

"There are some who have so much to give that they run themselves frazzled here and there, putting in hours whenever they can but then ignoring their own and their families' needs. In choosing an area, I do believe one gets a feeling, a calling, you might say, that they should help that place because something hits you, deep inside, and shouts at you to just say you'll do it!" she said.

Heather also explained that Luke 12:48 has motivated her to serve. "From everyone who has been given much, much will be demanded; and from the one who has been entrusted with much, much more will be asked." Her service is an outward act of her inward faith and her appreciation to God for His blessings on her life.

"I don't honestly profess my faith outwards in words. I don't go around talking about being blessed, discussing sermons—that is not my style. My faith is inside and it calls me to say yes to others when I am needed. And, of course, I do have to say no once in a while! I don't have twenty arms and do need to sleep!" Heather said.

"But also, I think it is important to assess both your time and your skills and look for a needy area that best matches your abilities—and, more importantly, is it something you can commit to? Once (you settle) on a volunteer position, the people you serve will begin to count on you, so it is imperative that you realize you are in it for the long haul and shouldn't overcommit because then you may let people down," she said.

Extending your hands to the poor and needy not only requires identifying the needs that most tug at your heart, but it also requires a special touch. Once you recognize the need and hear the call, you have to decide how to best respond.

Laura Bush has time and time again drawn upon her special touch with children and her professional understanding of their emotional, intellectual, and physical needs, especially during a crisis. This former teacher has stepped up and spoken out to deliver many worthy messages during times of difficulty. She praised the efforts of schools that welcomed children who were displaced from their own homes and schools after Hurricane Katrina.

"So really, around the country, in almost every state, children who have been displaced because of Hurricane Katrina are starting school this week," she said during a visit with Mississippi families affected by the hurricane.

"It's really important for parents to make sure their children go to school. It's important for their children to have a normal life, to have the structure and the routine of going to school, and especially since many children have suffered really—have seen and suffered a lot of really terrible things," she continued.[11]

She responded in a similar way after terrorists attacked on September 11, 2001. One of the first actions Laura Bush took was to pick up a pen and write two open letters to young Americans. She wrote one for elementary school students and one for middle and high school students. Her letters, which the Web team posted on the White House kids' Web site on September 12, revealed the touch and tenor of someone who understands the minds and hearts of children.

"When sad or frightening things happen, all of us have an opportunity to become better people by thinking about others. Be kind to each other, take care of each other, and show your love for each other," she wrote to elementary school students.[12]

Less than a week after the attacks, Laura attended a memorial service in Stonycreek Township, Pennsylvania. She spoke words of comfort and hope.

"In hours like this, we learn that our faith is an active faith, that we are called to serve and to care for one another, and to bring hope and comfort where there is despair and sorrow," she said. "All of this is the work of the living."[13]

This first lady became known as the "comforter in chief" for extending her arms to those in need, but she also kept a watchful eye on the country that had fostered the terrorists. When she heard about the Taliban's brutality of Afghan women and children, she responded in a multifaceted way. Laura used her voice to speak out against the oppression.

"The plight of women and children in Afghanistan is a matter of deliberate human cruelty, carried out by those who seek to intimidate and control," she said in her solo radio address to the American people. She became the first first lady to deliver the president's Saturday morning radio address.[14]

In a radio address to the Afghan people and in two speeches at the United Nations, she continued to reveal the hard facts. One in four children in Afghanistan lacked health care and would not live past age five. Girls could not attend school past age eight, if at all. She also welcomed twelve Afghan women to the White House to get a better understanding of their experiences. She traveled to Afghanistan in March 2005 and announced a multimillion-dollar U.S. grant for building schools to educate children from kindergarten to twelfth grade.

"It is really in moments of crisis . . . that you see the true character of a first lady," historian Carl Sferrazza Anthony said of her response. "She has been good."[15]

Heather Cooper has also brought her serving hands to the White House. An enthusiastic Bush supporter, she began volunteering in 2001 and has given about 450 hours a year. She serves primarily in the visitors' office. She remembers the day when the delegation of Afghan women came to visit Laura Bush at the White House. One Afghan woman shared her unforgettable story with Heather.

"When I got off the plane, I thought, wow, God must love this country and these people and he must hate my country for making so many bad things happen there," the Afghan woman said. "I look around. I see people happy walking in the streets; there is no destruction. People open the door when I go places. People smile. Children are running and playing. I just hope that our country will have this like you have."[16]

"I seriously believe that much is expected from those who have been given so much by God, and also this great country. The Afghan woman (whom) I met at the White House reminded me of this when she said, 'God must love your country, and be so ashamed of mine,'" Heather said.

"I have always believed that we are responsible for giving back—giving back the happiness, the joy, the gifts we have received. And I don't know any soul who doesn't find giving to be more rewarding than receiving—it is the giving that makes us whole, makes us feel worthy, and makes us complete," she said.

Service sometimes goes beyond identifying a need and answering the call with your own special touch. Sometimes extending your hands to the poor and needy requires giving sacrificially, perhaps all you have.

When we think of first ladies, we think of women with access to numerous resources, especially financial ones. We don't think of first ladies as being like the poor widow with the two small copper coins. Mark 12 tells us that one day Jesus sat across from the temple at the place where people gave their offerings. He watched the crowd, noticing how each deposited his or her money. Many of the wealthy threw in large amounts. But a widow came by and gave two small copper coins, worth only a fraction of a penny. Jesus called together his disciples and told them, "I tell you the truth, this poor widow has put more into the treasury than all the others. They all gave out of their wealth; but she, out of her poverty, put in everything—all she had to live on" (Mark 12:43, 44).

In some ways, the giving hands of Ida McKinley are like those of that poor widow. By the time Ida became first lady in 1897, she had lost the energy of her youth. Though often ill, frequently depressed, and sometimes temperamental, Ida gave what she could.

This bedridden first lady crocheted more than 3,500 house slippers with leather soles. She made blue ones for Union sympathizers, gray ones for Confederate supporters, and red ones for orphans and widows. She contributed these slippers to charity auctions.

She also sent flowers from the White House's greenhouses to Washington's Metropolitan Church each Sunday. At her request, the church sent them to invalids after the service. She also gave flowers and delicacies from the White House kitchen to hospitals.

Some modern historians have made fun of Ida's house slippers and her depression, saying that her illness was merely a way to keep her husband's attention. One of Ida's friends saw her differently.

"Mrs. McKinley's greatest charm was her perfect sincerity and thoughtfulness for others. No day passed over her head without her doing something for someone . . . If she hears of an affliction of any kind overtaking anyone—no matter how much a stranger—she will immediately order something sent to that person, if nothing more than a bunch of flowers or a cheering message; in some way she conveys her sympathy and good wishes," Mrs. John Logan said.[17]

Mrs. Logan realized that Ida's crocheting not only raised money for the poor, but it also raised Ida's spirits, relieving her of her depression.

"It does not require an expert to figure that by her own hands Mrs. McKinley has earned a considerable sum for benevolent purposes. Her example of continuous employment demonstrates that occupation is the surest defense against ennui and depression of spirits and morbidness from enforced confinement, most of the time within doors," she said.[18]

Ida and Mrs. Logan understood what Grace Coolidge discovered: "In loving service there is acquired a strength and beauty of soul, which can be gained no other way."[19]

The idea of giving two copper coins became very real to many Americans in the 1930s. President Franklin D. Roosevelt suffered from polio and launched a foundation to fight the spread of the disease by funding research. Radio personality Eddie Cantor urged Americans to send their loose change to President Roosevelt in a "march of dimes to reach all the way to the White House."

Americans, particularly children, responded. The White House was flooded by so many envelopes of dimes, the staff had to recruit numerous volunteers to open and process the mail. The campaign and the foundation became known as the March of Dimes. The effort raised $18.9 million for polio research by 1945. The funding allowed Jonas Salk to develop a polio vaccine that eradicated the disease in the United States.

"A number of historians have credited this effort by FDR as being one of the major philanthropy landmarks in American history," said Michelle King, spokeswoman for the March of Dimes, which now focuses on preventing birth defects. "Roosevelt showed so many Americans that they, too, could be philanthropists."[20]

Giving sacrificially sometimes means a willingness to give even when others do not appreciate the gift.

"One more thing comes to mind when I think about the great need many Americans, and many women feel about giving to others. Our president and his father always have talked about the points of light out there and about giving back. We are criticized the world over because of our generosity. Some call it 'butting in.' Other countries mock us and criticize us for 'saving the world.' We will never be truly appreciated, and our country's wealth is also a source of condemnation, but I know, and you know, that our hearts are in the right place," Heather said.

Heather inherited the legacy of an immigrant's heart. Her father came to the United States from Germany when he was fourteen years old. He taught her that America's abundance of copper coins came from those courageous individuals who left the security of their homeland to come to the United States with a willingness to start with nothing and the determination to make it.

"This country is rich because of the immigrants who sacrificed everything and came to a foreign land, knowing no one, and succeeded. They started with little, were rewarded with much, and it is due to their sacrifice and efforts that this great country was formed and most of them . . . most of them . . . wish to spread the wealth and the happiness of freedom around the world," Heather said.

Identifying needs, responding with your own special touch, and giving sacrificially contribute to an intangible legacy. Matthew 6:19, 20 reminds us: "Do not store up for yourselves treasures on earth, where moth and rust destroy, and where thieves break in and steal. But store up for yourselves treasures in heaven, where moth and rust do not destroy, and where thieves do not break in and steal."

Harriet Lane had many copper coins. Her willingness to sacrifice them resulted in an earthly treasure beyond her imagination, one that she did not live to see. Several years after serving as first lady, Harriet married a wealthy man and had two boys. Both of her sons died of illnesses when they were young teens. Harriet realized that their doctors did not know enough about the special needs of treating children and youth. She used her multitude of copper coins to establish the Harriet Lane home as a clinic for children of all races, faiths, and circumstances. She left most of her fortune to the home and arranged for Johns Hopkins Hospital and Medical School to manage it after her death. More than 100 years later, *U.S. News and World Report* ranks the Johns Hopkins Children's Center as the third best in the nation.

Harriet's charitable copper coins also show that life's most important investments can often turn a fallow field into a fruitful vineyard.

CHAPTER SEVEN

Investment Inklings

"She considers a field and buys it; out of her earnings she plants a vineyard" (Prov. 31:16).

R OBERT LOUIS STEVENSON" understood the investment inklings of little boys. He captured their wonderment of trees when he wrote this poem, "up into the cherry tree, who should climb but little me? I held the trunk with both my hands, and looked abroad on foreign lands."[1]

Will people come?" Helen Taft wondered for the thousandth time as she dashed about her dressing room in the White House.

"Which hat should I wear?" she said.

After a quick glance at her collection, she chose one with a broad brim ornamented by a rainbow of silk flowers, ideal for a sunny April afternoon. Its width was the perfect foil to her noticeably long nose and face.

Where are my best gloves? she wondered.

Helen selected a pair of pristine kid gloves. She slid them onto her hands and buttoned them.

"But what if no one comes? What if I have no one to wave to from the car?" She mumbled while walking over to her full-length mirror to check her appearance.

Even though the idea was hers, Helen knew the success or failure of today's ceremony and surprise announcement would reflect on her husband, President William Howard Taft. With the skill of a director staging a play, the first lady had spent a month planning the dedication of the park and speedway along the Potomac River. Her opening-day jitters were worse than she would dare admit to anyone, even her husband.

"You look like a queen," President Taft called cheerily as he walked into the room.

"Thank you," she said, as he kissed her on the cheek and stood behind her. The mirror reflected a pair of opposites. His three-hundred-pound frame dwarfed her slender size. His joy countered her intensity.

"Don't worry. Throngs of people will be there, in automobiles, carriages, on horseback, on foot. Throngs will be the headline," he said.

"How did you know what I was thinking?"

"My dear, it is 1909. A quarter of a century has passed since we met. You won me over at our actors' troupe in Cincinnati. You were orchestrating dramatic readings then and just as worried about having an audience for our performances."

Helen smiled. She treasured those days when she met and married William, an up-and-coming legal mind. Their shared love of theater and politics attracted them to each other. She had every reason to be grateful to him. His public service career spanned many positions, from judgeships to his most recent post as secretary of war under President Theodore Roosevelt. She especially enjoyed their time when he was governor of the Philippines, a U.S. territory. She loved strolling along Manila's grand park, the Luneta, and touring other Asian sites.

Her husband's inauguration as the twenty-seventh president of the United States was the pinnacle of their own script. She told her family she felt like Cinderella the first day she entered the White House as first lady. Seeing the president's seal on the White House floor for the first time and realizing her husband held the title engraved in its upper arch was one of the most thrilling moments of her life.

The presidency was as much a fulfillment of her hopes as it was his. Helen had dreamed of being first lady since she was sixteen, when her family stayed at the White House as guests of President and Mrs. Hayes. That visit planted a seed in her mind. She knew then that she had the administrative skills and instincts to be first lady. Now she was living the starring role she had long dreamed of playing.

Helen looked at her reflection in the mirror. She adjusted her hat. Then her critical eye scanned her husband's appearance.

"Your mustache could use a quick trim," she said.

President Taft rotated his face from side to side and studied his mustache in the mirror.

"You are right. I could use a trim, but it's not so bad, it will do," the former judge said, overruling her.

Helen sighed, accepting his verdict.

"No one will notice my mustache. Besides, if it hadn't been for my mustache, all of the men working here would have lost theirs, if you had had your way," he said with a wink. "You have certainly assumed your new role with gusto, my dear."

"Perhaps I have been a bit ambitious."

Helen believed she could not be mistress of the White House if she did not take an active interest in running it. She thought clean-shaven butlers would make a better impression on guests and requested that all of the butlers shave their facial hair. The head usher responded coolly to the idea. She relented when he reminded her that the president wore a mustache.

She took consolation in her more successful efforts. Within six short weeks, she had assumed the bookkeeping duties, updated the housekeeping staff's job descriptions, and hosted a dinner nearly every evening. Helen knew all of these were good investments, but they would only last as long as her husband was president. She hoped the dedication and announcement would be a more lasting contribution.

"Are you ready?" she asked. "Do you have what you need for the announcement?"

"I have the cablegram and an umbrella for you."

"An umbrella?"

"It's rather gray outside, could rain," he said.

"Rain!" she said. "It was so sunny earlier this morning."

Helen raced over to the window facing the south lawn of the White House. In the distance she could see the Potomac River, the backdrop for her event. Hovering over the river was a mass of clouds, grayer than her husband's mustache.

She glanced at the mantel clock.

"There's not enough time for the clouds to pass before the band starts its concert. This weather will scatter even the most enthusiastic crowd," she said worriedly.

"If you and I are the only ones there, the event will be a success," he said. "Don't worry. People will come. A few clouds won't deter them. Archie has popularized the idea in the press."

"I hope you're right, but as efficient as Archie is, he can't keep away a storm."

Helen had tapped Archie, her husband's military aide, as the assistant producer for the event. "I'm surprised no one has thought of it before," he had said on the morning she told him her idea of creating a public gathering place along the Potomac. She envisioned band concerts, polo games, and picnics. She wanted Potomac Drive to rival the Luneta in Manila and Hyde Park in London. Archie drove her immediately to the speedway, the wide elliptical stretch of road by the river. Within an hour she had chosen the spot for the bandstand and selected the date for the opening. By noon, her husband had invited the Marine Band to play at the dedication. After Archie told the press, she planned the surprise for opening day.

"You said you had the cablegram?" she asked.

"Yes, in my pocket. Let's go," President Taft said. "The motorcar is waiting."

The first couple walked from their living quarters to the White House driveway. The Tafts were more modern than the Roosevelts before them, preferring motorcars to horse-drawn carriages. They got in their Pierce-Arrow landaulet, one of the smaller vehicles in their fleet, and began the short drive to the Potomac River. Helen glanced at the clouds a dozen times as they rode.

The clouds are darker than they were at the White House, rolled around in her mind just before they approached the bridge leading to the park.

Helen closed her eyes as if she was praying while the car chugged over the narrow wooden bridge. When the car reached the other side, she opened her eyes. She was so excited she wanted to cry. Before her was a throng of people on the lawn. The crowd was so large she could barely see the green grass and swards of splendor that gave the park its lushness. To her delight, motorcars and carriages were parked two deep along the speedway. Yet the speedway was still wide enough to allow vehicles to pass in opposite directions.

"Everyone has come," she said, noticing the eclectic mix of both the fashionable and the frugal. "You have quite an audience now for your announcement."

"An excellent crowd," Taft said as they entered the speedway.

They waved as their motorcar drove past the crowd and parked on the speedway near the bandstand. Helen waved at Archie, who stood with the newspaper reporters.

"Hello, Ambassador Bryce," Helen said to the British ambassador and his wife as they passed by in their horse-drawn carriage.

She waved to the couple following behind in an electric roundabout and then turned her attention to the crowd. She watched as people laughed, talked, and waved at each other.

These are the same friendly exchanges that always made the Luneta such a pleasant meeting place, she thought.

Although she was thrilled with the crowd's size, she still felt more nervous than Shakespeare as she waited for her husband to deliver his opening day lines and announce his surprise.

When the band finished playing, President Taft left the car and walked to the bandstand. He thanked the crowd and began his remarks.

"Today, I have two proclamations. First the road here known as the speedway shall now be called Potomac Drive," he said. "Every Wednesday and Saturday there will be a public band concert here at the park, and I intend to come to each performance."

The crowd clapped enthusiastically.

"When my wife and I lived in the Philippines, we had the chance to visit Japan. We saw Japan's dearly loved cherry blossom trees in full bloom. Helen observed that the climate along the Potomac is suitable for planting these trees here. I have in my pocket a cablegram from the mayor of Tokyo. He has learned of our interest in beautification and has offered to send two thousand cherry blossom trees to plant here along these riverbanks. His gift will enhance the growing friendship between the United States and Japan. We have accepted his generosity."

The crowd's continual clapping and cheering meant as much to Helen as the mayor's gift. She glanced at the still gray sky and smiled. The clouds had withheld their rain. Opening day and her husband's surprise announcement were a success. Then Helen closed her eyes and tried to picture starry white and pink flowers adorning trees along the park.

I wonder if any of the trees will attain the magnificent growth of the ancient cherry trees of Japan, she reflected. *But will people come to see them? I hope so!*[2]

Come they did. Helen Taft's decision to plant cherry blossom trees was a wise long-term investment with a big payoff. Today, nearly 3,700 cherry trees adorn the monument grounds along Washington, D.C.'s tidal basin and Potomac Park. More than seven hundred thousand people come each year to enjoy the beautiful blossoms and celebrate the beginning of spring. A century has passed since Helen first had the idea to plant those trees, but she waited for the right opportunity to nourish her investment. When the time was right, she turned a handful of tree saplings into a flowering diplomatic gesture of friendship.[3]

Much like Helen Taft, we know the woman in Proverbs 31 was an investor. Verse 16 tells us that "she considers a field and buys it; out of her earnings she plants a vineyard." Perhaps this woman took some of the money she made from selling sashes and invested it in a simple field. Maybe her purchase was so successful that she used her profits to turn the field into a fruitful vineyard. By investing in real estate, she increased the value of her portfolio.

In a similar way, perhaps she saw the many facets of her life as an investment. Her eager hands, entrepreneurial spirit, and thoughtful decisions allowed her to invest in her family, business, coworkers, employees, and the poor and needy. Her investments were long term. They were valuable.

How and where you invest your life matters to God. You may never have the visibility or platform of a first lady. You may have no interest in gardening or diplomacy, but you can plant your own version of cherry blossom trees. Your time, treasure, and talents are your best assets. They are the seeds of your legacy and branches of your purpose in life. God wants you to incorporate your investment inklings into his business plan for you. Whatever portfolio he has given you, he wants you to view your life as an investment. Investing requires a willingness to use your talents, the humility to admit your shortcomings, the confidence to make sound decisions, and a commitment to reinvesting.

Before you begin investing, you have to appreciate the gifts God has given you. Helen Taft dreamed of becoming first lady because she visited First Lady Lucy Hayes in the White House and watched her do the job. Helen realized that the first lady needed to have good management skills, and she knew she had the gift of administration. Helen also had a vision for what she would do as first lady. After seeing how the cherry blossom trees in Japan brought beauty to the community while also bringing the community together, she hoped they would have the same effect in the United States. She waited for the right opportunity to employ her eager and capable hands. Then she invested them in cherry blossom trees.

Grace Coolidge also had accepted the gifts God had given her. When she became first lady in 1923, someone asked her to name her favorite book. Grace gave an unusual, almost strange answer. "People," she said. Grace was no bookworm, and she didn't pretend to be. She knew her warmth made her a natural to work with people. After college, she chose to become a teacher to deaf children. Her compassion for people with disabilities never waned. Later, she saw an opportunity to highlight the accomplishments of a woman who lived a full life despite her blindness and deafness. She invited Helen Keller to the White House.[4]

Grace also used her talent for people to nurture her own children. She believed her sons were the best long-term investment she ever made.

"It seemed to me that my own training had been very wholesome, and it was my aim to give my children the same background insofar as it was possible under somewhat different circumstances. I gave my entire time to it, and I know of no investment which yields such large and satisfactory returns," Grace wrote.[5]

Your talents are valuable tools for investing in the opportunities the Lord brings your way. One of the Bible's most popular teaching tales is the parable of the talents. A master called his servants together before he left on a journey. He gave one five talents of money, another two, and another one. He gave them each according to their ability. Then the master left on his trip.

The one with five talents put his to work and gained five more. The one with two talents also doubled his investment. But the man with one talent dug a hole in the ground and hid it. When the master returned from his journey, he asked each one what they had done with their talents. To the servants who invested their talents, he said, "Well done, good and faithful servants, come and share in your master's happiness." The other servant explained that he was afraid and hid his talent. He put his jewel back into the ground and covered it up with mud. For this the master called him wicked and lazy. He said the man would have done better to put his money in the bank and let someone else invest it.

"Take the talent from him and give it to the one who has the ten talents. For everyone who has will be given more, and he will have an abundance. Whoever does not have, even what he has will be taken from him," the master said. Then he threw out the lazy servant" (Matt. 25:14–30).

It doesn't matter how much talent you have. God values the talents he has given you and wants you to invest them.

Investing also requires a willingness and humility to admit what you don't know. In the parable, the master told the man with the one talent that he would have been better off letting the bank do the investing if he was unwilling. God places resources and people in our lives with other talents to help us when our own abilities fall short.

Julia Grant encountered this problem when she went shopping in New York one day. When she entered a store on Broadway, the owner asked her if her husband, President Grant, was going to veto the finance bill Congress was debating at the time. The man told her the bill would absolve the government's responsibility for honoring the war bonds. "Yes," she answered. "The president will surely veto any bill that is infamous or any bill that would reflect dishonor on the country."

When Julia returned to her hotel, she met several people in the lobby. They asked her whether her husband would sign a bill that would free the nation from debt and bring great prosperity. She answered, "Yes, of course, he would, if it was to bring prosperity and good to the country, I was quite sure he would sign it."

When she returned to the White House, she received several letters and, to her horror, she discovered the bills were the same piece of legislation.

Julia was a smart woman, but she obviously didn't know what she didn't know. She told Ulysses about her problem. They sat on the sofa in the White House library and talked about it. After he explained both sides of the issue to her, he asked her what she thought. She thought he should veto the bill. He did.[6]

Once Julia admitted what she did not know, she consulted an expert on the subject. She relied on someone else's talents and knowledge when hers were not enough. Investing is much the same way. If you are going to invest in something or speak out on something that is beyond your abilities or knowledge base, you ought to go to people who know what they're doing. Then you can decide if it's time to veto the bill or sign it. When you make a major decision, such as getting married, having children, or starting a business, do so with humility. Read books about the subject, and consult people who know what it takes to be successful in the area in which you want to invest.

The Proverbs 31 woman did not start out as an expert in real estate. She was a seamstress before she was a Realtor. Today, women in the United States can easily buy and sell real estate on their own. Hebrew women in the ancient world could legally trade and buy real estate, but only if they had the permission of their husbands. Whatever real estate purchases the first lady of Proverbs made, she made in her husband's name. Her earnings belonged to her husband unless they had made some other agreement.[7] We don't know what their arrangement was, but verses 28 and 29 tell us that her husband praised her and her accomplishments. "Her children arise and call her blessed; her husband also, and he praises her." Because of these accolades, it's safe to assume he trusted her investment inklings.

We know the woman of Proverbs 31 became a good investor in vineyards. She must have sought wise counsel before she purchased that first field. She probably learned from the expert which questions to ask. Was the soil fertile? Was it a sunny spot or a shady one? Which plants grow best in the field? This type of humility leads to wisdom. Another proverb defines knowing what you don't know like this: "When pride comes, then comes disgrace, but with humility comes wisdom" (Prov. 11:2).

Investing not only requires a willingness to use your talents and the humility to admit your shortcomings, but also a commitment to making sound decisions.

Historians often describe Bess Truman as a reluctant first lady. She canceled her first and only press conference and then answered reporters' questions in writing, mostly using yes or no answers. But Bess was not a wallflower—quite the contrary. She was, as her husband Harry said, "a full partner in all my transactions—politically and otherwise."[8] Bess's ability to make good decisions contributed to his success. She helped Harry behind the scenes throughout his career. When he suddenly became president after the death of Franklin Roosevelt, she worried she would lose the partnership they had labored to create. When Bess saw the multitude of advisers surrounding her husband, she wondered if her talents were still useful to him.

But Harry valued Bess's insight and missed her suggestions. It wasn't long before the Trumans returned to their routine. They spent many evenings together, going over his speeches, schedules, and legislation. According to Margaret, their daughter, Bess gave her opinion on an issue only once and then let it go. She didn't nag. She didn't second-guess him or stew about it when he didn't take her advice. "Bess never hesitated to try to influence Harry Truman's decisions. But she never attempted to control him," Margaret wrote.

President Truman valued her decision making. He told a White House news correspondent that Bess was part of all his major decisions during his presidency. He said, "She never made a suggestion that wasn't for the welfare and benefit of the country and what I was trying to do."[9]

The first lady of Proverbs 31 also was a good decision maker. Verse 16 says, "She considers a field and buys it." It doesn't say, she considered a field and worried about it. It doesn't say she wondered whether she was smart enough or pretty enough to buy the field. She could not have dwelled on thoughts that she was untalented, incapable, or unloved by God. She didn't sit on a decision, wondering whether a better field would come along. Such untruths would have paralyzed her. No, she simply made a thoughtful, reasonable evaluation. The field was bountiful. She had the cash. She was ready. She bought it.

Decision making matters to God. When the Lord instructed the Jews to build a temple, he ordered them to create a special vest for the high priest. "Fashion a breastpiece for making decisions—the work of a skilled craftsman. Make it like the ephod: of gold, and of blue, purple and scarlet yarn, and of finely twisted linen" (Exod. 28:15).

Then he told them to decorate it with valuable jewels. "In the first row there shall be a ruby, a topaz, and a beryl; in the second row a turquoise, a sapphire, and an emerald; in the third row a jacinth, an agate, and an amethyst; in the fourth row a chrysolite, an onyx, and a jasper. Mount them in gold filigree settings" (Exod. 28:17–20).

These rubies, emeralds, and precious stones were symbols of worth because each represented a tribe of Israel. The stones showed the high priest that God valued decisions that affected his people, and the breastplate's heaviness reminded him of the seriousness of seeking God's counsel. The breastplate was God's way of saying, "Decisions are important. I want you to bring them to me."

Maybe you are like Bess Truman or the woman in Proverbs 31, and decision making is easy for you. You may be confident when you make decisions, or perhaps you'd rather watch television, listen to the radio, scream, or eat chocolate—anything to avoid making a significant decision. Viewing your life as an investment requires good decision making and a commitment to think truthfully about your talents and the circumstances of your life.

Investing not only requires decision making based on truth, but also a commitment to reinvesting. The most valuable investments in life are perpetual.

The Proverbs 31 woman analyzed her investments and decided whether it was time to reinvest. Verse 18 explains how she watched over her investments. "She sees that her trading is profitable; and her lamp does not go out at night." This imagery of a lamp burning appears to mean that she worked twenty-four hours a day. What a discouraging thought, to live life sleep-deprived! Although this woman was diligent, she did not stay up all night studying her portfolio or researching the marketplace. The phrase "her lamp does not go out at night" is a reference to a Jewish cultural and religious icon, the perpetual lamp.

The perpetual lamp was a glass vessel that held a wick burning in olive oil. Perpetual lamps were found in Jewish temples and synagogues. The lamp's continuous burning symbolized life and prosperity.[10] King David said, "You, O LORD, keep my lamp burning; my God turns my darkness into light" (Ps. 18:28). His son Solomon said, "The lamp of the LORD searches out the spirit of a man, it searches out his inmost being" (Prov. 20:27). Perpetual lamps also symbolized God's presence in Israel. "I will give you one tribe to his son so that David my servant may always have a lamp before me in Jerusalem, the city where I chose to put my Name" (1 Kings 11:36).

The story of Helen's cherry blossom trees shows the power of perpetual investing. President Taft announced the mayor of Tokyo's gift on April 17, 1909. Three years later, Helen Taft and Viscountess Chinda, wife of the Japanese ambassador, planted the first two cherry blossom trees in Washington in a ceremony. Three years after that, the United States government reciprocated by donating flowering dogwood trees to the people of Japan.

First Lady Lady Bird Johnson, a proponent of beautification and the environment, continued Helen's investment. She accepted 3,800 more trees from Japan in 1965. The cycle of giving and investing came full circle in 1981, when Japanese horticulturalists took cuttings from the Washington trees to replace some trees in Japan that had been destroyed by a flood.[11] Helen's original idea has been invested and reinvested over the years. Her cherry trees have blossomed in the light of a perpetual lamp of diplomacy.

When I think of a modern-day woman who understands the value of reinvesting, I think of Karen Hughes. I first met Karen in 1998. As I mentioned earlier, my husband had expressed interest in working in politics and government, so we began looking for jobs as he neared completion of his PhD. When I found out Governor Bush's press office was hiring someone to develop his Web site, I conducted research and read hundreds of newspaper articles about him. I wanted to make sure I agreed with the governor on the majority of his positions before I tried to work for him. I also learned as much as I could about Web site development. Then I designed a five-page Web site, put it on a floppy disk, and mailed it to Karen Hughes.

When Karen interviewed me, I told her that I wanted to communicate the governor's message through the Web site. I am forever grateful to Karen because she gave me a chance to invest my communication talents. She hired me, even though I had scant political connections and even less political experience.

From day one of working for Karen in the Texas governor's office, I could tell she was a devoted wife and mother. She often arranged and rearranged her schedule around her son Robert's soccer games. I also realized that her dedication to George W. Bush was more than just a job. She had invested her talents in a leader who had earned her complete trust and confidence. She had a passion for communicating his message of reforming education, limiting government, and lowering taxes. Over the years, I watched in amazement as Karen pursued both of her perpetual investments with passion and persistence.

Her investment in the governor resulted in a series of open doors, each leading to more opportunities to invest in public service. When he ran for reelection as governor, Karen led his communication team and coordinated his campaign communication strategy. When he ran for president, she again invested her talents in a high-powered, high-stress campaign. Because traveling across the country took her away from home so often, she asked if Robert could travel with her in the last few months of the campaign. Bush agreed.

When President Bush asked her to serve as White House Counselor, she moved her family to Washington and invested in her country. As a result, many members of the media described Karen as the most powerful woman in Washington. They called her Bush's alter ego because she was so effective at articulating his message in clear and relevant terms. The reason she could easily explain his policies to soccer moms was simple. She was a soccer mom.

Karen also lived her life in the light of God's perpetual lamp. She kept a watchful eye on her family and her professional investment.

Karen soon realized that her husband and son were not happy living in D.C. The transition from the Texas capital to the nation's capital never came for them. When her son told her that living in the same house with her in D.C. was a lot like going to boarding school, she knew she had to reassess her most valuable investment. She decided to give up her White House job because her family, her top priority, needed reinvesting. She told President Bush that she needed to move her family back to Texas. He agreed, and Robert finished high school in his hometown.[12]

Karen's decision had a far-reaching impact, inspiring women across the United States. I have met dozens of women who have told me how much they admire Karen Hughes. Many of them would agree with one political commentator, who described Karen's choice in a Proverbs 31 way.

"To Karen and her husband, finding a way to spend more time with their son isn't a sacrifice. It's an investment in a child's life. Hughes's choice also speaks volumes about priorities. At a time when many children are tossed into daycare, sometimes for selfish reasons, and many married couples split up, again often for selfish reasons, Hughes has struck a powerful blow for doing the right thing," wrote Cal Thomas, the syndicated columnist.[13]

After Robert graduated from high school, Karen received an opportunity to reinvest in her country. President Bush appointed her as undersecretary of state for public diplomacy. She spoke at the State Department shortly after her nomination and reflected on her decision to reinvest in her family.

"As most of you know, I left Washington almost three years ago to spend more time with my family and to allow my son to attend high school during those critical years in Texas. Other than marrying my husband that was the best decision I think I've ever made," she said.[14]

At her swearing-in ceremony, President Bush explained Karen's role as an ambassador investing in diplomacy. Her job is to communicate America's message to the world by refuting the lies of terrorist propaganda and by proactively conveying the nonnegotiable demands of human dignity: the rule of law, limits on the power of the state, respect for women, private property, free speech, equal justice, and religious tolerance.

"We're in a war on terror. We are still at war. And to succeed in this war, we must effectively explain our policies and fundamental values to people around the world. This is an incredibly important mission. And so I've asked one of America's most talented communicators to take it on," President Bush said.

"Karen Hughes has been one of my closest and most trusted advisers for more than a decade. She understands the miracle of America. She understands what we stand for. After all, she's lived it," he said, noting that her grandfather was a Pennsylvania coal miner and that she was a working mom who rose to the highest level of government.

"Karen will deliver the message of freedom and humility and compassion and determination. She knows that freedom is not America's gift to the world. She knows that freedom is the Almighty God's gift to every man, woman, and child in this world," President Bush said.[15]

God's gift of freedom comes with a responsibility to invest. Just as the parable of the talents shows, burying talents and investments comes with a price. What happens when you fail to reinvest your talents or investments? Your life becomes a blank.

Sarah Polk made the investment of a lifetime when she married the short but dashing James Polk. Their journey took them through the doors of the White House in 1845. When he failed to win a second term as president, they didn't care too much. Although childless, this devoted couple looked forward to spending many years together at their home in Nashville.

James died within months of leaving the presidency. Sarah was only forty-six. "Life," she said, "was then a blank."[16] But Sarah lived another forty-two years. What is startling to me is how Sarah lived the rest of her life. She wasn't ill, but she lived as a recluse. She rarely left home. She did no charitable work. She rested on the laurels of her earlier life. She failed to reinvest.

Lara Holloway, a nineteenth-century biographer of first ladies, had access to people who knew Sarah. Holloway's work is well respected by historians. She wrote:

Mrs. Polk, though ever willing to converse, and always enriching the conversation from her ready store of information and observation, is remarkably reticent in regard to her own life . . . She is never seen in public except at church. The visits of chosen friends are grateful to her, but she does not return them, and no attraction is sufficient to draw her far away from the home where cluster so many dear and sacred memories.[17]

A modern-day biographer was less polite in his interpretation. He wrote, "Sarah Childress Polk undertook nothing and achieved nothing in the second half of her life, although she continued to be honored."[18] What a waste! I can understand how devastating James's loss was for her. But Sarah never got on with life. She stopped investing.

Sometimes the power of the perpetual lamp yields unimaginable returns. When Stacey and Ken Ankele moved from Maryland to Austin, Texas, they planted seeds and put down roots. The Ankeles joined a church and invested their time in a small group with other couples who met for Bible study and fellowship. The Ankeles put in their time each week, expecting little in return. But when Stacey gave birth to their third son, Jacob, in April 2004, they discovered the value of investing in others and keeping their decisions focused on the truth.

Stacey knew something was wrong almost immediately after his birth. Jacob struggled to breathe. The nurses put him on a ventilator and whisked him away for a million tests. The doctors diagnosed Jacob with infantile myofibromatosis, which are noncancerous fibroid tumors. In most cases, these tumors are harmless, appearing under an infant's skin and dissolving over time. Jacob's case was very serious. The tumors were in his liver and lungs, blocking his airways by 75 percent.

The prognosis for infants with so many of these tumors in the internal organs is not good. Because the disease is rare, little data exists about treatment. Case studies pointed the doctors to chemotherapy. Within his first twenty-four hours of life outside the womb, Jacob underwent chemotherapy.

"I felt so helpless as a human to be able to do anything. We knew we had great doctors and nurses, but that's no guarantee. They were the first ones to say, 'We don't know if he's going to make it,'" Stacey said.[19]

The church immediately responded to the Ankeles by starting a twenty-four-hour prayer network. Church members signed up at all hours of the day to pray for Jacob. One of the Ankeles' perpetual investments reaped a harvest of support.

"Some friends set their alarm for 4:30 a.m. They got up and prayed for Jacob at that time. For the first week of his life, someone was praying for Jacob every hour. It was just awesome to feel that we had this huge support without asking. It wasn't our idea to have a twenty-four-hour prayer watch. It was just done," Stacey said.

The church also provided meals and cared for the older Ankele boys to allow Stacey and Ken to be at the hospital. Ken created a Web site for Jacob so their friends and family could know what was happening and what specifically needed prayer.

"The power of the spiritual support we received from our church was incredible. We received so many messages of support that just made me cry. People we didn't even know at our church shared stories to give us encouragement," Stacey said. "So many people passed on Jacob's story to their family and friends that Jacob probably had thousands of people praying for him across this country."

She also realized she needed to keep her mind steadfast on the truth.

"Some people said, 'Oh, I can't believe how well you're handling this.' I didn't have a choice. Going insane wasn't going to help anybody," Stacey said.

"This was the first time I was able to completely surrender something to God. I think that was key for me in growing in my faith. You can have peace if you can truly give something to God," she said.

Jacob's condition was touch and go for many weeks. They had to wait and see how Jacob responded to the chemotherapy. The Ankeles could barely touch Jacob because the doctors wanted him as sedated as possible. When Jacob was a month old, Stacey and Ken were finally able to hold him. He stayed in the hospital for nine weeks and received chemotherapy once a week for six months. A year after his birth, Jacob became one of three miracle children chosen by the Children's Medical Center Foundation of Central Texas. Ken and Stacey made it through the ordeal because of their faith.

"On a practical level, I think we could have asked our church for anything, and it would have been provided for us. I've never felt such an outpouring of love and support," Stacey said.

"We never expected to have needs such as these, but what an amazing return on an investment! The time and effort we have spent forming relationships within the church body is nothing compared to the outpouring of love and support that we received from our church family at our greatest time of need," she said.

God values our investments. As the great investor, he has invested talents in you. He wants you to evaluate your decisions and investments in the light of his truths. He sees your life as a perpetual investment and wants you to continue to invest in the work he has given you and the people surrounding you. And to prepare for life's emergencies, he has another plan. He wants you to invest in scarlet.

CHAPTER EIGHT

Blizzards and Terrorism

"When it snows, she has no fear for her household; for all of them are clothed in scarlet" (Prov. 31:21).

S UCH BUTCHERY! What terror!" Louisa Adams said as her Russian carriage clip-clopped along the German road past the famous battlefield.

Through the carriage window, Louisa studied the remains of uniforms, boots, hats, and bones, bleaching the plane in all directions. A sign among the small mounds and crosses along the side of the road caught her eye. She learned that more than ten thousand had died on this spot two years earlier.

Louisa had heard the story from the innkeeper in the previous town. Once-loyal German soldiers had turned against Napoleon, the French emperor seeking to conquer Europe. He was so angry at their revolt that he ordered his army to fight to the death and butcher them. But the battle only emboldened Napoleon's opponents. They later joined together to defeat Napoleon, exiling him to an island.

"Lord, what is man that he should thus destroy?" Louisa whispered, tasting bitter saliva surfacing in her mouth. She fought nausea's overture by swallowing several times. Fearing she would faint,

Louisa took a deep breath. Then she tightened her coat around her dainty body, feeling the nudging comfort of her passport hidden inside her coat pocket.

"What terror! How barbaric!" Louisa said. "Such deadly sickness."

Her heart throbbed as she began to think about the tortures, suffering, and anguish of the men who died on the field. She caught a glimpse of a detached skull. The sight was too much. She covered her mouth and turned her head away from the window.

The innkeeper had warned her about the open graveyard, but she had no alternative route. Louisa took several deep breaths. She had traveled too far and had risked too much to turn back to St. Petersburg now. Nothing, not Napoleon himself, would keep her from feeling her husband's safe embrace in Paris.

Louisa glanced at the passengers in her care. She first focused on the bench across from her where Madame Babet sat. With her chin tucked against her neck and her eyes closed, Madame Babet appeared to sleep. Louisa wondered if the nurse was truly asleep or merely hiding her nerves. Louisa then looked at the back of the carriage where she had made a bed for her son for their terrestrial travels. Six-year-old Charles stirred slightly, pulling his Russian fur blanket over his head.

I wish I could have shielded Charles completely from the other horrors of this journey, she reflected.

"Do you think it's true?" Madame Babet said, her eyes suddenly popping open.

"What?" Louisa answered knowingly.

"That Napoleon is coming out of exile? I heard the innkeeper's wife talking about it."

"It's a rumor, nothing more," Louisa said sharply.

"If it is true, then he's headed for Paris. We'll be right in his path. You've seen how he butchers Germans. He'll not hesitate to kill those riding in a Russian carriage," Madame Babet said.

But I'm an American, and I will not be deterred by rumors, Louisa thought.

"Perhaps we'll learn more at the next town. If we are in any danger, I am certain Mr. Adams would warn me by sending a messenger. He is quite practical that way," Louisa said of her husband, John Quincy.

Louisa glanced out the window. When she saw a pristine pasture, she knew they had passed the worst of the battlefield.

The carriage's six horses trotted along at a steady pace. Louisa tried not to think about the rumor of Napoleon's return. Instead she turned her mind to John Quincy. The thought of seeing him again gave her hope and determination.

She could hardly believe it was March 1815. Nearly a year had passed since John Quincy had left their home in St. Petersburg on a peace mission for President James Madison. She was proud of her husband's service as the U.S. ambassador to Russia. However, Napoleon's terror had rippled throughout the world like an earthquake, his tremors reaching as far as the United States.

Napoleon was indirectly responsible for the United States' war against Britain. British captains had stormed American ships to kidnap sailors, forcing them to fight in the Royal Navy against Napoleon. As a result of this and other issues, President Madison declared war against Britain in 1812.

After Napoleon went into exile, the president asked John Quincy to go to Brussels to negotiate a treaty to end the war. Although saying good-bye was heartbreaking, Louisa knew if anyone could negotiate with the British, John Quincy could. She believed he had both the practicality and stubbornness the job needed. But sometimes she wondered if he was too practical.

Louisa stared out the window and contemplated her current circumstances. She was not surprised that her husband had successfully brokered a treaty with Britain last December. Nor was she shocked when President Madison appointed him as the new ambassador to Great Britain. What surprised her was John Quincy's request for her to break social norms. He had asked her, not a male secretary as was customary, to sell the furniture, hire a carriage, and make the travel arrangements. Worse, he wanted her to travel to Paris to meet him.

What other member of my sex spends nearly forty days traveling across a thousand miles of frozen tundra in war-torn Europe without her husband or another male protector? Louisa thought.

Louisa had understood John Quincy's reasons for not returning to accompany her and Charles. Travel was expensive. Brussels was too close to London for John Quincy to justify returning to St. Petersburg. Boat travel was impossible in the winter. His plan was practical. From Paris, they would travel to London together.

Like other women of her social class, Louisa had no more experience selling goods and making travel arrangements than men had in nursing babies. Without knowing where she would stay or what she would encounter along her journey, she had decided to be as prepared as possible.

Louisa ran her fingers along the edges of her cushioned seat. Underneath she kept a stash of gold coins and Madeira wine. She smiled at her secret treasure. Not even the drivers knew of her reserves. She had packed plenty of blankets, mostly Russian furs, for warmth. Louisa also had made a final unspoken pledge. She had decided that no matter what happened, she would keep her mind steadfast and her faith firm.

"Nothing but the buoyant hope of soon embracing John Quincy sustains me," she said under her breath. "And the promise of Providence's guiding hand."

Louisa thought about the rumor.

Has Napoleon escaped exile? Is he en route to Paris? Are we in danger?

The possibility of Napoleon's return concerned her, but she could not make a reasonable decision until she knew the truth. Louisa closed her eyes and rested.

When they reached the next town, they had difficulty obtaining fresh horses, but not a place to stay. Louisa asked the tavern keeper what had happened to the town's horses.

"Napoleon, Madame. Men are leaving town to join the emperor. He's marching to Paris to regain his throne," he said.

"But Napoleon is in exile," she replied in fluent French, which she had learned as a schoolchild. Years of practice allowed her to speak the language without an accent.

"Not any more."

It is true. Napoleon has slipped the bonds of exile. Her mind flashing to the horror of the battlefield and the detached skull.

"Where do you think he is? Is he ahead of us?" she said calmly, hiding her alarm.

"You are ahead of him, by a handful of days," he said.

"Thank you," she said.

Louisa ordered dinner from the tavern keeper and saved some bread for their ride the next day. As she helped Charles onto the tavern's mattress palette to go to sleep that night, she could hardly believe her journey had come to this point. She was nearing Paris just as Napoleon was coming back to power. She knew enough about France's politics to realize she could find herself in the crossfire of a civil war.

How many more emergencies can I face? Louisa wondered, as she stretched out next to Charles. Madame Babet was already snoring across the room.

As Louisa closed her eyes, her mind retraced the steps of her journey. Her travels had already been more terrifying than she had expected. Near the beginning, when she left Russia's borders, she had to choose whether to cross a frozen lake or travel around it. Because it was so late in the day, if she went around the lake, she might not find shelter for the evening. She chose to cross, trusting Providence's hand and the tapping sticks of her guides. The carriage began to break through the ice just as it came upon solid land on the other side. The horses reacted violently but pulled the carriage to safety.

At another town Louisa learned that a murder had recently been committed on the road she was about to take. Seeing no other option, she proceeded. Then her driver became lost on that road. They wandered around in a wild German forest under a starless night until midnight before finding shelter at a farmer's house.

After these and other difficulties, Louisa was surprised at how calm she was when she first heard the rumor of Napoleon's return. She didn't know why, but she felt strong—somewhat afraid, but also strong.

Should we proceed? We could try to hide in a town and wait for Napoleon's army to pass or we could try to stay ahead of him. Whatever I choose, I will not panic, she determined.

Louisa prayed and then went to sleep.

"It is better to get to Paris as soon as possible before the armies can regroup. Each day of delay puts us in more danger," she explained to Madame Babet the next morning.

Louisa found herself trying to calm the nurse's nerves a thousand times over the next week as they traveled from town to town and crossed the border into France. They followed a routine of staying in a tavern, acquiring fresh horses, and leaving early in the morning.

When they reached Epernay, a town in France's champagne country, Louisa learned she was not as far ahead of Napoleon's army as she hoped. The tavern owner expected Napoleon's troops to pass through the next day. The weather was sunny, and the roads were quiet. Louisa decided the conditions were good for proceeding and staying ahead of the army.

Louisa led Madame Babet and Charles into the carriage. Charles sat next to her and Madame Babet sat across from them. Louisa kept her arm around Charles as they rode along. She talked to Charles about how much John Quincy was looking forward to seeing them again.

"What's that noise?" Madame Babet asked about a mile after leaving town.

Louisa listened. She could hear rhythmic trotting.

"Horses. Horses," she said, remembering how quiet the road was when they left Epernay.

Louisa closed her eyes and listened to the trotting, which became louder and louder like a mounting thunderstorm. Then she heard shouts in French, military chants.

"It appears we are no longer ahead of Napoleon's troops but in the midst of them," Louisa said as she looked through the window. "There's also a mob of women lining the side of the road."

As they began to pass the mob, Louisa could hear their curses.

"Tear them out of the carriage. They are Russians. Take them out, kill them!" they shouted.

Louisa glanced at Madame Babet, whose face was as pale as her handkerchief. The nurse's whole body trembled. Louisa looked at Charles. His eyes were glued open like a marble statue. She drew him tightly to her side and turned her head to the window.

Louisa saw uniformed men on horses galloping next to the carriage. She heard someone shout at her driver to stop.

"What's happening? What's happening?" Madame Babet screamed.

"The soldiers have seized the horses. They have turned their muskets against the drivers," she answered.

The carriage came to a violent and sudden halt, throwing them from their seats.

Lord, what should I do? Louisa prayed as she helped Charles back into his seat. She heard the soldiers yelling at the drivers to unload all of the bags from the carriage.

Someone banged loudly on the passenger door.

Louisa saw a bayonet pointed at her through the window. Just as she was about to panic, Louisa heard a quiet voice whisper to her, "Take out your passport." She reached into her coat pocket and pulled out her papers.

An officer threw open the carriage door.

"Madame, you are surrounded by Napoleon's Imperial Guard."

"Here are our papers, sir," she said, handing him her passport. By this time the cursing crowd had surrounded the carriage. Louisa sat in silence as the officer read her papers. All she could hear were the mob's cries to kill the Russians. She glanced at Madame Babet. Tears ran down the nurse's cheeks while she clasped her hands together. Louisa pulled Charles as close to her side as she possibly could. Her heart was racing so fast she thought it would burst. With her free hand, Louisa patted her cheeks just below her eyes to wipe away her own tears. But to her surprise, her face was dry.

"This is just an American lady going to meet her husband in Paris," the officer shouted to the crowd.

Louisa took a deep breath and exhaled with relief. The mob grew quiet for a moment. Then the crowd and the soldiers began shouting over and over again, "Vive les Americains! Long live the Americans."

The officer jerked his head toward Louisa.

What does he want? Went through her mind. *Ah, I know.*

Louisa reached into her coat pocket and pulled out a handkerchief.

"Vive Napoléon! Long live Napoleon. Long live Napoleon," Louisa called out in perfect French while waving her handkerchief. She had to protect her son and get to Paris.

"Vive les Americains!" they shouted. "Ils sont nos amis. (They are our friends)."

The officer ordered a group of soldiers to march in front of Louisa's horses.

"My men will fire on you immediately if your horses go any faster than a walk. They will escort you to the next town. Your situation is very precarious, Madame," the officer said, returning her passport.

"The army is totally undisciplined and may not obey orders. You should always seem perfectly at ease and unconcerned. Whatever they shout at you, respond with 'Long live Napoleon.' The whole army is in motion to greet the emperor. I suggest you take a more circuitous route to Paris."

"Thank you for your kind attention. I will follow your advice," Louisa said.

"You speak French very well, Mrs. Adams. No accent. Your knowledge of the language will contribute to your safety. No one will suspect you are a foreigner."

Accompanied by Napoleon's imperial guards, Louisa and her passengers traveled to the next town. The soldiers pointed their bayonets at Louisa's drivers and yelled brutal threats every half hour.

For miles Louisa saw intoxicated men and women lining the roads and chanting threats.

When Louisa arrived safely at a tavern in the next town, she found something to laugh about. Because she relied on six horses to pull her carriage and was the only female traveling to Paris, a rumor had spread that she was one of Napoleon's sisters.

Just call me Princess Stephanie, went through her mind each time she waved from her carriage until she reached Paris a few days later. She shouted, "Long live Napoleon" as many times as she thought about John Quincy.

Louisa arrived safely at her husband's hotel in Paris. His embrace never felt better, and she was pleased when John Quincy reacted with astonishment to the stories of her journey. He assured her that had he been aware of Napoleon's return, he would have come to her. They were both thrilled when Napoleon suffered defeat in a battle called Waterloo, which returned him to exile.

Louisa later realized how well she came through the ordeal. As soon as they arrived in Paris, Madame Babet left the Adams' employment to live with nearby relatives as she had planned. Two months later, Louisa, John Quincy, and Charles left for London. Louisa visited Madame Babet shortly before their departure. She was horrified when she saw that the woman was still severely depressed and bedridden because of the journey. Louisa realized the value of keeping her mind steadfast on the promises of Providence.[1]

It snows in Israel, especially in the mountains. The rainy season brings with it snow, the same chilling snow that Louisa faced on her journey from St. Petersburg to Paris. Louisa knew she would encounter snowstorms and icy lakes, so she brought along Russian fur blankets for warmth and Madeira wine and bread for sustenance. She also prepared for other types of storms, ones of insecurity and uncertainty. Louisa was ready for a blizzard of hazards because she had clothed her heart and mind in scarlet.

Proverbs 31:21 provides a principle for facing life's storms. "When it snows, she has no fear for her household; for all of them are clothed in scarlet." This Hebrew term for scarlet thread is *shaniym*. Scarlet is a color, an adjective in English, but scarlet functions as a noun in this verse, denoting something made from scarlet thread. Here, scarlet most likely refers to a red wool cloak or a blanket.[2] *Shaniym* is also plural. Verse 21 could read "for all of them are clothed in scarlets." The plural could simply mean that she had cloaks or wool blankets for everyone in the family, or it could translate to double-layered cloaks.

Another proverb shows us that sometimes one garment is not enough during a snowstorm. "Like one who takes away a garment on a cold day, or like vinegar poured on soda, is one who sings songs to a heavy heart" (Prov. 25:20). Garments are protection against the cold. Double garments provide even more protection. Perhaps each member of the family had a double-layered coat or several blankets. One principle for protecting against life's storms is to clothe your heart and mind in something that is multilayered.

Another principle is found in the color. Red is significant. Why take the time to dye a coat used for snowstorms, which is something that doesn't happen every day? Why not keep it the color of the wool and save time? And why choose red? Some scholars suggest she chose red because it retained heat, but others have found no evidence for this practice in the ancient world.[3]

Because the woman in Proverbs 31 loved fabrics and textiles, she knew which dyes wouldn't fade and may have chosen scarlet for its durability. Scarlet was one of the most durable dyes of the ancient world. It was also very easy to make. All you had to do was boil a bug. By placing a female grub worm, which was found near oak trees, in boiling water, a beautiful and durable red dye appeared. Fabrics dyed with scarlet would not fade in the rain or melted snow. A red garment would also stand out on a snow-covered hill. Another principle for protecting against life's storms is to clothe your mind and heart in something durable.

Durability is also an important characteristic of gemstones. Durability separates jewels from other minerals. Some minerals are beautiful but are too soft and scratch easily. A gemstone is not only beautiful and rare, but it is also durable and resistant to abrasion, fracture, corrosion, and chemical reactions. Diamonds are the hardest of minerals, four times harder than the second-hardest minerals: sapphires and red rubies. No wonder the woman in Proverbs 31 was worth more than rubies and diamonds, and no wonder she chose something durable to protect against corrosion.

Like a ruby, a scarlet cloak was not only multilayered and durable, but it was also valuable. Scarlet robes were worn by the wealthy and warriors. Artisans used cords of scarlet for making temple tapestries. The curtain in the inner sanctuary was a tapestry woven with threads of white, blue, scarlet, and purple. Glittering scarlet indicates value, worth, and intensity.

Three different Hebrew words for scarlet appear together in Isaiah 1:18. "'Come now, let us reason together,' says the LORD. 'Though your sins are like scarlet (*shaniym*, as in Proverbs 31:21), they shall be as white as snow; though they are red (*'adem*) as crimson (*tola'*), they shall be like wool.'" The shedding of animal blood was part of the ancient Hebrew practice of offering sacrifice to God in atonement for sin. Crimson was a symbol of blood. The first lady of Proverbs 31 chose something dyed in scarlet as a valuable offering of her faith to protect her family from snowstorms.

The scarlet principle means that you can prepare for life's storms by clothing yourself and your family in multiple, durable, and valuable layers. Some layers are practical, and some are attitudes of the heart and mind.

Louisa Adams clothed herself in scarlet to protect against the dangers she experienced on her journey. She surrounded herself with multiple layers of practical, durable household items: food, clothing, fur blankets, bags of gold, and her passport. Louisa took advantage of the gift God had given her for language. Her fluent French allowed her to communicate. She also kept her mind steadfast on God. Unlike the nurse who traveled with her, Louisa didn't wrap herself in panic or fear. By keeping her mind calm and her faith strong in adversity, she wrapped herself with the most valuable and durable protection available to her.

As soon as Louisa read John Quincy's letter asking her to sell their house and furniture and travel across the frozen Russian tundra, Louisa knew she would be facing a difficult journey. Travel was risky in 1815, and women didn't travel without a male protector. Louisa revealed her commitment to honor her family in her response to John.

"Conceive the astonishment your letter has caused me, if you can," she wrote. "This is a heavy trial, but I must get through it at all risks, and, if you receive me with the conviction that I have done my best, I shall be amply rewarded."[4]

By determining to honor her husband through the trial, she also clothed herself in her marriage vows, something valuable and durable. But she also wrapped another layer of commitment around her. Years after her experience, Louisa wrote a narrative of her journey. She cited God's guiding hand as the reason for her survival.

"When I retrace my movements through this long and really arduous journey, I cannot humble myself too much in thankful adoration to the Providence which shielded me from all dangers and inspired me with that unswerving faith which teaches to seek for protection from above," she wrote.[5]

She also reflected on the importance of keeping her mind and body strong. Her arms were strong for her tasks. "I was carried through my journey and trials by the mercy of a kind Providence, which never deserts us when we faithfully believe and trust and by the conviction that weakness, either of body or mind, would only render my difficulties greater and make matters worse," she wrote.[6]

Louisa was determined to persevere no matter what. She followed Isaiah 26:3: "You will keep in perfect peace him whose mind is steadfast, because he trusts in you."

One of the worst snowstorms in my life taught me how to make better decisions and keep my mind steadfast on God's truth. When my husband and I came to Washington, D.C., to work in the White House and the Bush administration, we decided it was time to invest in our family by expanding it. We had been married seven years and were ready to have children. My plan was to work in the White

House a year and then leave in a blaze of maternal bliss. Six months turned into twelve months. One year turned into two; still no baby. I left the White House for two reasons: to pursue writing and to lessen the stress on my mind and body. Two years turned into three. We pursued doctors and specialists, but no clear reason for the infertility emerged. Sometimes we felt we were chasing the wind.

I wish I could tell you that decision making came easily during this time, but it didn't. I worried constantly. I became so self-consumed that I couldn't be in the same room with a pregnant woman or a baby. I stopped attending baby showers.

A counselor at my church helped me to discover the treasure of this passage: "We demolish arguments and every pretension that sets itself up against the knowledge of God, and we take captive every thought to make it obedient to Christ" (2 Cor. 10:5). She encouraged me to write down my thoughts and feelings and compare them with what I knew to be the truth. When I was upset or struggling to make a decision about treatment or what step to take next, I wrote down my thoughts. I left blank spaces in between each thought. Then I compared my thoughts with the truth. If I felt abandoned by God, I wrote down the truth, "God loves me." If I felt hopeless, I countered with God's promise that he had a plan for me. If I dwelled on thoughts that I would never have a baby, I countered with the facts. No doctor had said I couldn't have biological children. I discovered that taking thoughts captive to Christ meant that I wasn't a fortune-teller.

Perhaps what I struggled with the most was that no Scripture in the Bible guarantees a woman that she will bear children. God doesn't promise us that we will definitely marry or have children, but He does promise to be with us wherever we walk. He wants to bless our investments. In Jeremiah 29:11, He promises that He has a plan for us, to prosper us and give us a future. When I focused my mind on God's truth, then I was better able to make decisions about my treatment.

Around the time I got a handle on decision making, God revealed his plan for me by allowing me to experience some significant daily pain. When I asked my specialist about it, he continued to push an expensive, invasive procedure that ignored my pain. I changed doctors. My new doctor diagnosed me with endometriosis, a disease that causes pain and infertility, and treated it with laser surgery. Within months of the surgery, God allowed us to become parents on our own. Four years after deciding we were ready to invest in our family by expanding it, I gave birth to a healthy baby boy. I also emerged a better decision maker and truth detector. By committing my mind to focus on God's truth, I wrapped my heart in a scarlet cloak.

Louisa's in-laws, John and Abigail Adams, also turned to their faith and Scripture's durable promises to persevere in challenging times. John Adams took a moment to write Abigail from his desk at the Continental Congress in Philadelphia on September 16, 1774, when the Revolutionary War was at its infancy.

> Having a leisure moment, while the Congress is assembling, I gladly embrace it to write you a Line. When the Congress first met, Mr. Cushing made a Motion, that it should be opened with Prayer. It was opposed by Mr. Jay of N. York and Mr. Rutledge of South Carolina, because we were so divided in religious Sentiments, some Episcopalians, some Quakers, some Anabaptists, some Presbyterians and some Congregationalists, so that We could not join in the same Act of Worship. Mr. S. Adams arose and said he was no Bigot, and could hear a Prayer from a Gentleman of Piety and Virtue, who was at the same Time a Friend to his Country.[7]

The motion passed. An Episcopalian clergyman delivered several prayers to the Congress the next day and read from Psalm 35, which was the day's reading in the Episcopal Church's Book of Common Prayer. John Adams wrote to Abigail, "You must remember this was the next Morning after we heard the horrible Rumour, of the Cannonade of Boston. I never saw a greater Effect upon an Audience. It seemed as if Heaven had ordained that Psalm to be read on that Morning."

Because their home was so close to Boston, John was concerned about Abigail. Never before had the Adamses faced such danger. He was worried about her safety and "begged" her to read Psalm 35. By asking her to read something durable and valuable, he asked her to clothe herself in scarlet. He also encouraged her to share it with her father and their "churchmen."

We don't know if any particular verse stood out to John or Abigail. Because the lion is a longtime symbol for the British and John was serving in the assembly of an elected body—which later issued the Declaration of Independence—he may have found comfort and irony in these words. "O LORD, how long will you look on? Rescue my life from their ravages, my precious life from these lions. I will give you thanks in the great assembly; among throngs of people I will praise you" (Ps. 35:17, 18).

Dolley Madison was another first lady who experienced a blizzard of hazards. Her storm was a fury of fire and a torrent of terror. Perhaps you've heard of Dolley's drama. But you may not know how she wrapped herself in scarlet. She responded by clothing herself in a wedding veil, scarlet drapes, and a shawl.

Dolley had heard the terrible tales of British Admiral George Cockburn. In response to her husband's declaration of war against Britain in 1812, Cockburn behaved more like a pirate or a nineteenth-century terrorist than an admiral abiding by military codes. He terrorized the eastern shore of the United States by invading towns, taking horses, seizing supplies, and raiding homes. He had burned two-thirds of Havre de Grace, a town at the head of the Chesapeake Bay in Maryland. Dolley responded with indignation, not fear, at his desire to burn Washington and her home. She wrote of the admiral's plan in a letter to her cousin in May 1813.

> One of our Generals has discovered a plan of the British. It is to land as many chosen rogues as they can about fourteen miles below Alexandria in the night, who may arrive before day and set fire to the offices and President's House . . . I do not tremble at this, but feel affronted that the Admiral (of Havre de

Grace memory) should send me notice that he would make his bow at my drawing room soon.[8]

Dolley later heard another rumor. Not only did Cockburn want to burn the White House and the City of Washington, but he also wanted to capture her and parade her around like seized treasure. This threat to her dignity became a very real possibility in August 1814, when a massive British naval force landed off the shores of Maryland. The question was not whether they would attack, but where—Baltimore or Washington? President James Madison's top military adviser insisted the British would invade Baltimore because its bustling commerce and larger size made it a more valuable conquest than Washington. Dolley wasn't so sure. She prepared for an attack on Washington.

Throughout the ordeal Dolley thought more of her husband than herself. Like Louisa Adams, Dolley clung to the covenant symbolized by a wedding veil. She sought to bring James "good, not harm." On August 23, 1814, she started writing a letter to her sister, telling her that James had left the President's House (the White House) to be with the troops and militia. He asked her to be ready to leave at a moment's notice.

"He inquired anxiously whether I had the courage, or firmness to remain in the President's House until his return . . . and on my assurance that I had no fear but for him and the success of our army, he left me, beseeching me to take care of myself, and of the cabinet papers, public and private," she wrote.[9]

Dolley stayed at the President's House because of her commitment to her husband and her duty to her nation. She knew there was much hostility toward him and disillusionment over the war. She believed her presence at the President's House was an example to others who were leaving their firesides too quickly, as Dolley put it in her letter. She also saw the long-term benefit to her country by sacrificing her personal belongings and leaving room in the carriage for the most important papers of her husband's presidency.

At sunrise on August 24, President Madison received word that the British were marching toward Bladensburg, Maryland, less than seven miles from Washington. The nation's capital, not Baltimore, was their ultimate destination. James and the troops headed for Bladensburg. Dolley waited at the President's House for his return, pointing her spyglass through an upstairs window to watch for him. She stayed at her post, even after the hundred men guarding the President's House fled. The bad news came in the afternoon.

"Three o'clock—Will you believe it, my sister? We have had a battle or skirmish near Bladensburg, and I am still here within the sound of the cannon! Mr. Madison comes not, may God protect him! Two messengers covered with dust, come to bid me fly, but I wait for him," she wrote.[10]

Dolley didn't wait much longer. She knew it was time to leave. But as she stood in the dining room, her eyes glanced at the large portrait on the wall of George Washington. The painting was the first piece of art that Congress had purchased for the President's House. She couldn't leave it behind. She didn't hack it with an ax as legend has led us to believe. She asked a servant and the gardener to remove it. A gentleman from New York, who had stopped by to check on Dolley, arranged for its safe transport out of town. With her handbag on one arm, Dolley walked through the President's House. She slipped a few pieces of silverware into her purse. She also asked a servant to retrieve her favorite red velvet curtains, which had been packed away for the summer. With scarlet drapes in one hand and the knowledge of the portrait's safety in the other, Dolley Madison left the President's House for the last time as first lady. British Admiral Cockburn arrived a few hours later. His men burned the President's House and Capitol but failed to capture Dolley. She had escaped.

A few days later Dolley received a letter from James at her hiding place in Virginia. He told her it was safe to return. A hurricane had struck Washington the night the British burned the city. The storm's high winds had killed many British sailors and frightened the entire bunch out of town. Disguising herself as a farmer's wife by wearing a simple shawl, Dolley approached the shore of the river to cross back into Washington. She asked the ferryboat driver to row her across, but he told her that he was under orders to take no passengers to Washington. When she revealed her identity as the president's wife, he swiftly sailed her to the other side.

Dolley's rescue of the portrait of George Washington is one of the few heroic stories from the burning of Washington and the War of 1812. Her courage made her husband look good, both in their lifetime and in the history books. She chose not to live in fear and made decisions that she knew would reflect well on her husband. In a time of terror she brought James much "good, not harm" (Prov. 31:12).

I haven't found any documentation that Dolley's determination to stand up to fear came from her faith, other than her prayer for God's protection of her husband. But when war broke out against her and an army wanted to seize her, she reacted like King David did when his own son threatened his life. David made a commitment to stand up to fear, writing, "I will not fear the tens of thousands drawn up against me on every side" (Ps. 3:6). He also wrote this song:

The LORD is my light and my salvation—whom shall I fear? The LORD is the stronghold of my life—of whom shall I be afraid? When evil men advance against me to devour my flesh, when my enemies and my foes attack me, they will stumble and fall. Though an army besiege me, my heart will not fear; though war break out against me, even then will I be confident. One thing I ask of the LORD, this is what I seek: that I may dwell in the house of the LORD all the days of my life, to gaze upon the beauty of the LORD and to seek him in his temple. For in the day of trouble he will keep me safe in his dwelling; he will hide me in the shelter of his tabernacle and set me high upon a rock (Ps. 27:1–5).

I first heard of the terror attacks while I was buying breakfast in the cafeteria of the Eisenhower Executive Office Building shortly after nine o'clock on the morning of September 11, 2001. A woman standing in front of me in line told me that a plane had struck the World Trade Center. I raced upstairs. The one-sentence Associated Press headline in my e-mail confirmed the disaster. I called my husband and then went back downstairs to a colleague's office. We began to think about how to practically respond on the White House Web site, such as posting the phone numbers of blood banks and the airlines. While we were talking, I glanced at the television in his office. The news was reporting that our building was on fire and showed a video of dark smoke swirling into the sky from our building. We had no idea that this was an optical illusion. The smoke was coming from the Pentagon, more than a mile away on the other side of the Potomac River.

The Secret Service ordered an evacuation of our building. I left on the side that faces the West Wing and the White House. The guards had flung open the White House complex gates and told us to run. I remember watching my colleagues with longer legs get far ahead of me. My five-foot frame can't run very fast, and I remember the guard telling me to take off my shoes and run as fast as I could. I later realized he had been told that a hijacked plane was en route to the White House.

I started walking along the streets of Washington, D.C., not sure what to do. I tried walking to my husband's office on the other side of town, but when I saw people flooding out of the FBI building, I decided to take a cab home. The driver, not knowing what was going on, headed back to the White House and got stuck in traffic. For a half hour I sat in a cab facing the Treasury building, which is directly east of the White House. While I was in the cab, my cell phone rang. My husband was safe. I also heard on the cab's radio that a plane had crashed in Pennsylvania. When I arrived home, I hugged my dog, cried, thanked God, and called my parents. Then I watched the rest of the day's events unfold.

I wish I could tell you I wasn't afraid to return to work the next day, but I was. I thought about September 11 every day for weeks. Over time, my fear subsided. Although I no longer work at the

White House, I still live in the Washington, D.C., area. Sometimes when I get on a subway car or see a plane flying over the Potomac as I drive into Washington, I think about the possibility of another attack. I take comfort in God's durable promises found in Scripture. I know He will be with me wherever I go, whatever happens. I am learning to wrap my heart and mind in God's durable truths and the promises of His word.

A friend of mine from Texas, Hilary White, responded to September 11 in a proactive way. I met Hilary when I worked in then Governor Bush's office in Texas and she worked for the Texas agriculture commissioner. We had a lot in common: support for Bush, an education from Baylor University, and a belief and faith in God.

After the United States overthrew Saddam Hussein's regime in 2003, Hilary decided to join the coalition to help rebuild Iraq. She worked as a civilian in communications in Hilla, Iraq. Her job was to communicate the progress being made on the ground. She sent out press releases of the good news stories. When a women's center opened to provide job training for Iraqi women, Hilary coordinated the press and media. She sent press releases heralding the opening of a democracy center, which drew hundreds to its doors. Her work caught the attention of ABC's *Nightline* and the Fox News Network.

Hilary knew she was living in a danger zone, but she prepared the best way she could, both practically and spiritually. Her multi-layered scarlet cloak took the form of a bulletproof vest, boots, prayer, and a special psalm. She also looked to God to provide her comfort and protection.

"The reality of Iraq was that it was scary sometimes. In some of my scariest moments, some of my most emotional moments, where I was in the process of losing it or thought I was about to lose it, the Lord provided people at a compound that could minister to me. That's amazing," Hilary said.[11]

One of the practical ways that Hilary dealt with the danger of a war zone was by learning how to wear a bulletproof vest. When she first put one on, she realized she had to make some adjustments. The vest was too big for her. It hung off of her like a size two woman wearing a man's forty-two-size coat. She had to use safety pins to raise it up so that the protective part of the vest covered her major organs.

Hilary also found herself having to make unusual decisions about her footwear. Each day she had to decide which shoes to wear: sandals, loafers, or military boots. She needed to wear sandals to fit in with the culture of women in Iraq. If she got into a situation where she needed to run fast, she needed her loafers, but her loafers wouldn't protect her from flying glass and debris if her convoy was attacked. Boots were better protection, but not culturally acceptable for women. Hilary made her choices based on what she was going to be doing that day, whether it was traveling, staying in the compound, or interacting with Iraqis. She also kept her boots by her bed in case her compound was hit in the middle of the night.

Hilary's need to wear military armor paints a picture of what it means to clothe your mind and heart in scarlet. Ephesians 6:13–18 uses armor as a metaphor for faith:

> Therefore put on the full armor of God, so that when the day of evil comes, you may be able to stand your ground, and after you have done everything, to stand. Stand firm then, with the belt of truth buckled around your waist, with the breastplate of righteousness in place, and with your feet fitted with the readiness that comes from the gospel of peace. In addition to all this, take up the shield of faith, with which you can extinguish all the flaming arrows of the evil one. Take the helmet of salvation and the sword of the Spirit, which is the word of God. And pray in the Spirit on all occasions with all kinds of prayers and requests.

Hilary also dealt with threats to her compound by finding comfort in the multiple, durable verses of Scripture. A friend shared with her a passage that had helped him stay strong.

"I remember one time our compound was under threat, and you learned to deal with threats, but I was not used to it. I had never done anything like this before, so sometimes it was unnerving. I asked a friend who had more experience with threats and danger. His response was that I should read Psalm 91," Hilary said.

"This big, strong, tough guy read Psalm 91 every night before he went to bed, and to know he did that gave me comfort. When I got scared, I read Psalm 91; it's very comforting," she said.

Hilary had been in Iraq for nearly eight months when she came back to Washington to attend some meetings. Her plan was to return to Iraq. While she was gone, her roommate Fern Holland was assassinated along with two others in an ambush. Fern had worked tirelessly for women's rights in Iraq. Hilary was suddenly very personally affected by the war.

Hilary and I met to talk while she was in Washington. She was still in shock and grieving over Fern's death. She was also weighing whether to return to Iraq. Fern's death was the beginning of the insurgents' ambushes, kidnappings, and bombings. Because she had already spent so much time in Iraq, Hilary was not obligated to return. Those closest to her wanted her to stay, of course, but she told me that her work wasn't finished. She knew there were good news stories taking place, and she wanted to share them. She also believed in President Bush's mission to spread democracy. More than anything she believed God wanted her to return and finish the job she had started.

Hilary told me that Psalm 91 helped her to grieve Fern's death and also gave her courage to go back. She returned to Iraq clothed in scarlet and finished her work. She sent me an e-mail after she arrived safely.

"We pulled into the compound, and with large smiles the Iraqis welcomed us to our home in Hilla. My Iraqi interpreters were the first to greet me . . . bestowing hugs, something they usually reserve only for men. They'd written a huge welcome sign, then more Iraqis rushed into the office, more hugs by tribal leaders who typically only give me a handshake. I felt welcomed by dear friends," Hilary wrote.

Less than three months later, her work concluded when the coalition turned authority over to the Iraqis. Hilary returned to Washington.

My mom also directed me to Psalm 91:1—"He who dwells in the shelter of the Most High will rest in the shadow of the Almighty"—shortly after September 11. Perhaps reading a verse referenced as "911" is what first attracted so many others and me to this passage's pearls of wisdom. Here is Psalm 91:1–16:

> He who dwells in the shelter of the Most High will rest in the shadow of the Almighty. I will say of the LORD, "He is my refuge and my fortress, my God, in whom I trust." Surely he will save you from the fowler's snare and from the deadly pestilence. He will cover you with his feathers, and under his wings you will find refuge; his faithfulness will be your shield and rampart. You will not fear the terror of night, nor the arrow that flies by day, nor the pestilence that stalks in the darkness, nor the plague that destroys at midday. A thousand may fall at your side, ten thousand at your right hand, but it will not come near you. You will only observe with your eyes and see the punishment of the wicked. If you make the Most High your dwelling— even the LORD, who is my refuge—then no harm will befall you, no disaster will come near your tent. For he will command his angels concerning you to guard you in all your ways; they will lift you up in their hands, so that you will not strike your foot against a stone. You will tread upon the lion and the cobra; you will trample the great lion and the serpent. "Because he loves me," says the LORD, "I will rescue him; I will protect him, for he acknowledges my name. He will call upon me, and I will answer him; I will be with him in trouble, I will deliver him and honor him. With long life will I satisfy him and show him my salvation."

Golden strands of faith weave together scarlet cloaks. Gold is a valuable material in the jewelry world. This precious metal is durable and valuable like a red ruby, but it also has an important characteristic that pearls and jewels do not have. Gold is ductile. Gold is the most malleable of metals. At the hands of an artisan, gold can be hammered into incredibly thin foils or drawn into fine wires. Our faith is like gold: malleable, pliable, and supple. Storms in life shape our faith just as fire turns gold into a beautiful necklace.

"In this you greatly rejoice, though now for a little while you may have had to suffer grief in all kinds of trials. These have come so that your faith—of greater worth than gold, which perishes even though refined by fire—may be proved genuine and may result in praise, glory, and honor when Jesus Christ is revealed" (1 Pet. 1:6, 7).

One more point. When storms come in life, accept help. If you lose something or someone because of a terrible tragedy, such as a hurricane, terrorism, or a blizzard, accept help from those who offer you scarlet cloaks. Be receptive to those who want to meet your practical needs for food, clothing, shelter, transportation, and employment. Don't reject God's provision for you. If you find yourself depressed, humble yourself and go to a counselor or support group as many times as you need to. Embrace those who can shower you with love, respect, and faith. Take refuge in the scarlet cloaks the Lord provides for you.

The 1917 Russian Revolution prompted poet Aleksander Blok to reflect on the political blizzard that had enveloped his country. His poem has a Proverbs 31 quality to it.

And before, with banner red, through the blizzard snow unseen, all unharmed by hail of lead. With a step like snow so light, showered in myriad pearls of snow, crowned in wreath of roses white, Christ leads onward as they go.[12]

Wearing scarlet not only shields us from storms and molds our faith, but it also helps us to put on a funny face in the future.

CHAPTER NINE

Laugh Out Loud

"She is clothed with strength and dignity; she can laugh at the days to come" (Prov. 31:25).

ONE MORNING President Ulysses Grant, the famous general who led the Union to victory in the Civil War, asked his wife a question.

"Julia, I have a new conundrum for you," he said.

"Yes?" she said.

"Why is victory like a kiss?"

"Why is victory like a kiss?" she repeated, at a loss for an answer.

"Why," the general said. "It is easy to Grant."

"Ah, that is charming!" she said.

And they laughed out loud.[1]

Barbara Bush looked around the long thin dining room. From her seat at the head table she beheld a grand view of three tables running the room's length. She observed that she was surrounded mostly by American and Japanese businessmen at this state dinner hosted by Kiichi Miyazawa, the prime minister of Japan. She glanced at the room's crown, where a camera crew rested on the balcony. Once again her every move was in view of the lens. The event was one of several economic summit events hosted by Japan.

Tonight, she and her husband, President George Bush, were the guests of honor.

Barbara had enjoyed her morning, especially meeting the angelic two-month-old granddaughter of Japan's emperor. Her visit to an American fair at a popular Japanese department store was also quite fun. Her husband's schedule did not end as well. After a game of afternoon tennis, President Bush returned to their hotel room because he felt poorly. He consulted his doctor and took a nap before dinner.

Barbara looked at the head agent of her husband's Secret Service detail. He sat at a table halfway down the room.

He's not taking his eyes off George, she thought.

Barbara glanced at her husband, who sat between Prime Minister Miyazawa and his wife.

And George certainly doesn't look well, she thought.

Barbara saw George lean over toward the prime minister as if he was whispering. Before she could blink, she saw George's eyes roll back in his head. He vomited and passed out.

If her hair had been any other color, the shock alone would have turned it white. She rushed to her husband's side and wiped his face so quickly that she hardly knew what she had done.

"You stand there and guard your president," a strong voice called out. Barbara looked up and saw a large agent charging down the middle aisle.

Barbara realized the Secret Service's medical team had surrounded them. She stepped away to let them do their job.

"Give him air," someone hollered and removed his tie.

Somewhere in the confusion, Barbara saw her husband wake up.

"Maybe you better roll me under the table, let me sleep, and you just go on with your dinner," George said.

"I can't lift him," the head agent said.

"You have my leg," Prime Minister Miyazawa said quietly.

Barbara watched as the agent stopped trying to lift both heads of state at the same time. She then heard the agent explain to George that they were going to put him on a stretcher.

"Absolutely not," George said, motioning for his tie.

After more than forty-five years of marriage, Barbara knew what her husband meant.

He's going to walk out of this room by himself, she figured. Then she watched in amazement as her husband put on his tie while lying on the floor. She noticed his face was still paler than a tablecloth.

George stood up, smiled at the audience, and began to walk out of the room. Then he turned to Barbara and said, "Can you give the toast for me?"

Barbara instantly agreed, but she felt her heart tighten when she saw him leave the room. She desperately wanted to go with him.

What should I do? Barbara thought. *If I leave, people will think he is really ill, but I have no idea how sick he is. Will our children see this on television before I can tell them how he's doing?*

A thousand thoughts ran through her mind as she realized that it was she, not her husband, who would speak tonight.

Prime Minister Miyazawa stood at the head table and resumed the dinner.

"Mrs. Bush, would you like to say a few words?" he said, turning to her.

Barbara stood up. She smiled and turned toward the audience.

"Mr. Prime Minister and Mrs. Miyazawa, I rarely get to speak for George Bush," she said. "But tonight I know he would want me to thank you, on behalf of the members of his administration and the American businessmen who are here, for a wonderful visit and for a great friendship, on my part, for a lovely day, and I think for a wonderful day for all of you."

She stared at the audience, who seemed uncertain of how to respond to her. They still looked shell-shocked over the president's illness and sudden departure.

"You know, I can't explain what happened to George because it never happened before. But I'm beginning to think it's the ambassador's fault," she said, hearing some chuckles from the Americans in the audience.

"He and George played the emperor and the crown prince in tennis today, and they were badly beaten. And we Bushes aren't used to that," she said.

The audience's laughter grew. The Japanese seemed to be catching on to her American-style humor.

"So, he felt much worse than I thought."

The audience roared, and Barbara felt relieved.

"But General Scowcroft is going to speak for the president. And thank you very much for a wonderful visit."

Barbara took her seat. She was worried about George and wished the dinner was over so she could go to him. The first lady couldn't remember much of what she had said, but she knew the audience had laughed.

Sometimes, somebody up there just leans down and the right thing happens, she pondered.[2]

President George Bush had the flu and nothing more came of it, other than some serious laughter for late-night comedians. Although one of the cameras had remained on and their daughter first learned of the incident from television, Barbara maintained her sense of humor about that night. She wrote about it in her memoirs and ended the story with this:

Dear Mrs. Bush,

Tell Mr. President not to be embarrassed that he threw up on international TV. I once threw up on my dog.

Love,
Jennifer[3]"

Japanese television anchors called Barbara's impromptu comedic act "phenomenal." One anchor was so impressed with Barbara that he replayed her speech, which was unusual back then. T. R. Reid of the *Washington Post* gave his eyewitness report on the evening in an article published the following day. Under the headline, "One Flu over the State Dinner; Japanese Warm to First Lady's Cool," T. R. described the sequence of events and then praised Barbara's Bob Hope–like performance:

> The First Lady accepted the mission, and she fulfilled it in an ad-libbed presentation that was marked with old-fashioned Yankee virtues: a stoic calm in crisis, a gentle eloquence, a self-effacing wit.
>
> Her soothing presence and carefully timed jokes served to calm the troubled room, reassure the television audience both here and at home, and put the Tokyo summit back on an even keel.
>
> More important, perhaps, Barbara Bush's speech gave the people of Japan—a country where wives of officials generally say nothing and still walk two respectful steps behind their husbands—an unforgettable picture of an American woman taking charge in time of need.[4]

I was in the middle of writing this story when I had an opportunity to attend the fifteenth anniversary celebration of the Americans with Disabilities Act in July 2005. Former President George Bush spoke at the reception. He made a joke about the time he threw up on the prime minister of Japan. Although his humor had nothing to do with the ADA, he made everyone laugh. Sometimes you just need to laugh out loud.

Of all the twentieth-century first ladies, Barbara Bush has probably made more people laugh than any other. Humor is integral to her outlook on life.

"You really only have two choices; you can like what you do or you can dislike it. I choose to like it, and what fun I have had," she said.[5]

By laughing at the past, the woman known for wearing pearl necklaces has been able to look to the future with hope. With each new political campaign for her husband and then her sons, Barbara has used humor as her pearls of wisdom for diffusing tense times. She inherited her ability to laugh out loud from her father, Marvin Pierce. She is a fourth cousin once removed from President Franklin Pierce. Barbara has called humor "a fence you hide behind." She often makes fun of her grandmotherly appearance in designer clothes.

"One of the myths is that I don't dress well. I dress very well— I just don't look so good," she has said a thousand times with a wink and a smile.

Barbara may not think she would wow the pages of *Vogue* (although her granddaughters Jenna, Barbara, and Lauren have), but she is adorned by something valuable: strength and dignity. Proverbs 31:25 puts it this way: "She is clothed with strength and dignity; she can laugh at the days to come."

Perhaps one reason Barbara can laugh at the days to come is that she clothes herself in strength by exercising. Barbara is a swimmer. Exercise not only develops muscles, but it also produces a healthier outlook on life. Physical exertion causes the body to produce endorphins or chemicals that reduce emotional tension and stress.

Physical strength is one of the principles of Proverbs 31. Verse 17 tells us: "She sets about her work vigorously; her arms are strong for her tasks." Although this woman didn't have the scientific proof that we have today about endorphins, somehow she made the connection between physical strength and emotional calm. Perhaps one day she was upset about a conflict with one of her servant girls. Maybe she took a walk by herself to draw water from a well and think about her problem. Then she decided to take the long route back, the one going uphill. By the time she returned, she felt better. Perhaps she felt so much better that she was able to find the humor in her problem. She clothed herself in strength so she could laugh at the days to come.

Exercise keeps our bodies strong and functioning. By taking care of the outside, we show our respect for one of God's greatest gifts. "Do you not know that your body is a temple of the Holy Spirit, who is in you, whom you have received from God?" (1 Cor. 6:19).

Clothing ourselves in physical strength gives us emotional strength to laugh and enjoy life.

Grace Coolidge was also an exerciser. She walked to keep her image polished. As the wife of the vice president, especially in the age before television, her face was fairly anonymous. She often walked unnoticed around the reflecting pool near the Lincoln Memorial. She loved to watch the pinky purple haze of the sunset behind the monument. Sometimes she walked in downtown D.C.

Shortly after becoming first lady, she took a walk to the shopping district and discovered an opportunity to laugh at her newfound identity. Grace walked into a store to buy a hat. She described what she was looking for, and the saleswoman brought her a selection of hats.

The saleswoman looked at Grace closely and said, "My, but you look like Mrs. Coolidge!"

Grace smiled pleasantly but acted uninterested in the comment.

The woman left and quickly returned with more hats.

"Did anyone ever tell you before that you look like Mrs. Coolidge?" she asked.

"Yes," Grace replied simply, trying not to laugh out loud.

Grace chose a hat and signaled for her secretary to give the woman her address. Then she departed before the woman had a chance to see that the hat was to be sent to 1600 Pennsylvania Avenue, the White House's address.

"We all had a little laugh together," Grace wrote about the excursion.[6]

Clothing ourselves in physical strength is one of two Proverbs 31 principles for enjoying life. The second principle is wearing the jersey of dignity. Sometimes life's hard times make us emotionally strong for our tasks, enabling us to laugh at the days to come.

A group who became the first ladies of the basketball court in 2005 grew in both strength and dignity. Their arms became strong for their tasks by their willingness to learn from their mistakes and their ability to carry themselves with dignity in times of difficulty.

Women's basketball coach Kim Mulkey-Robertson had not seen Abiola Wabara play. But when she looked at the young woman's hands, the coach saw gold. Abiola's arms were strong for Kim's task: turning Baylor University's once-losing women's basketball team into a national champion.

"I shook her hand, and her hand was very large, and I thought, 'Hmm, that's a good sign,'" Kim said. "And when she stood up, she was cut and just had a great body."

Abiola's aunt, a student at Baylor's seminary, e-mailed Kim about her niece. Although she received hundreds of recommendations, Kim had a hunch about Abiola. There was a problem. Abiola didn't have a game tape, and under NCAA rules, she couldn't demonstrate her skills for Kim. But the rules allowed them to meet.

At their meeting, Kim told Abiola she liked her personality.

"Coach, I'm Italian, we talk with our hands," Abiola said with a smile.[7]

Kim's hunches about Abiola's hands and the hands of the other young women she recruited paid huge dividends during her first five years as coach. In the first year, Kim took a team with a previous 7–20 record and turned it into a winner. The team ended the 2000–01 season with a record of 21–9.

The Lady Bears' success on the court required great physical strength and training. Muscles grow strong by contracting or squeezing, which causes them to shorten and lengthen. Over time this movement makes muscles firm and strong. While her players were strong enough to win more games than they lost, they faced two huge hurdles that forced them to exercise a different set of muscles. They had to exercise dignity.

The summer of 2003 brought tragedy to the Baylor basketball program. A player on the men's basketball team murdered a teammate. Baylor stood in the ugly, glaring spotlights of tragedy and the national news.

Kim didn't want the women's team to lose hope and focus. She wanted them to be leaders and champions both on and off the court. She knew their actions and attitude could make a difference to the men's team and other students. At their first team meeting after the tragedy, Kim motivated her players to be a "shining light."

On the court they donned their green and gold jerseys and played with dignity. Off the court, they also demonstrated dignity and wore T-shirts with the shining light slogan. The idea spread throughout campus, and the Lady Bears made a difference in that time of tragedy by the way they carried themselves.

Kim's own life had taught her how to walk with dignity. As a student, she played at Louisiana Tech. She starred on a team that won two national championships. Kim devoted her career to her alma mater as an assistant coach for fifteen years. With the promise of becoming head coach one day, she turned down offers from other schools. When Louisiana Tech finally asked her to become the head coach, the initial three-year deal fell short of the five-year contract offered to most head coaches. Kim maintained her dignity. Baylor took notice and hired her in 2000.[8]

When a reporter asked the Lady Bears' starting five to describe Kim in one word, they said:

"Tenacious," Steffanie Blackmon said.

"Intense," Chameka Scott replied.

"Intense," Abiola Wabara stated.

"Intense," Sophia Young uttered.

"Intense," Chelsea Whitaker reiterated.[9]

Through Kim's tireless energy and intense focus, the Lady Bears continued to succeed. Their strong arms led them to the NCAA playoffs' Sweet Sixteen round in 2004. Although they led in double digits for most of their game against Tennessee, the Lady Bears found themselves with only a two-point lead with two-tenths of a second left. The referee called a foul. Tennessee beat Baylor 71–69.

Kim was so upset that she couldn't go into the locker room and comfort the girls after the game. She only watched the tape once, at home by herself. When a team loses by such a close margin, the players often blame the other team for cheating or the referees for unfairness. But the Lady Bears reached deep inside and admitted the truth. They had lost the game, not in the final second, but by allowing Tennessee to close the double-digit gap. They responded by wearing the uniform of dignity. The team members willingly took summer school so they could practice together and strengthen their weaknesses. They worked to build consistency.

Their efforts paid off the following spring when they swept into the NCAA's Final Four. Baylor had never been in the tournament until Kim became the coach, and on the fourth trip, Baylor made it to the national championship game. The players approached the game with Michigan with strength, dignity, and consistency. At the end of the game, the Lady Bears held the NCAA women's basketball championship.

The next day's headlines praised the women of Baylor and Kim Mulkey-Robertson. The reports were also witty. "Baylor 84, Michigan State 62: Far from your Average Bears"[10] and "Got Mulk? Then You're a Champion."[11]

Clothing yourself with strength and dignity is important in the game of life. The jersey of dignity worn over the arms of strength gives you the ability to laugh at the future, the unknown. Dignity is a form of inner beauty, which is "of great worth in God's sight" (1 Pet. 3:4). Dignity shows that you "can do everything through him who gives you strength" (Phil. 4:13). By exercising both your physical and spiritual muscles, you can better laugh at the days to come.

Who knows what the future will bring? Some days may feel better than winning the NCAA national championship in women's basketball. Other days are just as happy, the times when you walk into a store and laugh about buying a hat. Some days make you want to throw up. And other days are simply boring.

Abigail Adams had an antidote for those days of solitude. While traveling in Connecticut, she wrote a letter to encourage her bored husband, who was at home by himself in Massachusetts.

"I hope you will be in good Spirits all the Time I am gone, remembering Solomon's advise that a merry Heart was good like a medicine,"[12] she wrote. Her suggestion came from the proverb: "A cheerful heart is good medicine, but a crushed spirit dries up the bones" (Prov. 17:22).

Abigail knew from experience what it was like to be at home alone and bored, and she didn't want to come home to a Boston crab.

When days bring times of criticism, laughter provides a healing balm.

If anyone experienced criticism during her years in the White House, it was Nancy Reagan. Nothing was off-limits: her wardrobe, her personality, her taste, her love for her husband, and her spending habits. In her first few weeks as first lady, Nancy discovered that so many pieces of White House china had broken over the years that she could not host a White House dinner without mixing and matching china patterns. When she accepted a 220-piece china set, valued at two hundred thousand dollars, from a private foundation, she was shocked at the criticism she received. Nancy took more heat for that private gift than any White House oven could ever produce.

Nancy helped herself and her husband by diffusing the criticism with humor. She rinsed off some mud by laughing at herself. At the annual national press dinner called the Gridiron, Nancy dressed in secondhand clothes and rags and sang the 1920s Fanny Brice song, "Secondhand Rose." The song was a hit for its reworked lines, such as "I'm wearing secondhand clothes, secondhand clothes. They're quite the style in the spring fashion shows" and "even though they tell me I'm no longer queen, did Ronnie have to buy me that new sewing machine?"

"That song, together with my willingness to sing it, served as a signal to opinion makers that maybe I wasn't the terrible, humorless woman they thought I was—regal, distant, disdainful. From that night on, my image began to change in Washington," Nancy wrote.[13]

Laughing at the days to come is also effective medicine for accepting old age.

Old age was respected by the Hebrew culture. Solomon said, "Gray hair is a crown of splendor; it is attained by a righteous life" (Prov. 16:31). Sometimes it isn't easy to accept the aging process, no matter which side of it you're on. Perhaps that is why Solomon also wrote this proverb: "Listen to your father, who gave you life, and do not despise your mother when she is old" (Prov. 23:22).

Laura Bush traveled back and forth to Midland, Texas, in the spring of 2004 to help her mother move into a retirement home. Her father, who suffered from Alzheimer's, had died several years earlier.

"We closed her house down and went through everything, and it was a passage, really, for both of us. It was also a wonderful time for both of us. We went through everything together. We laughed. We talked. It brought back a lot of memories . . . And she doesn't have Alzheimer's but at the same time just the idea of her aging and moving on to this time of life is a grief for me, because it also indicates something for my life."[14]

Laughter helped both of them to get through the change.

By the time Martha Washington was an old lady, she had much to laugh about, but she also had experienced much sadness. She outlived all of her four children, several grandchildren who died as infants, a niece and nephew who were close to her, and both of her husbands. She also watched her husband lead a war that would have cost him everything had he lost. Failure would have resulted in the loss of their estate, and his reputation certainly would have ended as a traitor. Martha's steadfastness served her well throughout her life. As a result, she approached old age with strength, dignity, and laughter.

"I am still determined to be cheerful and to be happy in whatever situation I may be, for I have also learnt from experience that the greater part of our happiness or misery depends upon our dispositions, and not upon our circumstances; we carry the seeds of the one, or the other about with us, in our minds, wherever we go."[15]

Laughter is not only the result of strength and dignity. It is more than just an antidote for the difficulties in life. Laughter is a freedom.

"I believe in freedom of the press," former President George Bush said. "But now I rejoice in freedom from the press."[16]

The freedom to laugh comes from our freedom of speech and freedom of the press. Cartoons are protected speech. Jokes are protected. Laughter is protected.

It's hard to imagine that anyone would want to prohibit laughing, but some governments have tried. Prohibiting laughter was part of the Taliban's brutality of the Afghan people.

"Life under the Taliban is so hard and repressive, even small displays of joy are outlawed—children aren't allowed to fly kites; their mothers face beatings for laughing out loud," Laura Bush said when she delivered the President's Saturday morning radio address on November 17, 2001.[17]

I can't imagine not being able to laugh out loud. Laughter eases the burdens of humanity, and for some, laughter is a gift. Karen Hughes explained in her autobiography that she has the gift of joy. She nicknamed President Bush's first campaign for governor the "Campaign of Joy." She knew laughter was a great way to handle the stress of an intense political race. Karen also passionately believes in the freedom to laugh and in the one who gave us laughter.

"Freedom is the universal hope of the human heart, instilled not by any country or government but by the Creator, who cares for each of us and wants us to learn to care for one another," she said in remarks at the State Department.[18]

Our freedom to laugh comes from the one who created it. He knows its therapeutic power, its ability to heal our wounded spirits, lift our bored bodies, temper our angry tones, and ease our aching bones. God values laughter so much that he commanded the Jews to laugh out loud. When he gave Moses instructions for establishing the Hebrew government, he required the people to laugh and rejoice. "There, in the presence of the LORD your God, you and your families shall eat and shall rejoice in everything you have put your hand to, because the LORD your God has blessed you" (Deut. 12:7).

Go ahead and laugh out loud. It's free!

CHAPTER TEN

Gemstone Fire

"Charm is deceptive, and beauty is fleeting; but a woman who fears the Lord is to be praised" (Prov. 31:30).

ANNE RYUN and a friend sat on a beach several years ago. They were reflecting on their lives as wives, mothers, and grandmothers, when her friend said, "You know Anne, I think I've figured it out. When you're sixteen and you're not so pretty because you're an awkward teenager, that's really not your fault. That's part of maturity and growing. But when you're sixty and not pretty, then that is your fault."

The grand dame of Washington high society tiptoed over the threshold and into the back of the church. The day was Tuesday, not Sunday, but when she heard the bishops were coming to oversee the special service on July 15, 1845, this first lady knew her time had come.

Traces of her youth—her flashing smile and flirty blue eyes—peered past the wrinkles on her face. At age seventy-seven, Dolley Madison was still a beauty, but a beauty of a different kind. With her niece, Anne Payne, by her side, Dolley looked toward the front of the church. She saw the other early arrivers sitting in the first few pews.

I wonder what they will think when they see me at the altar? she thought.

"Hello, Mrs. Madison," Mr. Pyne called cheerily as he walked down the aisle to greet her.

"Congratulations on your appointment, Mr. Pyne," Dolley said as she handed the new rector a slip of paper.

"Thank you," he said with surprise. He held Dolley's note with care, as if he were holding a thousand dollars. "I'm glad you have come. Bishop Whittingham will give instructions soon. Please join the others at the front."

Dolley glanced around the church as she walked down the ruby red aisle, which was lengthened during a renovation to form a Latin cross shape. She remembered the days before the addition of the steeple and the extension, when the church's interior formed a Greek cross with equal arms.

She felt nervous as she sat down, but the familiar red buttoned cushion gave her comfort. After thirty years of attending services at St. John's, the pew pillows seemed custom made for her, but the cup of Holy Communion had yet to touch her lips.

"Mrs. Madison," the man in the pew in front of her said. He looked over his shoulder and smiled. "Pleased to see you today."

Dolley instantly recognized him, his wife, and daughter.

"What a pleasure to see you, Lieutenant Herndon, Mrs. Herndon," she said, waving at his wife and their eight-year-old daughter, Nell, who smiled shyly.

"So you have come today?" he said.

"Yes, I have."

Dolley quickly surveyed the number of people sitting in the pews. After years of hosting parties, she could easily assess how many were in a room.

"I believe we are part of three dozen who have come," she said, taking comfort in knowing that she was surrounded by so many others of the same mind.

Three robed gentlemen walked in front of them and interrupted their conversation. Mr. Pyne nodded his head knowingly at Dolley and smiled.

"What did your note to him say?" Anne whispered to Dolley.

"I told him that I wished to be with him on this day, the occasion of confirmation, and asked if he had any advice," she said.

Bishop Whittingham of Baltimore, Mr. Pyne, and another man stood in front of the first pew and faced the group. Bishop Whittingham welcomed Mr. Pyne on his first service as the rector of St. John's and introduced the guest preacher, George Washington Doane, the bishop of New Jersey. Then he gave instructions to the group. He asked them questions about their readiness and understanding of the Gospel, and concluded in prayer. With the pre-service meeting completed, Dolley and the others waited for the remaining worshipers to arrive so the service could begin.

Dolley could still remember the first day she stepped through the doors of the charming yellow church across the street from the President's House. She remembered how the smell of fresh paint and plaster overpowered her nostrils that day. It was sometime in 1816, the year St. John's opened. She also remembered standing on the church's steps after the service and studying the progress of the President's House, which was being rebuilt after British sailors burned it during the War of 1812. The President's House was much like her own life, a phoenix rising from the ashes.

Dolley glanced at Anne.

"You look quite lovely today, Anne," Dolley said.

"Thank you, and so do you," she said. "I am glad we're here together."

Her niece wore her hair parted down the middle and pulled it into a tight bun at the base of her head. Dolley noticed how Anne's dress collar climbed up her neck, while her A-line wide skirt hid her feminine shape.

A more severe style, but it's the fashion. If Anne's clothes had been the norm when I was younger, I might still be a Quaker, Dolley thought with a laugh.

Dolley patted her turban to make sure it was still secure on her head. Although few others wore them, she liked her turban because it hid uncooperative strands, especially gray ones.

She thought about the changes in dress since her days at the President's House, when lower cut bodices, empire waists, and straighter Greek-style skirts were in vogue. She missed her chignon hairstyle, with its soft ringlets framing her face. At least she could still wear a turban, although it wasn't as tall as it was when it reached its peak of chic.

Dolley watched the pews around her fill with worshipers. Her mind drifted to her earliest memory of pews and religion. It wasn't her choice to be a Quaker, a member in the Society of Friends, but she knew nothing different growing up. Her loyal parents took refuge in Quaker colonies, moving from Virginia to North Carolina and back before finally settling in Philadelphia. Each move was their attempt to escape the corrupting influences of society while pursuing economic stability among the Friends. What Dolley remembered most about the Quakers were the rules, especially the don'ts.

She thought about how the Friends had controlled her entirely; barring her from so many advantages and pleasures that Philadelphia had to offer, such as parties and balls. Then the Quakers expelled her father because his business failed, thrusting him into debt. Dolley believed that true friends would not have abandoned someone in their greatest hour of need. But she remained in the fold, marrying a Quaker named John Todd.

Her questions about the Friends—and dare she admit it, God himself—multiplied when yellow fever struck Philadelphia, forcing her to flee the city in panic with her two sons. The epidemic nearly destroyed the city. No family escaped its grip. She lost her husband, one of her two sons, and her in-laws to yellow fever. By the time she was twenty-seven years old; she had sat on many pews and stood by many gravesides, including her father's and three brothers'.

"James," she whispered.

"What?" Anne asked.

"James, I wish he were here. I wonder what he would think knowing his Quaker wife had finally decided to fully embrace his religion," she said.

"He would be happy."

"Yes, he would be happy, but his mother would be happier," Dolley said. "She was the one whose Bible was the most worn in our household."

Dolley remembered the day she took her second wedding vow. When she said, "I do," to James Madison, an older man savvy in the world of politics and the father of the Constitution, she said good-bye to the Friends. Although she expected the Quakers to expel her for marrying an Episcopalian, the hurt was worse than a hundred lashings. She remembered how she felt each time she ran into an old Friend, whose critical words or disagreeable eyes revived terror in her heart of legalism.

Rules without grace, she mused. *That's what's kept me in the pew and not at the altar all these years.*

Dolley looked around her and saw that the pews were nearly full. Because James had served as president, she knew her face was familiar to most in the congregation.

Although there was a time in life when she wanted to be the center of attention, such as the inaugural ball when she wore a yellow velvet gown, multiple strands of pearls, and a Parisian turban with a bird of paradise plume in her hair. Today, she wasn't so sure how she felt about the attention.

Nerves, she thought. *I must bid them fly.*

Dolley noticed the hum in the room had hushed to a silence. She looked at the altar on the east wall and saw the two bishops and rector take their places. Dolley quickly glanced at Anne, who smiled back knowingly. They had talked for quite some time about confirming their belief in Christ. Dolley had worried that she wasn't worthy of membership in the church, but Anne had convinced her otherwise.

After several Scripture readings, Bishop Doane stood and began his sermon. Dolley had heard he was a fine preacher.

"First, the blade. Then, the ear," he said, explaining the parable of the growing seed. He talked about how the soil produces a grain, followed by a stalk, and then a head. When the full kernel appears, the harvester comes.

"What an allegory of Confirmation!" he continued. "Years of understanding. Years of discretion. Years of affection. Years of devotion. The opening mind. The ripening heart."

Dolley felt her nerves ease as his words rang true in her heart.

She listened to Bishop Doane talk about Pentecost, the day when the apostle Peter addressed a crowd of three thousand. He talked about how they received the Holy Ghost, their day of confirmation. He pointed out that the new believers had everything in common, selling their possessions and goods and giving to those in need.

He's a beautiful champion for charity, as her mind flashed to 1 Corinthians 13.

"True charity suspects not, thinks no evil," she whispered to herself, thinking of the suspicious ways of her Friends.

When Bishop Doane concluded his message, Bishop Whittingham stood to lead the next part of the service. He recited the confirmation service's introduction found in the Book of Common Prayer. Then he asked all to be confirmed to come forward. He sat in the bishop's chair, located in the middle of the aisle.

Dolley and Anne stood, left their pews, and formed a line along the wings of the church. As Dolley took her place, she noticed she was second in line and Anne was third.

"Do ye here, in the presence of God, and of this congregation renew the solemn promise and vow that ye made or that was made in your name, at your Baptism; ratifying and confirming the same?" Bishop Whittingham said to the group. "And acknowledging yourselves bound to believe and to do all those things which ye then undertook, or your sponsors then undertook for you?"

"I do," Dolley answered along with the others.

"Our help is in the name of the Lord," he said.

"Who hath made heaven and earth," they responded in unison.

"Blessed be the name of the Lord," he said.

"Henceforth, world without end."

"Lord, hear our prayer."

"And let our cry come unto thee."

"Let us pray," he said.

Dolley bowed her head and listened to the bishop's prayer.

"Almighty and ever living God, who hast vouchsafed to regenerate these thy servants by water and the Holy Ghost, and hast given unto them forgiveness of all their sins; strengthen them, we beseech thee, O Lord, with the Holy Ghost, the comforter; and daily increase in them thy manifold gifts of grace; the spirit of wisdom and understanding, the spirit of counsel and ghostly strength, the spirit of knowledge and true godliness; and fill them, O Lord, with the spirit of thy holy fear, now and forever. Amen," he said.

Amen, she prayed.

Dolley watched as the woman in front of her in line walked over to the bishop's chair and knelt in front of him. He placed his hands on her and spoke to her.

When he finished, Dolley felt more nervous than the day she married James. She walked over and knelt in front of the bishop. Her heart was racing until his hands touched her head.

"Defend, O Lord, this Thy servant with Thy heavenly grace; that she may continue thine forever; and daily increase in thy Holy Spirit more and more, until she come unto thy everlasting kingdom. Amen," he said.

Amen, again went through her mind.

Dolley returned to her pew more relaxed than she had left it. Anne knelt before the bishop and then joined Dolley. They watched and listened as the bishop repeated the blessing one by one to the rest of those standing in line for confirmation.

When he finished, Bishop Whittingham said to the congregation, "The Lord be with you."

"And with thy spirit," the congregation answered.

"Let us pray," he said.

Dolley knelt and repeated the familiar words, "Our Father, who art in heaven, Hallowed be thy name. Thy kingdom come. Thy will be done on earth, as it is in heaven. Give us this day our daily bread. And forgive us our trespasses, as we forgive those who trespass against us. And lead us not into temptation; but deliver us from evil. Amen."

She started to lift her head, but lowered it as the bishop began another prayer.

"Almighty and ever living God, who makest us both to will and to do those things which are good, and acceptable unto thy divine majesty; we make our humble supplications unto thee for these thy servants, upon whom, after the example of thy holy Apostles, we have now laid our hands, to certify them, by this sign, of thy favor and gracious goodness toward them."

Yes, she thought. *Thy favor, not the Quakers', not my father's, not my husband's.*

"Thy favor," she whispered.

"Let thy fatherly hand, we beseech thee, ever be over them; let thy Holy Spirit ever be with them; and so lead them into the knowledge and obedience of thy Word, that in the end they may obtain everlasting life through our Lord Jesus Christ, who with thee and the Holy Ghost liveth and reigneth, ever one with God, world without end. Amen," the bishop said.

"Amen," Dolley repeated, feeling more agreement in her heart than ever before.

The bishop continued.

"O Almighty Lord and everlasting God, vouchsafe, we beseech thee to direct, sanctify, and govern both our hearts and bodies in the ways of thy laws, and in the works of thy commandments, that through thy most mighty protection, both here and ever, we may be preserved in body and soul; through our Lord and Savior Jesus Christ. Amen," he prayed.

"The Blessing of God Almighty, the Father, the Son, and the Holy Ghost, be upon you, and remain with you forever. Amen," he concluded.

With the confirmation portion of the service complete, Dolley looked up and smiled. Her heart felt different, renewed. Peace had finally washed over her. Her lips were free to drink from Holy Communion's cup.[1]

George Washington saw faith in God as the essence of life and prosperity. In his Farewell Address to the nation, he wrote, "Of all the dispositions and habits which lead to political prosperity, religion and morality are indispensable supports."[2]

His wife shared his faith. She was the great-granddaughter of the first pastor of Bruton Parish Church in Williamsburg, Virginia.

Martha's faith was important to her, and grew deeper as her life progressed.[3] Ellen McCallister Clark, who wrote the introduction for a book of Martha's correspondence, noted her reverence for God.

"Her letters reveal a God-fearing woman of deep religious convictions, with a strong belief in the hereafter, and a faith that her God was always doing what was best," she wrote.[4]

Historian Mary V. Thompson explained that Martha found time each day to practice her faith, even though she was busy entertaining many visitors and managing her duties.

"She regularly retired to her bedroom between nine and ten o'clock each morning, 'for an hour of meditation[,] reading, and prayer, and that hour no one was ever allowed to interfere with. She and Nelly, the granddaughter she and George Washington raised at Mount Vernon, also prayed, read the Bible, and sang hymns in the evening in preparation for bed," she said.[5]

Martha's Book of Common Prayer and a large Bible, which she purchased in New York at the beginning of George's presidency, are part of the collections at Mount Vernon. Her prayer book features an inscription by her great-grandson, which indicates that Martha read from the book twice a day from the time she acquired it until her death in 1802.

As the previous chapters illustrate, many first ladies were women of noble character. Their lives show us that they were worth far more than rubies. Their priceless pearls of wisdom illustrate principles of faith and reverence for God. Historians have documented the denominations of presidents and first ladies, but they usually don't delve too deeply into their religious beliefs. Often we know that a president or first lady believed in God, but we don't always know what they believed about God. Their lives, letters, and legacies sometimes give us clues to their deeper beliefs. Their ripest fruit, however, often shows the roots of faith.

Julia Grant's memoirs are laced with biblical references. She was the granddaughter of a Methodist minister. Helen Taft described herself as a strict Presbyterian. Anna Harrison's letters often refer to Scripture and reflect her Presbyterian viewpoints. After their retirement, Mamie became involved in a Presbyterian church.

Ida McKinley met her husband, future President William McKinley, while they crossed paths walking to church in Canton, Ohio. She attended Presbyterian services and he attended Methodist ones. After passing each other several times, he suggested they attend the same church. They did for the rest of their lives.

Harriet Lane's protestant doctrine was so grounded that her uncle told her he doubted she would convert to Catholicism when he sent her to finish her education at a convent. "Your religious principles are doubtless so well settled that you will not become a nun."[6] She later reflected that the nuns helped her to develop her philosophy for charity and giving.

Sometimes scholars and editors will try to hide a person's statements of faith. I first came across Louisa Adams's narrative of her journey from St. Petersburg to Paris at the Library of Congress. I read her handwritten manuscript on microfilm. *Scribner's* magazine printed this manuscript in October 1903 but, for whatever reason, the editors omitted Louisa's clearest statement of faith, an insult to her and their readers. No wonder it's sometimes difficult to know what someone believed. Here's the paragraph *Scribner's* deleted, a jewel of insight into Louisa's beliefs:

> "And when it is his will that I lay me down to sleep, that sleep from which we wake no more in this world; may I die in my Savior Jesus Christ and the full hope of those divine promises, which lead the purified soul to heaven for evermore."[7]

The editors of Grace Coolidge's republished autobiography didn't try to hide her faith.

At one place in her lovely narrative she remarks what it meant, quite literally, in the old days, to "face the music." She was willing to do that because of her very considerable faith. When the president and his wife were aboard the presidential yacht, the *Mayflower*, and the day was Sunday, the Coolidges held church services. Three-quarters of a century later one can almost hear Mrs. Coolidge's voice, lustily singing the hymns.[8]

One of Abigail Adams's clearest statements of her faith and reverence for God comes from a letter she wrote to John after her mother's death in October 1775.

I am not left to mourn as one without hope. My dear parent knew in whom she had Believed, and from the first attack of the distemper she was perswaded it would prove fatal to her. A solemnity possess'd her soul, nor could you force a smile from her till she dyed. The voilence of her disease soon weakened her so that she was unable to converse, but whenever she could speak, she testified her willingness to leave the world and an intire resignation to the Divine Will. She retaind her senses to the last moment of her Existance, and departed the World with an easy tranquility, trusting in the merits of a Redeamer. Her passage to immortality was marked with a placid smile upon her countanance, nor was there to be seen scarcly a vestage of the king of Terrors.

. . . Forgive me then, for thus dwelling upon a subject sweet to me, but I fear painfull to you. O how I have long'd for your Bosom to pour forth my sorrows there, and find a healing Balm, but perhaps that has been denied me that I might be led to a higher and a more permamant consolater who has bid us call upon him in the day of trouble.[9]

Presidents and first ladies have faced the challenge of balancing their public role with their private faith. They are respectful of other religions, often inviting different groups to the White House around times of celebration. Occasionally they have found ways to candidly express their faith.

A debate among the Republican presidential candidates took place in Des Moines, Iowa, on December 13, 1999. John Bachman, one of the moderators, asked the candidates a simple question, "What political philosopher or thinker, Mr. Forbes, do you most identify with and why?" he said.

Candidate Steve Forbes used seventy-nine words to name John Locke and Thomas Jefferson as the thinkers he most identified with. Candidate Alan Keyes used 145 words to express his views on the founders but failed to name anyone specifically.

Candidate George W. Bush, however, used only six words to say, "Christ, because he changed my heart."

The moderator, perhaps slightly stunned, said, "I think the viewer would like to know more on how he's changed your heart."

Bush replied, "Well, if they don't know, it's going to be hard to explain. When you turn your heart and your life over to Christ, when you accept Christ as the Savior, it changes your heart. It changes your life. And that's what happened to me."[10]

Exactly a year later after he spoke so frankly about his faith, George W. Bush received the news that he would be the next president. The five-week postelection recount dispute ended when the U.S. Supreme Court issued a ruling on December 13, 2000, triggering a concession from Vice President Al Gore.

Election night 2000 is still vivid in my memory. I remember standing on a packed street in front of the Texas capitol in the cold rain. When one of the jumbo outdoor screens showed a news report declaring Bush the winner, the crowd went wild. At the same time, the Gore crowd became increasingly despondent on the big screen. Then, when the networks recalled the decision, and Vice President Gore decided not to concede, the jumbo screens showed the Gore camp cheering while our faces turned blanker than the cold wind and rain pouring down on us.

By the time the Supreme Court made its decision, the desire to block off the streets of Austin for another rally had waned. In the end, it was to a house of prayer that the Bushes turned to celebrate. The service was quite memorable for its simplicity and respectful spirit.

I remember sitting on a pew surrounded by cheery yellow walls at Austin's Tarrytown United Methodist Church, where three hundred of us had gathered for the post-recount prayer service. With the excitement of watching a bride and groom walk down the aisle, I remember seeing President-elect Bush and Laura Bush walk to the front of the church and take their seats. Three ministers, all close to the Bushes, led different parts of the service. Country singer Larry Gatlin sang a song he wrote for the occasion. The Scripture readings came from Exodus 14:10–16, when Moses parted the Red Sea and Romans 8:31–39, where Paul reminded the Romans that nothing, not even a postelection mess, could separate anyone from the love of God. Perhaps the most powerful statement of faith at this "christening" of a president was the prayer of intercession printed in the program:

> Almighty God, by whose mercy we have come to the gateway of a new era for our country: Grant that we may enter it with humble and grateful hearts; and confirm our resolution to walk more closely in your perfect will and labor more faithfully in your service. Forgive our shortcomings and our sins; purify our hearts to see and love the truth; give wisdom to our leaders, especially President-elect George W. Bush and Vice President-elect Dick Cheney; and give steadfastness to our people. In the time of prosperity, fill our hearts with thankfulness, and in the day of adversity, do not let our trust in you fail. Guide us as we seek to do your will. Amen.

Although President Bush made bold statements about his faith during the campaign, Laura Bush was the one who worked to plan this service. In the aftermath of September 11, 2001, her statements of faith brought meaning to that intercessory prayer's plea, "in the day of adversity, do not let our trust in you fail."

"I'm blessed to be married to a man who is strong enough to bear great burdens, and humble enough to ask God for help. We draw on our faith in times of joy and also in times of uncertainty. This was especially true in the days after September 11," Laura Bush reflected at a New York prayer breakfast in May 2004.[11]

"On the Sunday after those attacks, the president and I attended church at Camp David. Remarkably, the psalm outlined in the lectionary for that September Sunday was Psalm 27. It reads, 'Thy face, LORD, do I seek. I believe that I shall see the goodness of the LORD in the land of the living,'" she said.

"Given the week's tragic events, the words carried enormous meaning—because that's exactly what we saw. We witnessed a handful of people commit an unbelievable atrocity, but we saw millions more commit acts of care and compassion. Because of this, I chose Psalm 27 for our first White House holiday card. This was a small way to pay tribute to the resiliency and the goodness of the American people," she said.

President Jimmy Carter and Rosalynn Carter also have been candid about their faith throughout their years of public service. He is known for teaching Sunday school, and they both have written about their beliefs. Rosalynn expressed her faith in her autobiography, *First Lady from Plains.* She wrote:

> God was a real presence in my life. We were taught to love him and felt very much the necessity and desire to live the kind of life he would have us to live, to love one another and be kind to and help those who needed help, and to be good. We were also taught to fear God, and though I loved him, I was afraid of displeasing him all my young life. I didn't think about him as a forgiving God but as a punishing God, and I was afraid even to have a bad thought. I thought if we were good he would love us, but if we weren't, he wouldn't.[12]

Rosalynn's explanation of her youthful understanding of fearing the Lord is a common struggle. Fearing the Lord and respecting Him through our actions does not mean forfeiting His love and forgiveness. When her father died at an early age, Rosalynn had many questions about the God she feared. She later came to understand that His love for her was not conditional.

"Didn't God love me anymore? I had doubts about God, and I was afraid because I doubted. That was long before I knew that God is a loving God who cares for us and loves us, who suffers when we suffer, and who knows that we are going to have doubts, and that we're not always going to do what is right, but he loves us anyway," she wrote.[13]

Hundreds of passages in both the Old and New Testaments of the Bible employ the phrase "fear of the Lord," including a verse in Proverbs 31. "Charm is deceptive, and beauty is fleeting; but a woman who fears the LORD is to be praised" (Prov. 31:30). Only one verse describes this woman's relationship to God. Her fear of the Lord was her statement of faith.

The concept of fearing the Lord is difficult to understand to our modern way of thinking. Fear is something that entertains us in horror movies. Fear shows up on the nightly news and on reality television shows. We have turned phrases, such as Franklin Roosevelt's edict, "The only thing we have to fear is fear itself," into mottos. We've humanized God so much—sometimes seeing Him as a giant genie or a jolly Santa—that we have a hard time relating to this concept of fearing God. Like Dolley's experience with Quakerism of the nineteenth century, we revolt when grace and forgiveness disappear from the equation of the dos and don'ts resulting in legalism.

Carol Blair, an adjunct English teacher at a Christian college, came face-to-face with fear phobia. As was the custom at her school, she began each lecture with a devotional. One day she read from Proverbs 1:7, "The fear of the LORD is the beginning of knowledge, but fools despise wisdom and instruction." Carol talked about the fear of the Lord and how the concept permeates both the Old and New Testaments.

One by one the students reacted negatively, saying that God was not to be feared. He was their pal, their buddy, and a friend. They nearly shouted Carol down, and she abruptly stopped the devotional.

"I had many other problems with that class—academics, discipline, attendance, and more," Carol later said. She wondered if the root of these problems was in her students' inability to view God as worthy of their fear.[14]

Much like today, fear in the ancient world meant terror and apprehension, but fear also meant reverence, respect, and piety. Just as a child fears and respects his parents, the fear of the Lord means a fear of God and a humble reverence for His authority. It also means a love for God, a respect for Him.

The first lady of Proverbs 31 would have known the law's command to fear the Lord. "And now, O Israel, what does the LORD your God ask of you but to fear the LORD your God, to walk in all his ways, to love him, to serve the LORD your God with all your heart and with all your soul, and to observe the LORD's commands and decrees that I am giving you today for your own good?" (Deut. 10:12, 13).

As a result, the first lady of Proverbs 31 lived her life in a way that respected the Lord. Her respect or fear motivated her to work with eager hands, to lead by example, to speak with wisdom, and to give to the needy. Her actions were offerings of respect to God.

Wisdom is a result of fearing the Lord. "The fear of the LORD is the beginning of wisdom; all who follow his precepts have good understanding. To him belongs eternal praise" (Ps. 111:10). "Then you will understand the fear of the LORD and find the knowledge of God" (Prov. 2:5). In Proverbs 1:29–33, Solomon warns that those who fail to fear the Lord will "eat the fruit of their schemes" but those who do will "live in safety and be at ease, without fear of harm."

Dolley Madison demonstrated her respect for the Lord when she stepped across that threshold and into the confirmation service at St. John's Church on July 15, 1845. Dolley was a Victorian version of a celebrity. Everyone had heard about her. Those who attended church with her probably assumed she had been confirmed years earlier, unless they noticed that she had never participated in Holy Communion.

In a letter to her nephew, Dolley explained that she and Anne had been thinking about confirmation for a while. Although her early religious life was shaped by the beliefs of her father and husbands, she made a decision to publicly confirm her private faith in Jesus Christ on her own. Her decision to be confirmed was both a humble and courageous step, a statement of faith made with her own two feet. I can only imagine the peace this Victorian beauty queen must have felt when she publicly embraced the beauty of the Lord. As the bishop prayed that day, "Fill them, O LORD, with the spirit of thy holy fear, now and forever."

In thinking about this concept of fearing the Lord and openly declaring faith, a friend of mine suggested I talk to Anne Ryun about her faith story and Proverbs 31. I had met Anne briefly and in our thirty-second conversation, I could see beauty and joy radiating from her. I asked to interview her about her perspective on what it means in Proverbs 31:30 to fear the Lord. The timing was perfect, because she had been studying this concept and talking about it with her friend, Carol Blair, whom I mentioned earlier.

"To fear the Lord is to hold Him in awe and in respect, and to honor Him and to know that he's Lord and I am not," Anne said. "One side of God is tenderness and compassion. But there's that side of God that says, 'I'm a just God. I'm sovereign. And I will do what I have said that I will do.'"

Anne and I met in her husband's congressional office, where framed copies of his photograph on the cover of *Sports Illustrated* and other leading magazines decorated the paneled walls. I knew she was married to Kansas Congressman Jim Ryun, but—I'm sure this will insult the many sports fans out there—I was too young to know who Jim Ryun was. I didn't know Jim Ryun set the world's record in 1967 for running the mile in three minutes and 51.1 seconds. He held that record for years. I didn't know Jim Ryun won the silver medal for the 1,500-meter race in the 1968 Olympics. Anne shared with me what it was like for her to be the wife of such a successful athlete. His running shoes brought her to her knees.

"I had thought pretty well of myself, arrogantly, pridefully, and haughtily until I got married to the world record holder in the mile. And then when I married him, people didn't know my name. If they acknowledged me at all, it was Mrs. Ryun," she said.

Living in a track star's shadow made her question her own worth. People didn't know her first name was Anne and that it was spelled with an "e" on the end. When Jim began losing races shortly after their marriage, his coach came to her and said, "Anne, you've got to do something more to help Jim other than to distract him." Anne said that sports writers would write things like, "Ryun's wife brings him down."

At first, Anne didn't care. She was happy. She had married the man she loved, and it was no big deal to her that he was the world record holder in the mile. She said she wasn't this Proverbs 31 wife who was encouraging her husband and supporting him. She was totally into herself. But then Anne began to think, "Wait a minute. Am I a person of value? Do I count? Am I of any worth? I have never done anything great or world renown."

Even as recently as a few years ago, Anne went to the Ford dealership to pick up their car and received a reminder of her past.

Sam, the salesman, recognized her as the wife of Jim Ryun.

"My girlfriend and I hate you," Sam said.

"Can you tell me why?" she said, surprised at his candor.

"You dismantled our idol," he said.

"Well, Sam, I'm so grateful to God," she said, explaining how Jim's downfall as a runner brought them to God. She handed him a copy of *In Quest of Gold*. The Ryuns distribute thousands of these pocket-size foldouts to people they meet each year. *In Quest of Gold* shares how Jim's quest for Olympic gold brought Jim and Anne to their knees so they could one day walk on God's streets of gold.

As Jim struggled to win races again to prepare for the 1972 Olympics, he and Anne realized that they needed help. They began meeting people and other athletes who said they were born-again Christians. The Ryuns started studying the Bible. Thirty days later on May 18, 1972, they knelt with friends and prayed to receive the Lord into their lives.

"My initial relationship with the Lord was as a friend who would come alongside of me and help me," Anne said, noting that she didn't understand the concept of fearing God at first.

She later came to another crisis point that showed her both sides of God, as a friend and comforter and as one who demanded humility. At the time, Anne had three children under age three, Jim was traveling extensively with professional track, her parents were living in another state, and she needed encouragement.

"One night everybody was asleep. Jim was gone. I had just finished mopping the kitchen floor. I literally fell down on the floor—but I knew it was clean," she said, laughing.

"I'm sobbing. I'm just exhausted. I'm really overwhelmed. I opened my Bible and read through Psalm 27. And Psalm 27:4 has been my life verse ever since. There's one thing that I want and one thing only, that I might dwell in the house of the Lord all the days of my life to inquire of the Lord and to behold His beauty," she said, paraphrasing.

Anne says that as she has matured, she has developed a deeper respect for God's sovereignty. When she was still nursing her youngest child, she joined a Bible study with women who were ten and twenty years older than she. They became her lifelong friends and mentors. Their influence helped her to learn to respect God. As her respect for God grew, she showed more respect to her husband and family.

She remembers one day when she and the children had planned to accompany Jim on a photo shoot several hours away. After the shoot they had planned to spend a couple of days with Anne's brothers. Jim was a professional photographer by this time. She had spent hours packing and preparing the children for a long car ride when Jim suddenly announced they weren't going. His camera equipment hadn't arrived, and he couldn't do the shoot. Anne remembers how her response was one of acceptance, even though the decision meant she would not see her brothers. Her reaction was quite different than her response to the criticism she received from Jim's coach and sportswriters years earlier.

"OK, we're not going," she remembers thinking without complaining. "And I have found great peace in my husband's leadership. That doesn't mean he doesn't have holes in the umbrella. It's my responsibility to patch and cover those holes."

Today, Anne participates in Bible studies with other wives whose husbands serve in Congress. They learn from each other as their families navigate the murky waters of Washington politics, from the big votes on the Hill to losing the employment of cherished and loyal staff members. These are all reminders of God's sovereignty in a world where control and power dominate.

"We really do live on the battleground. We don't live on a playground. Just as King David inquired of the Lord, I want to be that kind of person that says, 'OK, God, what is your heart? What is your mind? What is your idea for this circumstance?'"

Anne's respect for the Lord has led her to share her faith with others.

"I have such a burden that people are looking for Christ, and they don't know how to find Him. I knew growing up there was a God who loved me, but I had no idea there was a relationship to be had," she said.

My story of faith is a little different from Anne's, but the ending is the same. I grew up in a secure home. My parents took me to church and talked to me about God and Jesus. One Easter Sunday, when I was eight years old, I told my parents I wanted to walk down the aisle at church. They took me home and asked me questions to make sure I understood the basics of Christianity. I knew that God loved me. But like other humans, I did wrong things. Death was the ultimate result of Adam's and Eve's sin, and everyone since then. I knew our sins separated us from God in the long run. But God had a remedy. He sent his Son, Jesus Christ, who was without sin, to die in my place so I might have eternal life.

That Easter Sunday on my parents' couch, I said a prayer not unlike Dolley Madison's confirmation prayer or Anne Ryun's prayer. I told God I was sorry for my sin, asked His forgiveness, accepted His loving remedy, and committed my life to Him.

When I talked with Anne that day in her husband's office, I thought about where I had come since first accepting Christ as my Savior. Did I mostly think of God as my buddy, as I did when I prayed as a child, or did I really fear Him as Proverbs 31:30 says?

Candidly, I think I'm somewhere in the middle of that spectrum. I hope when I'm closer to sixty than sixteen, I'll reflect his beauty because my life reveals an abiding respect for Him.

I discovered I had two other things in common with Anne. We have both had to accept our shortcomings, literally. I am only five feet tall. Anne and I talked about how one of the results of fearing and respecting God is accepting who you are and the gifts He has given you, being comfortable in your own skin.

"My legs are a little short. I think God was distracted and gave those three extra inches to my husband," Anne said with a smile.

"Being comfortable in your own skin is not self-esteem. It's being confident of who we are in Christ, that our old lives have died, and Christ now lives in us and through us. It's being comfortable in who we are and the way He has created us with our giftings and talents," she said.

Something else I have in common with Anne is a love for giving tours of the White House. One of my joys when I worked at the White House was giving tours to friends. I loved sharing with them little-known anecdotes, some I have shared in this book, as I took them through the public rooms of the White House.

As the wife of a congressman, Anne also enjoys giving tours of the White House to Jim's constituents. At the end of her tours, she shares the prayer by John Adams inscribed in the fireplace mantel of the dining room. On his first night in the White House, the first time a president ever slept under its pillars, John Adams wrote a letter to Abigail.

"Before I end my Letter I pray Heaven to bestow the best of Blessings on this House and all that shall hereafter inhabit it. May none but honest and wise Men ever rule under this roof," Adams wrote.[15]

Although earthly beauty fades, the light of God radiates no matter how old you are. His love does not disappear as we age. As we mature, our respect for Him reveals our inner beauty. That is why "Charm is deceptive, and beauty is fleeting; but a woman who fears the LORD is to be praised" (Prov. 31:30).

The fire of a gemstone paints a picture of our worth and value in Christ. Jewelers rate gems on their ability to reflect light, which is called refraction. When a jewel, such as turquoise, has low refraction or a limited ability to reflect light, white light travels through it and emerges as white light with no sparkle or color. Jewels with high refraction showcase different colors of light. Blue light bends more than green light, which bends more than red light, and so on. When light scatters this way, colors flash within the jewel. Jewelers call these flashes of light the fire of a gemstone. Diamonds have the highest rate of refraction because their fire is more brilliant than any other gem. Much like a rainbow, the fire of a jewel is its ability to reflect the full spectrum of colors found in its light source.

The mother-of-pearl also appears to glow from within. Its luster rivals the fire of a ruby, diamond, or a sapphire. A pearl starts with an irritant such as a food particle inside an oyster. The oyster covers the speck with alternating layers of skin and crystals. Because a pearl's surface is round, it works like a convex mirror. As a result, light appears to emanate from within the pearl and creates an iridescent glow. The layers within the mother-of-pearl are like tiny prisms, refracting light's rainbow of colors.[16]

Because the Proverbs 31 first lady respected God, he wiped off the sin, mud, and imperfections that encased the jewel within her, polished her talents and abilities, placed her among others who needed light, and fueled the fire within her. Her fire rivaled a diamond and glowed more beautifully than mother-of-pearl. As this Psalm reminds us, she brought great joy to the jewelry maker: "The LORD delights in those who fear him, who put their hope in his unfailing love" (Ps. 147:11).

When we humble ourselves in respect for God and show we fear Him by declaring our faith in Jesus Christ, He reflects a fire of light within us. Our worth and value is intrinsic in Him. He gives us a rainbow glow that cannot fade with age. This inner beauty shines through us in every area of our lives and creates a patchwork legacy, much like a stained-glass window.

CHAPTER ELEVEN

Stained-Glass Windows

"Give her the reward she has earned, and let her works bring her praise at the city gate" (Prov. 31:31).

W HEN ARCHITECT Benjamin Latrobe, famous for rebuilding the Capitol and the White House, studied his latest accomplishment, St. John's Church, he marveled at the church's most attractive features, its exquisite proportions and Greek cross shape. He wrote his son, "I have completed a church that has made many Washingtonians religious who had not been religious before."[1]

St. John's has reminded many presidents over the years of the importance of faith. Every president since James Madison has attended at least one service within its walls. Today, if you walk into St. John's Church you can't help but notice the stained-glass windows. These jewels of color glisten as the sun lights them from the outside while lifted hearts and altar candles light them from within.

If you glance to the right, the side of the church facing the White House, you'll see a window depicting the resurrection of Christ. A closer inspection of this glass collage shows that God's love for man also reveals man's love for woman. The window's bottom panel features a long red rectangle with rounded corners. Inside the rectangle in yellow letters is this inscription: "To the glory of God and in memory of Ellen Lewis Herndon Arthur, entered into life January 12, 1880."

President Chester Arthur arranged for this stained-glass window to be placed in memory of his wife on the south side of the church so he could see it from the White House. Once again, Chester had publicly declared his love for Nell. Just as he put her photograph in the White House's state floor hallway, so he also placed her stained-glass window at St. John's to tell everyone about her. She was the little girl whose parents were confirmed in the service with Dolley Madison. She was the teenager who sang in St. John's choir. She was the young woman Chester married. She was the first lady of his heart.

To make Nell's window, the stained-glass maker used different chemicals to color the pieces of glass. The artisan employed copper for green, cobalt for blue, and gold for red. To build a window, the glass artisan put the pieces in a frame and poured lead or concrete into the frame to set the glass fragments. By themselves, the pieces of glass don't make sense, but together they tell a story. Sometimes the stained-glass maker chips the surface of each piece to make them rough, which helps the patterns to shine more brightly in sunlight.

Our lives and legacies are not too different from stained-glass windows. The combined pieces of our lives, tiles of chipped and jagged glass, form a mosaic. The stained-glass maker puts them together to tell our story.

By placing a stained-glass window in memory of Nell at St. John's, Chester praised his wife for her nobility. To him she surpassed all others.

Such blessings were common in ancient cultures. One blessing common to the Hebrews was a benediction of someone's personal character. These were thanksgivings for the manifestation of divine goodness on someone's life.[2] Proverbs 31 ends with a family benediction. "Her children arise and call her blessed; her husband also, and he praises her: 'Many women do noble things, but you surpass them all'" (Prov. 31:28, 29).

Grace Coolidge had Proverbs 31 in mind when she wrote about her philosophy of marriage and the legacy she hoped to leave:

Marriage is the most intricate institution set up by the human race . . . There are adjustments to be made from time to time, and each should make those which contribute to efficiency and permanency. And my humble opinion (is that) the woman is by nature the more adaptable of the two and she should rejoice in this and realize that in the exercise of this ability she will obtain not only a spiritual blessing but her own family will rise out and call her blessed.[3]

Today, we find ways to honor people, especially those we consider famous. And, of course, we have found ways to praise the first ladies, often before their legacy is complete.

Martha Washington began to receive praise from the American people very early in her husband's public life. Historian Mary V. Thompson says that Martha was mystified at the reception she received along the way to Philadelphia in the first year of the Revolutionary War. Martha wrote that she left the city "in a great pomp as if I had been a very great somebody."[4]

People began to name their children after George and Martha. The Washingtons received a portrait of twins, a boy named George and a girl named Martha, from a family they did not know. Ship owners named their boats after Martha. Songwriters wrote tributes to her. These tokens, Mary said, "suggest the love and respect, which she inspired in her countrymen, from very early in the war."[5]

Elizabeth Ellet, a first lady biographer, similarly described Martha: "Those who read the record of her worth, dwell with interest on the loveliness of her character. To a superior mind she joined those amiable qualities and Christian virtues which best adorn the female sect and a gentle dignity that inspired respect without creating enmity."[6]

Harry Truman continually praised his wife. Several years after leaving the presidency, the crowning achievement of his career, he wrote, "I've had several moments of great joy, but the greatest joy of them all was when my sweetheart from six years old consented to become Mrs. Truman."

First ladies often receive the most poignant praise after death.

When Bess Truman died in 1982, a private funeral took place at the Trinity Episcopal Church in Independence, Missouri, where she and Harry married in 1919. First ladies Nancy Reagan, Rosalynn Carter, and Betty Ford attended and heard Rev. Robert Hart's eulogy.

"Your presence as family and friends is a well-spoken word in testimony to a life well lived. Bess Truman was a Christian woman, a woman of integrity, graciousness, and intelligence," he said. "You know who she was and what she was. You know what she meant to you; what she meant to our city and state; to the nation, and to the church. Let us now lift her up to God in thanksgiving. Let us give thanks for her life and her witness among us."

Upon the death of Abigail Adams, Rev. Kirkland, who was president of Harvard at the time, said, "Ye will seek to mourn, bereaved friends, it says, 'as becomes Christians, in a manner worthy of the person you lament.' You do then bless the giver of life that the course of your endeared and honored friend was so long and so bright; that she entered fully into the spirit of those injunctions which we have explained and as a minister of blessings to all within her influences."[7]

Some first ladies have received praise specifically for the way they fulfilled their role as mother. Victorian-era biographer Lara C. Holloway praised Julia Grant for her family focus.

"To be approved by one's friends is comfort, but to be adored by one's children is to be crowned with the most imperishable of earthly diadems," Holloway wrote. "It is to her credit that her sons, grown to manhood, pay her marked attentions, and that she is to them the ideal mother."

Today, first ladies most often receive praise for their work and accomplishments.

For her contributions to environmental beautification, Lady Bird Johnson has received forty-seven awards and fifteen honorary degrees since 1958. These range from a variety of sources, from *Ladies' Home Journal's* Woman of the Year Award to the Theodore Roosevelt National Park Medal of Honor.

Many hospitals are named for Nancy Reagan because of her work to prevent drug and alcohol abuse among youth and her efforts to extend her hand to the elderly and emotionally disabled children. Her work and support for Alzheimer's research in memory of her husband also continues through the Ronald and Nancy Reagan Research Center of the Alzheimer's Association.

Perhaps the most touching praise Nancy ever received came in the form of letters from her husband. On Christmas Day in 1981, the first Christmas after the assassination attempt on his life, Reagan wrote a Proverbs 31–like letter to his wife.

"There are several much beloved women in my life and on Christmas I should be giving them gold, precious stones, perfume, furs, and lace. I know that even the best of these would still fall far short of expressing how much these several women mean to me and how empty my life would be without them," Ronald Reagan wrote.

Among Reagan's "much beloved women" was the first lady who brought grace and charm to whatever she did, making stuffy events fun. She was also the woman who reached out to "touch an elderly invalid with tenderness and compassion just as she fills my life with warmth and love." The other women were the gal who was a nest builder and the one who went to the ranch with him and the sentimental lady "whose eyes fill up so easily." Another was the woman who loved to laugh, even at his stale jokes.

"Fortunately all these women in my life are you—fortunately for me that is, for there could be no life for me without you. Browning asked: 'How do I love thee—let me count the ways?' For me there is no way to count. I love the whole gang of you—Mommie, first lady, the sentimental you, the fun you and the peewee power house you," Reagan concluded, signing his love note with, "Lucky me."[8]

Our nation's first ladies have made a difference. Like the woman in Proverbs 31, they deserved to be praised for their contributions, character, and work.

Sometimes, however, we focus too much on achievement. From a very early age, we teach children to participate in activities that will help them fill up the blanks on their college applications. College breeds more pressure for achievement. We tell students that a thousand activities on a resume will impress a future employer. We take jobs wondering how this position will help us to find a better job in the future. We live in a culture that often values achievement more than the achiever.

We sometimes supersize someone's success. We honor people for their outstanding achievements or the size of their wallet. If you invent something significant, you can have a school named after you. If you donate money, you can have a museum, hospital, or college building named after you. With so many awards and recognitions, it's easy to place our worth in our resumes, trophies, or degrees.

Government evaluates our lives based on our vital statistics. Forms often require us to list our status as married or unmarried, identify the number of children in our household, or state how much money we earn. No wonder we often find our identity in how we identify our lives.

Proverbs 31 honors its first lady for her accomplishments and successes, but it goes beyond bullet points on a resume and blue ink on a form. This proverb highlights character over career ladders, wisdom over waistlines, and faith over firsts. The author of Proverbs 31 tells us that her family praised her. The poet went a step further and added this to his benediction: "Give her the reward she has earned, and let her works bring her praise at the city gate" (Prov. 31:31).

The city gate was the most public place in the ancient Hebrew world. It was the marketplace and a public gathering place. City council sessions were held at the gate. Community leaders made announcements there. The gate was where it was happening. The books of Daniel and Esther reveal that the gate was the king's court.

In a tour of one of Solomon's cities, biblical historian Ray Vander Laan explained that the city gate became the place to meet the king. "If you wanted an audience with the king, the king would come down at a certain time and have an audience here in the compartments of the gate. So much so that the phrase in the biblical world to 'sit in the gate' is a synonym for to be a judge," Ray said.[9]

Because a gate surrounded cities, the term often meant the city itself. The city gate was a place where judges held court. To praise her at the city gate meant to recognize her in the most public way possible and to praise her before God, the ultimate judge.

"It also is taught in the Bible . . . that the last judgment, the final judgment, is held in the city gate," Ray said.[10]

"Let her works bring her praise at the city gate" means "Let the judge of the highest court judge her, for she is worth more than rubies to him." In the end, she was the first lady of God's heart. By fearing Him and allowing Him to shine through her, she was a first lady to those around her.

For Mother's Day in 2005, Catharine Ryun wrote a resume for her mother, Anne. She knew people were constantly asking her mother what she did as the wife of the congressman from Kansas or as the wife of the Olympic medalist.

"From a little girl I've always wanted to be a wife, a mommy and a teacher. And God has given me those three desires and abundantly more," Anne said, noting that wives and mothers don't usually sit down and write a resume of what they've done.

Catharine read her mother's resume out loud on Mother's Day in front of all of Anne's children and grandchildren.

"But when she read it, I thought, 'Oh Lord, how gracious you have been to me,'" Anne said, remembering years earlier when she was the anonymous wife of the world record holder of the mile. She realized how far she had come since she first discovered that God knew her name and that she spelled it with an 'e' on the end. As John 10:3 reminds us, "He calls his own sheep by name and leads them out."

Anne's life changed when she allowed God to uncover the jewel inside of her. She was better able to shine and sparkle in the hands of the Jewelry Maker.

God wants to praise us, just as He longs to wipe off the mud, the sin, the gunk in our lives. He wants to be the fire of our gemstones, allowing His rainbow of light to shine through our work, appearance, leadership, families, and service to others. He wants to hold us up to the light of His Son. He wants us to invest our talents, time, and treasure. He wants us to wear purple to parties and scarlet for safety. He wants us to laugh out loud. He wants us to model the sample pattern and mold a household with wisdom. He wants us to extend our hands to those in need. He wants our inner beauty to outshine the outer. He doesn't want us to throw our pearls to pigs, but He wants us to enter His pearly gates. He wants us to ask forgiveness for our sins and accept and believe in His Son.

Jesus compared the kingdom of heaven to finding a jewel. He said, "Again, the kingdom of heaven is like a merchant looking for fine pearls. When he found one of great value, he went away and sold everything he had and bought it" (Matt. 13:46). He also described heaven as a mansion. "In my Father's house are many rooms; if it were not so, I would have told you. I am going there to prepare a place for you" (John 14:2).

God wants to welcome you into His streets of gold and meet you at the city gate. He will even sing a song for you. "The LORD your God is with you, he is mighty to save. He will take great delight in you, he will quiet you with his love, he will rejoice over you with singing" (Zeph. 3:17).

Then He wants to take you to His mansion, His white house, to show you the picture He has of you hanging on the wall or the one sitting on a table in His hallway. He wants to show you a mosaic of your legacy, your stained-glass window. He wants you to remember that you are the first lady of His heart.

Bibliography

"Abigail Adams: First Lady Biography." National First Ladies Library,
http://www.firstladies.org/biographies/firstladies.aspx?biography=2
(accessed August 2005).

"Active on Esplanade." *Washington Post,* April 11, 1909.

"Anna Harrison: First Lady Biography." National First Ladies Library,
http://www.firstladies.org/biographies/firstladies.aspx?biography=9
(accessed August 2005).

"Approaching Centenary of Old St. John's Church, Worshipping Place of
Presidents and Notables for 100 Years. Will Be Event of Deep Historic
Interest." *Washington Post,* March 21, 1915.

"Busy With Esplanade." *Washington Post,* April 4, 1909.

"Careful that Dish Is Hot: At the Gridiron Dinner, Hams Glazed with
Condi." *Washington Post,* March 13, 2005.

"Death of Major Butt Mourned by Washingtonians." *Washington Times,*
April 19, 1912.

"Dolley Madison: First Lady Biography." National First Ladies Library,
http://www.firstladies.org/biographies/firstladies.aspx?biography=4
(accessed August 2005).

"Ellen Arthur: First Lady Biography." National First Ladies Library,
http://www.firstladies.org/biographies/firstladies.aspx?biography=22
(accessed August 2005).

"Hanau." Napoleon Guide. http://www.napoleonguide.com/battle_hanau
.htm (accessed August 2005).

"Harriet Lane: First Lady Biography." National First Ladies Library, http://www.firstladies.org/biographies/firstladies.aspx?biography=16 (accessed August 2005).

"Helen Taft: First Lady Biography." National First Ladies Library, http://www.firstladies.org/biographies/firstladies.aspx?biography=27 (accessed August 2005).

"Highlights of the ASAPS 2004 Statistics on Cosmetic Surgery." American Society for Aesthetic Plastic Surgery, http://www.surgery.org/press/procedurefacts-asqf.php (accessed August 2005).

"History of the Trees and Festival." National Cherry Blossom Festival. http://www.nationalcherryblossomfestival.org/cms/index.php?id=574 (accessed June 2005).

"Host on Parkway." *Washington Post,* April 18, 1909.

"How Long Does Gem Mining Take?" Sheffield Mine, http://www.sheffieldmine.com (accessed November 2004).

"Louisa Adams: First Lady Biography." National First Ladies Library, http://www.firstladies.org/biographies/firstladies.aspx?biography=6 (accessed August 2005).

"Martha Washington: First Lady Biography." National First Ladies Library, http://www.firstladies.org/biographies/firstladies.aspx?biography=1 (accessed August 2005).

"Military Service Record of Archibald Irwin Harrison, 8th Indiana Infantry." National Archives and Records Administration, 1861.

"Military Service Record of Carter B. Harrison, 51st Ohio Infantry." National Archives and Records Administration, 1861–64.

"Pearls." American Museum of Natural History, http://www.amnh.org/exhibitions/pearls/ (accessed September 2005).

"Purple Passion, May 15, 2001." *Jolique.* http://www.jolique.com/dyes_colorants/purple_passion.htm (accessed September 2005).

"Republican Presidential Candidates Participate in Political Debate in Des Moines, Iowa." Washington Transcript Service, December 13, 1999.

"Rosalynn Carter Deals with Defeat." *Chicago Tribune,* April 9, 1989.

"The Heart and Truth Campaign and the Red Dress Project." http://www.whitehouse.gov/firstlady/initiatives/womenandheartdisease2.html (accessed August 2005).

"The Order of Confirmation, or Laying On of Hands Upon Those That Are Baptized, and Come to Years of Discretion." *1789 U.S. Book of Common*

Prayer. The Society of Archbishop Justus. http://justus.anglican.org/ resources/bcp/1789/Confirmation_1789.htm (accessed August 2005).

"Washington Drive Opened: Mrs. Taft Leads Official Society Parade, Accompanied by the President." *New York Times,* April 18, 1909.

"Welcome to St. John's Flyer." Washington: St. John's Church, 2005.

Adams Family Papers: An Electronic Archive. The Massachusetts Historical Society. http://www.masshist.org/digitaladams/aea/index.html (accessed August 2005).

Adams, Louisa. "Mrs. John Quincy Adams's Narrative of a Journey from St. Petersburg to Paris in February, 1815. With an Introduction by Her Grandson, Brooks Adams." *Scribner's* magazine. 34, October 1903, 449–63.

———. "Narrative of a Journey from St. Petersburg to Paris." Microfilms of the Adams Papers, Library of Congress.

Adler, Cyrus, and I. M. Casanowicz. "Perpetual Lamp." *The Jewish Encyclopedia.* http://www.jewishencyclopedia.com (accessed June 2005).

Adler, Cyrus, Henry Cohen, and Kaufmann Kohler. "Dyes and Dyeing." *The Jewish Encyclopedia.* http://www.jewishencyclopedia.com (accessed June 2005).

Akers, Charles W. *Abigail Adams: An American Woman.* Boston: Little, Brown and Co., 1980.

All networks. "Excerpts of Evening Network News Broadcasts from the Week of 6/27/70 to 7/3/70." WHCA VTR Tape #3770. Nixon Presidential Materials, National Archives and Records Administration, College Park, MD, July 14, 1970.

Anderson, Judith Icke. *William Howard Taft: An Intimate History.* New York and London: W.W. Norton and Co., 1981.

Ankele, Stacey. Interview by Jane Cook, tape recording, Alexandria, VA. June 13, 2005.

Archer, Jules. *They Made a Revolution: 1776.* New York: St. Martin's Press, 1973.

Ariail, Dan, and Cheryl Heckler-Feltz. *The Carpenter's Apprentice: A Spiritual Biography of Jimmy Carter.* Grand Rapids, MI: Zondervan Publishing House, 1996.

Arnett, Ethel Stephens. *Mrs. James Madison: The Incomparable Dolley.* Greensboro, NC: Piedmont Press, 1972.

Associated Press. "For Bushes, Retirement Has Been Nice, But Not Quite A Rose Garden." *Chicago Tribune*, January 23, 1996.

———. "Letters to Friend Reveal the Private Bess Truman." *St. Louis Post-Dispatch*, February 19, 1995.

Blok, Alexander. "The Twelve." *The Columbia World of Quotations*. New York: Columbia University Press, 1996.

Bowles, Hamish, ed. *Jacqueline Kennedy: The White House Years*. New York: Little, Brown and Co., 2001.

Bryan, Helen. *Martha Washington: First Lady of Liberty*. New York: John Wiley and Sons, 2002.

Bumiller, Elisabeth. "Bush, Calling U.S. 'A Nation Guided by Faith,' Urges Freedom of Worship in China." *New York Times*, February 22, 2002.

Bureau of Labor Statistics. "Women's Share of Workforce to Edge Higher by 2008." U.S. Department of Labor, http://www.bls.gov/opub/ted/2000/Feb/wk3/art01.htm (accessed August 2005).

Bush, Barbara. *Barbara Bush: A Memoir*. New York: St. Martin's Paperbacks, 1994.

Bush, George W. *A Charge to Keep*, New York: HarperCollins, 1999.

———. "President Honors Ambassador Karen Hughes at Swearing-In Ceremony," U.S. Department of State, September 9, 2005.

Bush, George. "Remarks to the Staff of the Primary Children's Medical Center in Salt Lake City, Utah." Original Sources, http://www.originalsources.com, September 18, 1991.

Bush, Laura. "First Lady Laura Bush Delivers Remarks at New York Tenth Anniversary Prayer Breakfast." Washington Transcript Service, May 11, 2004.

———. "Interview by Larry King." *Larry King Live*, December 18, 2001.

———. "Letter to Elementary School Children." http://www.whitehouse.gov/kids/connection/letter2.html, September 12, 2001 (accessed August 2005).

———. "Mrs. Bush's Remarks During a Visit with Families Affected by Hurricane Katrina, September 8, 2005." Greenbrook Elementary School, Southaven, MS. http://www.whitehouse.gov/ (accessed September 9, 2005).

———. Radio address. November 17, 2001.

———. "Remarks by Mrs. Bush at 204th Commencement of Georgetown University, School of Nursing and Health Studies." Georgetown University,

http://www.whitehouse.gov/news/releases/2003/05/20030517-2
.html, May 17, 2003 (accessed August 2005).

————. "Remarks by Mrs. Bush at Memorial Service in Pennsylvania." Stonycreek Township, http://www.whitehouse.gov/firstlady/news-speeches/ speeches/fl20010917.html, September 17, 2001 (accessed October 2005).

————. "What do you say to children?: A New America." Delivered to the National Press Club, Washington, November 8, 2001.

Butt, Archibald. *Taft and Roosevelt: The Intimate Letters of Archie Butt Military Aide.* New York: Doubleday, Doran and Co., 1930.

Carter, Jimmy, and Rosalynn Carter. *Everything to Gain: Making the Most of the Rest of Your Life.* New York: Random House, 1987.

Carter, Rosalynn. *First Lady from Plains.* Boston: Houghton Mifflin Co., 1984.

Clemmer, Mary. *Ten Years in Washington: Life and Scenes in the National Capital, as a Woman Sees Them.* Hartford, CT: A.D. Worthington & Co., 1875.

Clinton, William. "Statement on the Death of Pat Nixon, June 22, 1993," http://www.originalsources.com (accessed August 2005).

Coates, Foster. "The Courtship of General Grant." *Ladies' Home Journal.* 7, October 1890.

Conkling, Margaret C. *Memoirs of the Wife of Washington.* New York: Miller, Orton and Mulligan, 1855.

Conroy, Sara Booth. "Martha-Bashing in Vogue, but Founding Mother Really Cool." *Houston Chronicle,* September 24, 1987.

Cook, Alison. "Women Leading the Way/Barbara Bush." *Houston Chronicle.* March 26, 1990.

Coolidge, Grace Goodhue. *Grace Coolidge: An Autobiography. Edited by Lawrence E. Wikander and Robert H. Ferrell.* Worland, WY: High Plains Pub. Co., 1992.

David, Lester. *The Lonely Lady of San Clemente: The Story of Pat Nixon.* New York: Thomas Y. Crowell, 1978.

Diamant, Lincoln, ed. *Revolutionary Women in the War for American Independence: A One-Volume Revised Edition of Elizabeth Ellet's 1848 Landmark Series.* Westport, CT: Praeger, 1998.

Doane, George Washington. *The Life and Writings of George Washington Doane . . . for Twenty-Seven Years Bishop of New Jersey. Containing His*

Poetical Works, Sermons, and Miscellaneous Writings; with A Memoir, by his son, William Croswell Doane. 4, New York: D. Appleton and Co., 1860–61.

Editorial, "Bess Truman's Role as First Lady." *Washington Post,* September 2, 1992.

Editors, "2008 Run, Abortion Engage Her Politically." *Washington Times,* March 12, 2005.

Eisenhower, Julie Nixon. *Pat Nixon: The Untold Story.* New York: Simon and Schuster, 1986.

Eisenhower, Susan. *Mrs. Ike: Memories and Reflections on the Life of Mamie Eisenhower.* New York: Farrar, Straus and Giroux, 1996.

Ellet, Elizabeth F. *The Women of the American Revolution* 2, Philadelphia: George W. Jacobs and Co., 1900.

Fields, Joseph E., ed. *'Worthy Partner': The Papers of Martha Washington: With an Introduction by Ellen McCallister Clark.* Westport, CT: Greenwood Press, 1994.

Foster, Kate. "A Beauty in the White House." *The Scotsman,* May 4, 2001.

Gelles, Edith B. *Portia: The World of Abigail Adams.* Bloomington, IN: Indiana University Press, 1992.

Ginzberg, Louis, and Julius H. Greenstone. "Dowry." *The Jewish Encyclopedia,* http://www.jewishencyclopedia.com (accessed June 2005).

———, and Lewis N. Dembitz. "Commercial Law." *The Jewish Encyclopedia,* http://jewishencyclopedia.com (accessed June 2005).

Givhan, Robin. "Condoleeza Rice's Commanding Clothes." *Washington Post,* February 25, 2005.

Gordon, Lydia. *From Lady Washington to Mrs. Cleveland.* New York: C.T. Dillingham, 1889.

Grant, Julia Dent. *The Personal Memoirs of Julia Dent Grant (Mrs. Ulysses S. Grant) Edited, with Notes and Foreword by John Y. Simon.* Carbondale, IL: Southern Illinois University Press, [1988], c1975.

Harnden, Toby. "'My Husband and I Get a Lot of Strength from Each Other' In An Exclusive Interview at the White House, Laura Bush Talks to Toby Harnden about How the Events of September 11 Redefined Her Role as First Lady-and How She Took Inspiration from the Royal Family." *The Daily Telegraph,* June 6, 2002.

Hill, Barbara. Interview by Jane Cook, digital recording. Fairfax, VA. May 31, 2005.

Hirsch, Emil G., and Caspar Levias. "Color." *The Jewish Encyclopedia*, http://www.jewishencyclopedia.com (accessed August 2005).

———, and Immanuel Benzinger. "Spinning." *The Jewish Encyclopedia*, jewishencyclopedia.com (accessed June 2005).

———, Kaufmann Kohler, Richard Gottheil, M. Gemann, Cyrus Adler, Gotthard Deutsch, and Joseph Jacobs. "Education." *The Jewish Encyclopedia* (accessed June 2005). http://www.jewishencyclopedia.com (accessed June 2005).

Hodge, Shelby. "Irish Magic Showers Women's Home." *Houston Chronicle*, March 19, 2003.

Holloway, Lara C. *The Ladies of the White House*. Philadelphia: Bradley and Co., 1881.

Hostetter, Ida L. K. "Harriet Lane," *Papers Read Before the Lancaster County Historical Society*, 22:6 (1929).

Hughes, Karen. *Ten Minutes from Normal*. New York: Viking, 2004.

———. "Remarks at U.S. Department of State." March 14, 2005.

Jacobs, Joseph, Kaufmann Kohler, Cyrus Adler, A. M. Friedenberg, and Lee K. Frankel. "Charity and Charitable Institutions." *The Jewish Encyclopedia*, http://www.jewishencyclopedia.com (accessed June 2005).

Jastrow Jr., Morris, and Wilhelm Nowack. "Blessing and Cursing." *The Jewish Encyclopedia*, http://www.jewishencyclopedia.com (accessed June 2005).

Jastrow, Marcus, and Caspar Levias. "Artisans." *The Jewish Encyclopedia*. http://www.jewishencyclopedia.com (accessed June 2005).

Joyce, Deshua. Interview by Jane Cook, tape recording. Springfield, VA. June 8, 2005.

Kalec, William. "In a Word, Mulkey-Robertson One 'Intense' Coach." New Orleans: *Times-Picayune*, April 5, 2005.

Kamen, Al. "Yuletide Greetings from Bush, Cheney Families." *Washington Post,* December 15, 2003.

Keil, C. F., and F. Delitzsch. *Commentary on the Old Testament in Ten Volumes, Vol. 6*. Grand Rapids, MI: Eerdmans Publishing Co., 1984.

Kilian, Michael. "Ladies First Smithsonian Takes a Serious Look at Lives of Presidents' Wives." *Chicago Tribune*, April 12, 1992, 12.

Kimutai, Vitalis. "Councillor Who Wanted to Marry Clinton's Daughter." *Kenya Standard*, July 21, 2005.

Kohler, Kaufmann, and Adolf Guttmacher. "Family and Family Life." *The Jewish Encyclopedia*. http://www.jewishencylopedia.com (accessed June 2005).

Laskas, Jeanne Marie. "The Most Important Part is Love." *Ladies' Home Journal*, 122, no. 4 (May 2005).

Leonard, Mary. "First Lady Takes a Leading Role in Re-election Bid: Bush Team Aims for Women Voters with Wife's Perspective." *Houston Chronicle*, May 23, 2004.

Lopez, John P. "Got Mulk? Then You're a Champion." *Houston Chronicle*, April 6, 2005.

Lossing, Benson J. *Mary and Martha: The Mother and Wife of George Washington*. New York: Harper and Brothers, 1886.

Lynch, Patrick. "Enthusiastic and Slightly-Exuberant Account of the New Administration: From the Irish American." *New York Times*, March 20, 1857.

Madison, Dolley. "A Letter to Mr. Pyne, July 15, 1845." An Autograph of Mrs. Madison on the day of her Confirmation. Baltimore: Archives of the Diocese of Maryland.

———. *The Selected Letters of Dolley Payne Madison*. Edited by David B. Mattern and Holly C. Shulman. Charlottesville, VA: University of Virginia Press, 2003.

Mansfield, Stephen. "The President's 'Secret Weapon.'" *Washington Times*, October 25, 2005.

Mathis, Nancy. "'Children, They Must Come First': U.S. and Soviet First Ladies Speak to Graduates at Wellesley." *Houston Chronicle*, June 2, 1990.

May, Peter. "Coach Gives Baylor the Loyal Treatment." *Boston Globe*, April 3, 2005.

Morris, Sylvia Jukes. *Edith Kermit Roosevelt: Portrait of a First Lady*. New York: Modern Library, 2001.

Nelson, Rebecca, ed. *The Handy History Answer Book*. Canton, MI: Visible Ink Press, 1999.

Nichols, Bonnie. Interview by Jane Cook, tape recording. Alexandria, VA. June 3, 2005.

Nichols, Daniel. Interview by Jane Cook, tape recording. Washington, DC. March 2004.

Nixon, Pat. "Remarks on Arrival at Jeorge Chavez Airport in Lima, Peru, with Mrs. Juan Velasco." Tape C-046, Nixon Presidential Materials,

National Archives and Records Administration, College Park, MD. June 28, 1970.

———. "Remarks Walking through Earthquake Area in Peru's Anta Valley." Tape C-047, Nixon Presidential Materials, National Archives and Records Administration, College Park, MD, June 29, 1970.

O'Keefe, Mark. "Benefactors in Chief; Since Jimmy Carter, Presidents Lead by Charitable Example." Newhouse News Service, *The Grand Rapids Press*, April 28, 2002.

Peacock, Virginia Tatnall. *Famous American Belles of the 19th Century*. New York: Books for Libraries Press, 1900, Reprint 1970.

Phelan, Jacqueline. Interview by Jane Cook, digital recording. Vienna, VA. May 24, 2005.

Reagan, Nancy. *I Love You, Ronnie: The Letters of Ronald Reagan to Nancy Reagan*. New York: Random House, 2000.

———. *My Turn*. New York: Harper Collins, 1989.

Reid, T. R. "One Flu Over the State Dinner; Japanese Warm to First Lady's Cool." *Washington Post*, January 9, 1992.

Romney, Lee. "Family, Faith Top Former First Lady's List; Speech: Barbara Bush Stresses Values in Address to Convention-goers in Anaheim. Audience Lauds Her 'Hilarious' and 'Wonderful' Style." *Los Angeles Times*, November 17, 1996.

Rosenberger, Homer T. "Harriet Lane, First Lady: Hostess Extraordinary in Difficult Times." *Records of the Columbia Historical Society*, 1966–68.

Ryun, Anne. Interview by Jane Cook, digital recording. Washington, DC. June 28, 2005.

Ryun, Jim, and Anne Ryun. *In Quest of Gold*. Testimony Pamphlet, 2005.

Sallee, Rad. "Former First Lady Promotes Literacy: Bush Urges Reading as Family Event." *Houston Chronicle*, March 15, 1995.

Scaasi, Arnold. *The Women I Have Dressed (and Undressed)*. New York: Scribner, 2004.

Schloessinger, Max, and Emil G. Hirsch. "Distaff." *The Jewish Encyclopedia*, http://www.jewishencyclopedia.com (accessed June 2005).

Schneider, Dorothy, and Carl J. Schneider. *First Ladies: A Biographical Dictionary*. New York: Checkmark Books, 2001.

Seale, William. *The President's House: A History*. Washington: National Geographic Society, 1986.

Smith, Marie. "Pat Ends Tour." *Washington Post*, June 19, 1969.

Stevenson, Robert Louis. *A Child's Garden of Verses and Underwoods*. New York: Current Literature, 1906.

Stickney Jr., W. H. "Baylor 84, Michigan State 62: Far From Your Average Bears: National Title Separates Baylor from NCAA Pack." *Houston Chronicle*, April 6, 2005.

Symmes, John Cleves. *The Intimate Letters of John Cleves Symmes and His Family*. Edited by Beverly W. Bond. Cincinnati: Historical and Philosophical Society of Ohio, 1956.

Taft, Helen Herron. *Recollections of Full Years*. New York: Dodd, Mead & Co., 1914.

Thomas, Cal. "White House Aide Sets Selfless Example." *Milwaukee Journal Sentinel*, April 24, 2002.

Thomma, Steven. "Attack on America: First Lady Makes Her Presence Felt." Knight Ridder News Service, *Milwaukee Journal Sentinel*, September 18, 2001.

Thompson, Mary V. " 'As If I Had Been a Very Great Somebody' Martha Washington in the American Revolution: Becoming the New Nation's First Lady." A Talk Given at the Annual George Washington Symposium, Mount Vernon, VA, November 9, 2002.

———. " 'An Old Fashioned Virginia House-keeper: Martha Washington at Home." A Talk Given to Phi Upsilon Omicron, the National Honor Society in Family and Consumer Sciences at the University Club, Washington, November 16, 2002, slightly revised November 27, 2002.

Truman, Harry. "Truman's Diary, June 5, 1945." President Truman Library, President's Secretary's Files, http://www.trumanlibrary.org/speaks.htm (accessed August 2005).

Truman, Margaret. *First Ladies*. New York: Random House, 1995.

Vander Laan, Ray. *That the World May Know*. Focus on the Family Films. 1995.

Washington, George. "Farewell Address, September 9, 1796." Original Sources, http://www.originalsources.com (accessed August 2005).

Weiss, Eric M. "There's No Shortage of Royalty." *Washington Post*, April 10, 2005.

Wharton, Anne Hollingsworth. *Martha Washington*. New York: Charles Scribner's Sons, 1897.

———. *Social Life in the Early Republic*, Philadelphia & London: J.B. Lippincott Co., 1902.

White, Hilary. Interview by Jane Cook, tape recording. Arlington, VA. April 2004.

Whittingham, William Rollinson. "Tuesday, July the 15th, 1845, St. John's Parish, Washington D.C." Thirty-seven Names Listed for Confirmation. Dolley Payne Madison is Second on the List. *Confirmation Journal*. Baltimore: Archives of the Diocese of Maryland.

Whitton, Mary Ormsbee. *The First First Ladies*. New York: Books for Libraries Press, 1969.

Wickell, Carly. "Gem Mining in Franklin, North Carolina." http://jewelry.about.com/cs/gemmining/a/nc_rubies.htm (accessed October 2004).

Willets, Gilson. *Inside History of the White House*. New York: The Christian Herald, 1908.

Wolf, Naomi. "The Sexes." *New York*, September 27, 2004.

Notes

INTRODUCTION
First Lady of His Heart

1. To write the fictionalized short story of a true moment in the life of Chester Arthur, the author consulted these sources: "Ellen Arthur: First Lady Biography." National First Ladies Library, http://www.firstladies.org/biographies/firstladies.aspx?biography=22 (accessed August 2005); William Seale, *The President's House*, 531, 425; Lydia Gordon, *From Lady Washington to Mrs. Cleveland*, 420–30.

2. Michael Kilian, "Ladies First Smithsonian Takes A Serious Look at Lives of Presidents' Wives," *Chicago Tribune*, April 12, 1992.

3. Ibid.

4. Alison Cook, "Women Leading the Way," *Houston Chronicle*, March 26, 1990.

5. Nancy Reagan, *My Turn*, 31.

6. "Rosalynn Carter Deals with Defeat," *Chicago Tribune*, April 9, 1989.

7. Sara Booth Conroy, "Martha-Bashing in Vogue, but Founding Mother Really Cool," *Houston Chronicle*, September 24, 1987.

8. Grace Coolidge, *An Autobiography*, 62.

9. Dan Ariail, *The Carpenter's Apprentice*, 85.

10. Naomi Wolf, "The Sexes," *New York*, September 27, 2004.

CHAPTER ONE
Romancing the Stone

1. Vitalis Kimutai, "Councillor Who Wanted to Marry Clinton's Daughter." *Kenya Standard*, July 21, 2005.

2. To write the fictionalized short story of a true moment in the life of Julia Grant, the author consulted these sources: Julia Grant, *Memoirs*, 48–55; Foster Coates, "The Courtship of General Grant," *Ladies' Home Journal*, 7, October 1890.

3. Louis Ginzberg, "Dowry," *The Jewish Encyclopedia*, http://www .jewishencyclopedia.com (accessed August 2005).

4. Harry Truman, *From Truman's Diary, June 5, 1945*. President Truman Library, President's Secretary's Files, http://www.trumanlibrary.org/speaks.htm (accessed August 2005).

5. "How Long Does Gem Mining Take?" Sheffield Mine, http://www .sheffieldmine.com/ and Carly Wickell "Gem Mining in Franklin, North Carolina," http://jewelry.about.com/cs/gemmining/a/nc_rubies.htm (accessed October 2004).

6. Foster Coates, "The Courtship of General Grant," *Ladies' Home Journal*, 7, October 1890.

CHAPTER TWO
Extreme Makeovers

1. Editors, "2008 Run, Abortion Engage Her Politically," *Washington Times*, March 12, 2005.

2. "Careful that Dish is Hot: At the Gridiron Dinner, Hams Glazed with Condi." *Washington Post*, March 13, 2005.

3. Robin Givhan, "Condoleeza Rice's Commanding Clothes," *Washington Post*, February 25, 2005.

4. To write the fictionalized short story of a true moment in the life of Harriet Lane, the author consulted these sources: "Harriet Lane: First Lady Biography." National First Ladies Library, http://www.firstladies.org/biographies/ firstladies.aspx?biography=16 (accessed August 2005); Patrick Lynch, "Enthusiastic and Slightly-Exuberant Account of the New Administration." *New York Times*, March 20, 1857; Homer T. Rosenberger, "Harriet Lane, First Lady: Hostess Extraordinary in Difficult Times." *Records of the Columbia Historical Society 1966–68*, 109–12; Gilson Willets, *Inside History of the White House*, The Christian Herald, 1908, 154; Ida Hostetter, "Harriet Lane," *Papers Read Before the Lancaster County Historical Society*, 33, no. 6, 97–112.

5. Barbara Bush, *Memoir*.

6. "Purple Passion, May 15, 2001." *Jolique*. http://www.jolique.com/dyes _colorants/purple_passion.htm (accessed September 2005).

7. Cyrus Adler, "Dyes and Dyeing," *The Jewish Encyclopedia*, http://www .jewishencylopedia.com (accessed June 2005).

8. Jacqueline Phelan, author interview, May 24, 2005.

9. Susan Eisenhower, *Mrs. Ike*, 4.

10. Arnold Scaasi, *The Women I Have Dressed*, 62.

11. Ibid., 8.

12. Hamish Bowles, *Jacqueline Kennedy: The White House Years*, 31.

13. Ibid., 117.

14. Ibid., 143.

15. American Society for Aesthetic Plastic Surgery, "Highlights on Cosmetic Surgery," http://www.surgery.org/press/procedurefacts-asqf.php (accessed August 2005).

16. Ida Hostetter, "Harriet Lane," *Papers Read Before the Lancaster County Historical Society*, 33, no. 6, 103, 104.

17. Homer T. Rosenberger, "Harriet Lane, First Lady: Hostess Extraordinary in Difficult Times." *Records of the Columbia Historical Society 1966–68*, 119.

18. Ibid., 150.

19. Ida Hostetter, "Harriet Lane," 98.

20. Ibid., 101.

21. Ibid., 102.

22. Barbara Hill, author interview, May 31, 2005.

23. "The Heart and Truth Campaign and the Red Dress Project," http://www.whitehouse.gov/firstlady/initiatives/womenandheartdisease2.html (accessed August 2005).

CHAPTER THREE
Eager Beavers

1. Grace Coolidge, *An Autobiography*, 45.

2. Ibid., 51.

3. To write the fictionalized short story of a true moment in the life of Abigail Adams, the author consulted these sources: Abigail Adams, "Letter to John Adams, December 13, 1778," and John Adams, "Letter to Abigail Adams, August 27, 1778." Adams Family Papers: An Electronic Archive. The Massachusetts Historical Society. http://www.masshist.org/digitaladams/ aea/index.html (accessed August 2005); Edith B. Gelles, *The World of Abigail Adams*, 37–49; Mary Ormsbee Whitton, *The First First Ladies*, 29.

4. Emil G. Hirsch, "Spinning." *The Jewish Encyclopedia*, http://www .jewishencyclopedia.com (accessed June 2005).

5. Bureau of Labor Statistics, "Women's Share of Workforce to Edge Higher by 2008," The U.S. Department of Labor, http://www.bls.gov/opub/ ted/2000/Feb/wk3/art01.htm (accessed August 2005).

6. Jacqueline Phelan, author interview, May 24, 2005.

7. Mary Leonard, "First Lady Takes a Leading Role," *Houston Chronicle,* May 23, 2004.

8. Sylvia Jukes Morris, *Edith Kermit Roosevelt,* 285–87.

9. Judith Anderson, *William Howard Taft,* 153–67.

10. Ibid., 153.

CHAPTER FOUR
Family Focus

1. Archibald Butt, *Taft and Roosevelt,* 39.

2. "Death of Major Butt Mourned by Washingtonians," *The Washington Times,* April 19, 1912.

3. To write the fictionalized short story of a true moment in the life of Anna Harrison, the author consulted these sources: "Military Service Record of Archibald Irwin Harrison, 8th Indiana Infantry." National Archives and Records Administration, 1861; "Military Service Record of Carter B. Harrison, 51st Ohio Infantry," National Archives and Records Administration, 1861–64; E-mail conversation with curator of Benjamin Harrison Home; John Cleves Symmes, *The Intimate Letters of John Cleves Symmes and His Family,* Cincinnati: Historical and Philosophical Society of Ohio, 1956, 140–67; Lara C. Holloway, *The Ladies of the White House.* Philadelphia: Bradley and Co., 1881, 346–65; Mary Clemmer, *Ten Years in Washington: Life and Scenes in the National Capital, as a Woman Sees Them.* Hartford, Connecticut: A.D. Worthington & Co., 1875, 219; Mary Ormsbee Whitton, *The First First Ladies.* New York: Books for Libraries Press, 1969, 152–76.

4. Barbara Mathis, "Children, They Must Come First," *Houston Chronicle,* June 2, 1990.

5. William Seale, *The President's House,* 574.

6. Kaufmann Kohler, "Family and Family Life," *The Jewish Encyclopedia,* http://www.jewishencylopedia.com (accessed August 2005).

7. Rad Sallee, "Former First Lady Promotes Literacy," *Houston Chronicle,* March 15, 1995.

8. Shelby Hodge, "Irish Magic Showers Women's Home," *Houston Chronicle,* March 19, 2003.

9. Daniel Nichols, author interview, March 2004.

10. Bonnie Nichols, author interview, June 3, 2005.

11. Emil G. Hirsch and others, "Education," *The Jewish Encyclopedia,* http://www.jewishencyclopedia.com (accessed June 2005).

12. Grace Coolidge, *An Autobiography*, 14.

13. George W. Bush, *A Charge to Keep*, 19.

14. Laura Bush, interview by Larry King, *Larry King Live*, CNN, December 18, 2001.

15. Deshua Joyce, author interview, June 8, 2005.

CHAPTER FIVE

Follow the Leader

1. Margaret Truman, *First Ladies*, 95.

2. To write the fictionalized short story of a true moment in the life of Martha Washington, the author consulted these sources: "Martha Washington: First Lady Biography." National First Ladies Library, http://www.firstladies.org/biographies/firstladies.aspx?biography=1 (accessed August 2005); Helen Bryan, *Martha Washington: First Lady of Liberty*, 214–21; Margaret C. Conkling, *Memoirs of the Wife of Washington*, 150, 151; Lara C. Holloway, *The Ladies of the White House*, 49; Mary V. Thompson, "An Old Fashioned Virginia House-keeper: Martha Washington at Home." (A talk given to Phi Upsilon Omicron in November 16, 2002, slightly revised November 27, 2002); Anne Hollingsworth Wharton, *Martha Washington*, 110, 111, 116–18; Mary Ormsbee Whitton, *The First First Ladies*, 12, 13.

3. Marcus Jastrow, "Artisans," *The Jewish Encyclopedia*. http://www.jewishencyclopedia.com (accessed June 2005).

4. Joseph E. Fields, *Worthy Partner*, 61–75, 126.

5. Max Schloessinger, "Distaff," *The Jewish Encyclopedia*, http://www.jewishencyclopedia.com (accessed June 2005).

6. Jeanne Marie Laskas, "The Most Important Part Is Love," *Ladies' Home Journal*, May 2005.

7. Stephen Mansfield, "The President's 'Secret Weapon.'" *Washington Times*, October 25, 2005.

8. Mary Clemmer, *Ten Years in Washington*, 227–29.

9. Susan Eisenhower, *Mrs. Ike*, 197.

10. Ibid., 195.

11. Ibid., 190, 191, 194.

12. Ibid., 194.

13. Ibid., 199.

14. Lester David, *The Lonely Lady of San Clemente*, 134.

15. Julia Grant, *Memoirs*, 175, 176.

16. Anne Hollingsworth Wharton, *Social Life in the Early Republic*, 137, 138.

17. George Bush, *Remarks to the Staff*, September 18, 1991, Original Sources, http://www.originalsources.com (accessed August 2005).

CHAPTER SIX

Charity Choices

1. To write the fictionalized short story of a true moment in the life of Pat Nixon, the author consulted these sources: All networks. "Excerpts of Evening Network News Broadcasts from the Week of 6/27/70 to 7/3/70." WHCA VTR#3770. Nixon Presidential Materials, National Archives and Records Administration, College Park, MD, July 14, 1970; Pat Nixon, "Remarks on Arrival at Jeorge Chavez Airport in Lima, Peru, with Mrs. Juan Velasco." Tape C-046, Nixon Presidential Materials, National Archives and Records Administration, College Park, MD. June 28, 1970; Pat Nixon, "Remarks Walking through Earthquake Area in Peru's Anta Valley." C-047, Nixon Presidential Materials, National Archives and Records Administration, College Park, MD. June 29, 1970.

2. Lester David, *The Lonely Lady of San Clemente*.

3. Julie Nixon Eisenhower, *Pat Nixon: The Untold Story*, 1986.

4. Lester David, *The Lonely Lady*.

5. William Clinton, "Statement on the Death of Pat Nixon, June 22, 1993," http://www.originalsources.com (accessed August 2005).

6. Mary V. Thompson, "An Old Fashioned Virginia House-keeper: Martha Washington at Home." (A talk given to Phi Upsilon Omicron in November 16, 2002, slightly revised November 27, 2002.)

7. Joseph Jacobs, "Charity and Charitable Institutions." *The Jewish Encyclopedia*, http://www.jewishencyclopedia.com.

8. Laura Bush, "Remarks by Mrs. Bush at 204th Commencement of Georgetown University, May 17, 2003," Georgetown University, http://www .whitehouse.gov/news/releases/2003/05/20030517-2.html (accessed August 2005).

9. Rosalynn Carter, *First Lady from Plains*, 95, 96.

10. Heather Cooper, author interview, September 2005.

11. Laura Bush, "Mrs. Bush's Remarks During a Visit with Families Affected by Hurricane Katrina, September 8, 2005," Greenbrook Elementary School, Southaven, MS. http://www.whitehouse.gov/ (accessed September 9, 2005).

12. Laura Bush, "Letter to Elementary School Children September 12, 2001," http://www.whitehouse.gov/kids/connection/letter2.html (accessed August 2005).

13. Laura Bush, remarks, September 17, 2001.

14. Laura Bush, radio address, November 17, 2001.

15. Steven Thomma, "Attack on America: First Lady Makes Her Presence Felt," Knight Ridder News Service, *Milwaukee Journal Sentinel*, September 18, 2001.

16. Heather Cooper, author interview, June 2005.

17. Gilson Willets, *Inside History of the White House*, 418.

18. Ibid.

19. Grace Coolidge, *An Autobiography*, 115.

20. Mark O'Keefe, "Benefactors in Chief," *The Grand Rapids Press*, April 28, 2002.

CHAPTER SEVEN

Investment Inklings

1. Robert Louis Stevenson, *A Child's Garden of Verses and Underwoods*, 1913.

2. To write the fictionalized short story of a true moment in the life of Helen Taft, the author consulted these sources: "Active on Esplanade," *Washington Post*, April 11, 1909; "Busy With Esplanade," *Washington Post*, April 4, 1909; "Helen Taft: First Lady Biography." National First Ladies Library, http://www.firstladies.org/biographies/firstladies.aspx?biography=27 (accessed August 2005); "Washington Drive Opened," *New York Times*, April 18, 1909, 2; Archibald Butt, *Taft and Roosevelt*, 39, 40, 56; Judith Icke Anderson, *William Howard Taft: An Intimate History*, 153–67; "Host on Parkway," *Washington Post*, April 18, 1909; Helen Herron Taft, *Recollections of Full Years*, 2, 6, 333, 361–363.

3. Eric Weiss, "There's No Shortage of Royalty," *Washington Post*, April 10, 2005.

4. Grace Coolidge, *An Autobiography*, 74.

5. Ibid., 41.

6. Julia Grant, *Memoirs*, 183, 184.

7. Louis Ginzberg, "Commercial Law," *The Jewish Encyclopedia*. http://www.jewishencyclopedia.com (accessed June 2005).

8. Editorial, "Bess Truman's Role as First Lady," *Washington Post*, September 2, 1992.

9. Ibid.

10. Cyrus Adler and others, "Perpetual Lamp," *The Jewish Encyclopedia*, http://www.jewishencylopedia.com (accessed June 2005).

11. National Cherry Blossom Festival, "History of the Trees and Festival," http://www.nationalcherryblossomfestival.org/cms/index.php?id=574 (accessed July 2005).

12. Karen Hughes, *Ten Minutes from Normal*, 289–311.

13. Cal Thomas, "White House Aide Sets Selfless Example," *Milwaukee Journal Sentinel*, April 24, 2002.

14. Karen Hughes, *Remarks at U.S. Department of State* (speech), March 14, 2005.

15. George W. Bush, "President Honors Ambassador Karen Hughes at Swearing-In Ceremony," U.S. Department of State, September 9, 2005.

16. Dorothy Schneider, *First Ladies*, 77.

17. Lara Holloway, *Ladies of the White House*, 422–23.

18. Dorothy Schneider, *First Ladies*, 76.

19. Stacey Ankele, author interview, June 13, 2005.

CHAPTER EIGHT
Blizzards and Terrorism

1. To write the fictionalized short story of a true episode in the life of Louisa Adams, the author consulted these sources: "Louisa Adams: First Lady Biography." National First Ladies Library, http://www.firstladies.org/biographies/firstladies.aspx?biography=6 (accessed August 2005); Louisa Adams, *Narrative of a Journey from St. Petersburg to Paris*, Microfilm of Adams Family Papers, Library of Congress; Louisa Adams, "Mrs. John Quincy Adams's Narrative," *Scribner's* Magazine. 34, October 1903, 449–63; Lara Holloway, *The Ladies of the White House*, 244–47; Rebecca Nelson, ed. *The Handy History Answer Book*, 95–97; Mary Ormsbee Whitton, *The First First Ladies*, 102–04; "Hanau," Napoleon Guide. http://www.napoleonguide.com/battle_hanau.htm (accessed August 2005).

2. Emil G. Hirsch, "Color," *The Jewish Encyclopedia*, http://www.jewishencyclopedia.com (accessed August 2005).

3. C. F. Keil, *Commentary on the Old Testament*, 334, 335.

4. Ibid., 449.

5. Ibid., 459.

6. Louisa Adams, "Mrs. John Quincy Adams's Narrative."

7. John Adams, "Letter to Abigail Adams, September 16, 1774." Adams Family Papers: An Electronic Archive. The Massachusetts Historical Society. http://www.masshist.org/digitaladams/aea/index.html (accessed August 2005).

8. Dolley Madison, *Selected Letters*, 176.

9. Ibid., 193.

10. Ibid.

11. Hilary White, author interview, April 2004.

12. Alexander Blok, "The Twelve," *The Columbia World of Quotations,* New York: Columbia University Press, 1996. http://www.bartleby.com/66/ (accessed September 2005).

CHAPTER NINE
Laugh Out Loud

1. Julia Grant, *Memoirs,* 178.

2. To write the fictionalized short story of a true moment in the life of Barbara Bush, the author consulted these sources: Barbara Bush, *Memoir,* 474–76; T. R. Reid, "One Flu Over the State Dinner," *Washington Post,* January 9, 1992.

3. Barbara Bush, *Memoirs,* 474–76.

4. T. R. Reid, "One Flu Over the State Dinner," *Washington Post,* January 9, 1992.

5. Barbara Bush, *Memoirs,* 474–76.

6. Grace Coolidge, *An Autobiography,* 68.

7. William Kalec, "In a Word, Mulkey-Robertson One 'Intense' Coach," *Times-Picayune,* April 5, 2005.

8. Peter May, "Coach Gives Baylor the Loyal Treatment," *Boston Globe,* April 3, 2005.

9. Kalec, "In a Word."

10. W. H. Stickney, Jr. "Baylor 84, Michigan State 62: Far From Your Average Bears: National Title Separates Baylor from NCAA Pack," *Houston Chronicle,* April 6, 2005.

11. John P. Lopez, "Got Mulk? Then You're a Champion," *Houston Chronicle,* April 6, 2005.

12. Abigail Adams, "Letter from Abigail Adams to John Adams, November 16, 1788," Adams Family Papers: An Electronic Archive. The Massachusetts Historical Society. http://www.masshist.org/digitaladams/aea/index.html (accessed August 2005).

13. Nancy Reagan, *My Turn,* 42, 43.

14. Jeanne Marie Laskas, "The Most Important Part is Love," *Ladies' Home Journal,* May 2005.

15. Mary V. Thompson, " 'As If I Had Been a Very Great Somebody' " (A talk given at the Annual George Washington Symposium, Mount Vernon, Virginia, November 9, 2002).

16. Associated Press, "For Bushes, Retirement Has Been Nice," *Chicago Tribune,* January 23, 1996.

17. Laura Bush, radio address, November 17, 2001.

18. Karen Hughes, remarks, March 14, 2005.

CHAPTER TEN
Gemstone Fire

1. To write the fictionalized short story of a true moment in the life of Dolley Madison, the author consulted these sources: "Approaching Centenary of Old St. John's Church," *Washington Post,* March 21, 1915; "Dolley Madison: First Lady Biography." National First Ladies Library, http://www.firstladies .org/biographies/firstladies.aspx?biography=4 (accessed August 2005); "The Order of Confirmation," *1789 U.S. Book of Common Prayer.* (In use in 1845. Revised in 1892); http://justus.anglican.org/resources/bcp/1789/Confirmation _1789.htm; "Welcome to St. John's Flyer," Washington, D.C.: St. John's Church, 2005; Ethel Stephens Arnett, *Mrs. James Madison,* Greensboro, N.C.: Piedmont Press, 1972; George Washington Doane, "Confirmation Sermons," *The Life and Writings of George Washington Doane.* New York: D. Appleton and Company, 1860–61, 4, 623–40; Conversation with Mary Klein, curator of The Diocese of Maryland; John Cleves Symmes, Dolley Madison, "A Letter to Mr. Pyne, July 15, 1845," Archives of the Diocese of Maryland; William Rollinson Whittingham, *Confirmation Journal.* Baltimore: Archives of the Diocese of Maryland; Anne Hollingsworth Wharton, *Social Life in the Early Republic,* 132.

2. George Washington, "Farewell Address September 19, 1796," Original Sources, http://www.originalsources.com (accessed August 2005).

3. Mary V. Thompson, "An Old Fashioned Virginia House-keeper: Martha Washington at Home." (A talk given to Phi Upsilon Omicron in November 16, 2002, slightly revised November 27, 2002).

4. Joseph E. Fields, *Worthy Partner,* xxxiii.

5. Mary V. Thompson, "An Old Fashioned Virginia House-keeper: Martha Washington at Home." (A talk given to Phi Upsilon Omicron in November 16, 2002, slightly revised November 27, 2002).

6. Ida Hostetter, "Harriet Lane," *Papers Read Before the Lancaster County Historical Society,* 22, no. 6 (1929).

7. Louisa Adams, *Narrative of a Journey from St. Petersburg to Paris,* Library of Congress.

8. Grace Coolidge, *An Autobiography,* xvi.

9. Abigail Adams, "Letter to John Adams, October 8, 1775." Adams Family Papers: An Electronic Archive. The Massachusetts Historical Society. http://www.masshist.org/digitaladams/aea/index.html (accessed August 2005).

10. "Republican Presidential Candidates Participate in Political Debate," Washington Transcript Service, December 13, 1999.

11. Laura Bush, "First Lady Laura Bush Delivers Remarks at New York Tenth Anniversary Prayer Breakfast," May 11, 2004.

12. Rosalynn Carter, *First Lady from Plains*, 10, 11.

13. Ibid., 19.

14. Carol Blair, "A Disturbing Experience with the Concept of the 'Fear of the Lord,'" unpublished data.

15. John Adams, "Letter to Abigail Adams, November 2, 1800." Adams Family Papers: An Electronic Archive. The Massachusetts Historical Society. http://www.masshist.org/digitaladams/aea/index.html (accessed September 2005).

16. "What Are Pearls?" American Museum of Natural History, http://www .amnh.org/exhibitions/pearls/ (accessed September 2005).

CHAPTER ELEVEN
Stained-Glass Windows

1. "Welcome to St. John's Flyer," St. John's Church, 2005.

2. Morris Jastrow, Jr., "Blessing and Cursing," *The Jewish Encyclopedia*, http://www.jewishencyclopedia.com.

3. Grace Coolidge, *An Autobiography*, 34, 35.

4. Mary V. Thompson, "'As If I had Been a Very Great Somebody'" (A talk given at the Annual George Washington Symposium, Mount Vernon, Virginia, November 9, 2002).

5. Ibid.

6. Elizabeth Ellet, *The Women of the American Revolution*, 29.

7. Lara Holloway, *The Ladies of the White House*, 122.

8. Nancy Reagan, *I Love You, Ronnie*, 155–60.

9. Ray Vander Laan, "That the World May Know," *Focus on the Family Films*, 1995.

10. Ibid.